McLibel

McLibel

burger culture on trial

JOHN VIDAL

THE NEW PRESS   NEW YORK

Library of Congress Catalog Card Number
97-69259 ISBN 1-56584-411-4

First published in the United Kingdom by Macmillan
Published in the United States by The New Press, New York
Distributed by W.W. Norton & Company, Inc., New York

The New Press was established in 1990 as a not-for-profit alternative to the large, commercial publishing houses currently
dominating the book publishing industry. The New Press oper-
ates in the public interest rather than for private gain, and is
committed to publishing, in innovative ways, works of educational, cultural, and community value that might not normally
be commercially viable. The New Press's editorial offices are
located at the City University of New York.

Production management by Kim Waymer, The New Press
Printed in the United States of America 9 8 7 6 5 4 3 2 1

A Preface

Three hundred and thirteen days of evidence and submissions. Eighteen thousand pages of court transcripts. Forty thousand pages of documents and witness statements. Twenty-eight pre-trial hearings. England's longest ever court case. One hundred and eighty witnesses. Appeals to Europe and the highest courts in Britain. One of the world's largest corporations. Two of the world's most determined and tenacious people. Some of the most contentious issues of the times. Humbug. Reputation. Tears. Tedium. Drama. Ideals. Six weeks to grasp it all and put this book together.

Entering this wilderness of claim and counterclaim was hazardous, and I needed exceptional guides. First and foremost, thank you Jay Griffiths and Philip George who both worked so hard on *McLibel*, the book. Griffiths was asked to be a fine writer, researcher, journalist, editor and friend. She was that and much more. I specifically asked George to research the case from McDonald's' point of view. The scale of his task was phenomenal. It was brilliant, painstaking work in difficult circumstances. *McLibel* the book was a team effort and to them fell the hardest work.

Thanks also to Keir Starmer, barrister, of Doughty Street Chambers whose legal overview was vital; to Dan Mills at the McLibel Support campaign whose grasp of the issues and unfailing helpfulness was fundamental. Franny Armstrong of documentary makers One Off Productions made many recordings and much research available. Thank you, too, the many witnesses, lawyers and others who provided much of the raw material – on both sides, and to the McDonald's and McSpotlight Internet sites, where there are now hundreds of megabytes of information.

Others contributed ideas, especially to the later chapters, which stretch the case beyond the confines of Britain and McDonald's. Their names are recorded at the very end, but thank you George Monbiot, Kevin Watkins, Nicholas Hildyard, Vandana Shiva, Ed Mayo, John Elkington and others. *McLibel* was written in a one-month sabbatical from the *Guardian*, so particular thanks to the editor Alan Rusbridger, Society editor Malcolm Dean, Rachel Mulligan and Zoe Sewell in the library, and environment correspondent Paul Brown who kept the shop in my absence.

A word on the relationship between the author and the two defendants. David Morris and Helen Steel feel they have been imprisoned by McLibel, the trial, for many years. They trusted me to write about them in some detail and made many papers available. Such was the tight publishing schedule that we only met on one occasion before the book was started and for a few minutes later on. They were in the High Court almost to the book's deadline, yet when exhausted and stressed beyond understanding they mostly found time to check and check again many of the facts. Respect and thanks. But I was never their ghost writer and I dare say this is not how they would have chosen to present their case; indeed, I do not share their politics nor, necessarily, their conclusions. The book is, I hope, a fair interpretation of a massively complex case.

McDonald's chose not to be involved. It was telephoned

on very many occasions before and after the case was closed and offered the right of reply and space to contribute to the very many debates that are raised. Mostly it did not respond. When it did, both Illinois and London were polite but firm. The corporation's policy was to comment only after the judge had delivered his verdict. Effectively this has meant a two-year blackout of detailed information about the case from the plaintiff. Indeed, by making its legal team unavailable for interview or for comment in either a personal or corporate capacity, portrayal of its side of the case has, I fear, been made more difficult. The corporation has promised to engage in debate after the judgements and I, for one, look forward to it.

Few people have had the time, energy or inclination to follow all McLibel and I make no apology for warning that some bits may seem of interest only to specialists. Others, though, were genuinely dramatic. The whole was somewhere between a public enquiry, a post-mortem on industrialism, a Greek tragedy and a *Carry On* . . . (and On and On) film. Whether read for detail or for wider meaning, it must be remembered that at the beginning and at the end McLibel, both trial and book, is about cultures.

But anyone who has come near this scarecrow of litigation sees quickly how barbarous and antiquated are the libel laws and how difficult the law has become for people wanting to – or having to – represent themselves. They ill serve the democratic process, freedom of speech and debate, and anyone without fabulous wealth is immediately put off. They can make a grotesque mockery of what reasonable people might call justice and they are open to vile abuse by all. They have cast a long shadow over both the subject and the content of this book to the point where I and others must censor ourselves, for not to do so is to court certain disaster. The laws need radical and immediate overhaul and if *McLibel* the book does nothing else but make this clear, then it will have served a purpose.

Thanks, finally, to Catherine Hurley at Macmillan. A quite extraordinary, far-sighted editor and compadre.

Contents

List of illustrations

Early Day Motion sponsored by Jeremy Corbyn, MP, lodged in
the House of Commons 26 May 1994

*'That this House opposes the routine use of libel writs as a
form of censorship particularly by US multinationals taking
advantage of the United Kingdom's more repressive libel laws;
notes that McDonald's has threatened or initiated libel actions
against numerous organizations including the BBC, Channel
4, the Guardian, Today, Scottish TUC, Green, vegetarian and
labour movement groups and individuals; notes that apologies
and damages have been obtained under false pretences after
McDonald's lied about their practices e.g. by denying using
beef reared on ex-rainforest land; believes that as McDonald's
spends over $1 billion annually on advertising and promotions
it should expect public criticism and should not seek to
suppress it; further notes that the House of Lords recently
ruled that in the interests of freedom of speech "governmental
bodies" would not be allowed to sue their critics for libel, and
believes that this ruling should logically be extended to cover
immensely powerful, wealthy and influential multinational
corporations.'*

A complaint lodged in the British courts 1990

*That McDonald's has been 'greatly damaged in its trading
reputation', and has 'been brought into public scandal, odium
and contempt' by a 'fact sheet' which has libellously alleged
that, among other things, McDonald's causes the evictions of
small farmers in the Third World, destroys rainforests, lies
about its use of recycled paper, misleads the public about the
nutritional value of their food, sells food high in sugar and*

salt to encourage an addiction to it, uses gimmicks to cover up that the food is of low quality, targets most of their advertising at children, are responsible for the inhumane treatment of animals, sells hamburgers likely to cause food poisoning, pay bad wages, are only interested in cheap labour etc. etc.... all of which are vigorously denied by the corporation.

Chapter One

Day 222

'It's almost as if there is an imaginary line straight down the middle of this court.'

— Mr Justice Bell. Day 222

27 February 1996: Dave Morris, single father, former post-man, has made breakfast for Charlie. It's a bright, cool London morning and by 9.25 he's walked his six-year-old son to school and is standing in the ticket hall at Turnpike Lane Underground station. He rifles through one of two plastic bags to find a fax that a Brazilian-based journalist sent him late the night before. He skim reads it and returns it. He delves deeper, draws out pages photocopied from a book about the Amazon rainforest. He flicks through them but he's not concentrating, keeps looking at the big wall clock. The North London commuters jostle him but he is oblivious. 'She's late,' he says to himself, as he thumbs through more paperwork, occasionally pencilling passages.

Helen Steel, a former London gardener and minibus driver who now works in a West End bar two nights a week, arrives a few minutes later. The two greet each other, go straight down the escalator and onto platform 1. They are friendly, warm but businesslike. This is a meeting held almost on the run between people who know each other well and have been meeting here for years. 'Guess what,' says Morris, non-chalantly, as the commuters compete for space on the plat-form, 'I got a fax from Mr Rampton. To my house.' Steel feigns being impressed: 'Oooh, you are honoured,' she says.

The tube train between Turnpike Lane and central London makes the worst legal chambers in Britain. As usual, there are no seats and Steel and Morris are hanging on to straps, jammed against the side of the train and tossed around in the human crush as they prepare to cross-examine witnesses. The tube must serve as an office because neither has the time or the resources to meet elsewhere. In fact today is only Average Bad on the Piccadilly Line. The woman hanging on to a strap next to Morris is failing to read a Barbara Cartland romantic novel; two people are almost managing a conversation about a TV soap, a man with a seat is flailing around with three sections of the *Guardian* newspaper. Mostly though, the train sways as it always does, faces loom out of armpits, bodies fall over each other, sweat mixed with deodorants and perfume with grimaces.

Steel: 'Well, what did the fax say?'

Morris: 'Take a look.'

They make a bit of space between each other, and with arms pinioned by the crowd on the train they speed read it together. It's twenty pages of memos that the US Agriculture Council had sent to Cargill's, a privately owned corporation that controls more than 50 per cent of the world's grain sales. Yesterday the original was in the briefcase of Mr Ray Cesca, the head of world trade of the $30 billion a year McDonald's Corporation.

Morris: 'I can't concentrate on this.'

By Holloway Road station they know they've hit silver, if not gold. Some of the information will further their case. Morris wonders why it was not disclosed to them years ago. He's furious at what he sees as obstruction but says there is no time for emotion. Steel asks him if he wants to cross-examine Ray Cesca first. Morris says he is not ready. They each read their papers as the train sways along.

Steel: 'I discovered something very interesting last night.'

Morris: 'Well, are you going to tell me?'

Steel: 'No. Wait.'

By Russell Square station the rush hour has thinned out. Morris is now sighing deeply, pencilling through Cargill passages, giving the impression of a harassed schoolteacher marking substandard fourth-form essays. A tourist, map in hand, wife on shoulder, leans heavily towards a recoiling Steel. When the train stops at Holborn Steel and Morris put their papers back in bags, get out and head to the crowded streets without so much as glancing at each other. Morris picks up the last conversation, wants to know what Steel has found out.

Steel (teasing): 'No, I want it to be a surprise. It's good to have surprises.'

Morris: 'Come on, it's a wet blanket, isn't it?'

Steel: 'Let's just say it's more of a sparkler than a stick of dynamite.'

The two dash like schoolchildren for the 171 bus and banter with the driver. By the time they reach the Royal Courts of Justice on the Strand both are working themselves up: Morris about what he says are the links between the fast-food industry and the Latin American military, Steel about litter. Hardly pausing for breath they sweep up the steps, hand their bags to the security guards to check and, with a cheerful 'Morning . . .' to the ushers and porters, they are in Britain's premier courts to defend themselves against charges of libel brought by McDonald's against them five years before.

George Edmund Street's Victorian Gothic fantasy is built on the scale of and in the style of one of Europe's medieval cathedrals. All it lacks is a high altar. One hundred yards down the central nave, past puffy-faced young men scuttling singly or in pairs over the grey flagstones with boxes of papers and bundles of legal briefs, Steel and Morris swing left. Another fifty yards and they go through double doors, then it's left and right again, up a short flight of stairs past the marble gaze of a stern Victorian Appeal Court judge, through more swing doors and into Court 35.

This is the two hundred and twenty-second day that Steel and Morris have been defending themselves against the world's largest food-service corporation. It is the second 27 February that Court 35 has been sitting. It's the second winter running that snow has fallen outside in the Strand as the case grinds on. The IRA has left London to cheers and returned with bombs, Bill Clinton has lost Congress but can contemplate a second term of office, the English cricket team has played and lost umpteen matches and South Africa has all but thrown off apartheid in the years since Steel and Morris came to court with McDonald's.

It is actually more than five years since they allegedly distributed a 'Factsheet' that claimed to tell the public 'the truth about McDonald's'. The six sides of paper that were distributed by supporters of a group called London Greenpeace so offended or worried the image-conscious fast-food corporation that its head office in Illinois, USA, felt it proper to spend whatever it needed (latest reckoning £10 million) to bring these two people to the courts without any prospect of realistic recompense or damages and no chance of an apology.

It is more than six years since the corporation sent spies into the group to identify who among them was responsible for the alleged libels and it's more than five and a half years since McDonald's issued writs and the two parties first locked horns in a marathon series of pre-trial hearings.

McDonald's maintained that the leaflets were so dangerous that they threatened to become common parlance and people everywhere might start to believe that, for instance, the corporation was responsible for cutting down rainforests. The Factsheet, they claimed, was a tissue of terrible untruths, and the allegations were damnable. Their last recourse, they said, was to go to law, but they had no option because they were defending themselves against lies and fighting for 'the truth'.

The two defendants push through the last pair of doors. Court 35 is elegant and austere, oak panelled and polished in institution-grade beeswax. It is like a pompous little side chapel of the vainglorious vaulted main cathedral building. Outside it are statues and busts and grey stone carvings and discreet directions to 'gentlemen advocates' robing rooms' and 'lady advocates' robing rooms'. Inside it is pure theatre: three Gothic windows rise behind the judge's high red chair. His desk is also divided into three. All the court architecture is designed to centralize the throne, to draw the eye and to keep it there in the symbolic dead centre of the two parties who will argue on either side of him.

It is part temple, part theatre, part library. The walls are lined with leather-bound *Weekly Law Reports* marked Supreme Court Library, and, like wallpaper stuck haphazardly onto other wallpaper, dozens of boxes of the proceedings of the trial stand piled in six-foot columns in front of the law reports. Boxes, more boxes and yet more; sixty-six in all, it has been counted, each with six fat files.

All are carefully labelled. Some of the transcripts of the proceedings are dated by court time, others by Christian day and date. There are said to be – but no one has kept count – 15,000 pages so far of daily transcripts of the proceedings. In other boxes there are 40,000 pages of documents and witness statements and all are classified first by bundle, then by document and then by page. And because the law must be accessible to all, there is a ladder to reach the highest shelves and boxes; and because everything in Court 35 must have a provenance and be marked, the ladder is correctly labelled 'ladder'.

Like the interminable case of Jarndyce vs. Jarndyce in Charles Dickens's *Bleak House*, McDonald's Corporation and McDonald's Restaurants Ltd. vs. Helen Marie Steel and David Morris drones on in claustrophobic judicial isolation, a bizarre backcloth to and commentary on the way life continues outside. Occasionally there are anniversaries or records broken but the public seldom enters in great numbers, and when it does it is mostly attracted by the case's longevity or weirdness value. There is not even a jury to give an air of normality, it having been deemed, controversially, years before that it would take too long, cost too much and – most importantly – be too difficult in parts for twelve ordinary men and women to comprehend.

At this point in the proceedings – remember we are now almost two years into the trial itself – there is no remote end in sight. So long-winded is this scarecrow of a case, so stuffed is it with fact and counter-fact, claim and counter-claim, that it is almost an institution itself, acquiring a crust of permanence in the Royal Courts of Justice. People, it is said, are becoming famous for having followed it even this far. Slowly, though, by dint of Steel and Morris's increasingly voluble and passionate supporters, the word is getting out that two people who earn at most £7,500 a year between them are not just defending themselves against one of the world's most powerful corporations but are scoring points.

By all possible measures, the case seems spectacularly unbalanced and stacked against Steel and Morris. McDonald's, it is said, is paying a crack legal team in the region of £6,000 a day to sledgehammer a nut. Apart from a leading libel silk estimated at £2,000 a day, the corporation employs a full-time barrister as his assistant (about £1,000 a day), with corporate lawyers on two continents backing them up, and a panoply of secretarial and other help. They have huge legal experience, skills of delivery and analysis and all that money can buy: access to a set of first-class legal chambers well versed in the intricacies of libel law, libraries, databases, communications systems and advisers. They have people to gather and brief witnesses, others to think only about their strategy, yet more to administrate and plug the tiniest legal points. They can pay people to come first class from anywhere in the world to give evidence on their behalf or travel halfway round the world themselves to brief their witnesses. They can get daily transcripts of the proceedings and help with their speeches just as they got help from private detectives to bring Steel and Morris to trial. And none of the McDonald's team, it is believed, has to use the Piccadilly line as their office.

Court 35 is the domain of the High Court judge Sir Rodger Bell, who is referred to as Mr Justice Bell. Promoted from recorder in 1993 – the same year as he started on the present case – this is his first libel trial. He is an Oxford University man, a college rower and, suitably, a long-distance running blue. He is Establishment but unassuming, a member not of the expected clubs like the Athenaeum or the Garrick, but discreet sporting ones like Achilles and Dacre.

There are, says one of his old masters, photographs of the eighteen-year-old Bell walking with the young Queen Elizabeth II when she toured Brentwood School in 1957 and he was the head boy. There, or in the wings, were Griff Rhys Jones, Noel Edmunds and the writer Douglas Adams. Rodger Bell, he remembers, 'was an outstanding sportsman, academic, a fine chap'. He passed easily into Oxford (Brasenose College), and then glided through law school and up to the bar aged twenty-four. He shows none of the arrogance, tetchiness or impatience that marks so many of his peers; indeed he has a long record of public service: Bell has been chair of an NHS mental health tribunal and is on the Parole Board. On the evidence of this case alone, he is one of the most patient, even-handed men in the world and he has a reputation for great kindness and sense.

Steel and Morris are not the first people in court today. Already there, adjusting power leads, is Mr Riley, the court usher. They nod to him, dump their bags on their bench, lay out their papers and pencil cases as if this were an exam. Morris turns round to see who's come for the morning show. Justin, who has a peroxide-blond Mohican cut and earrings, has come a hundred miles from Nottingham to help take notes. Also there is Dan Mills, a former City lawyer who was unhappy in the corporate world and now coordinates the McLibel Support Campaign. There are two people at the back of the court whom he does not recognize. Morris pulls at his reindeer-covered pullover, adjusts his spectacles and settles down. Steel is ready.

Enter, stage right, Richard Rampton. The McDonald's' QC's footsteps make slipper sounds as he pads to his pew. Rampton is one of Britain's most formidable libel lawyers, the star of several recent high-profile spats, and now, like Bell in his fifties, a legal heavyweight in the prime of his professional life. He comes from a family of philanthropists who made their money with mail-order catalogues.

Rampton has a reputation for being wily, for knowing the libel law inside out and being a powerful advocate and a great psychological judger of judges and reader of juries. He flops his wig over his head like a grocer putting on his apron, harrumphs gruffly, glares over his steel-rimmed spectacles to Steel and Morris, sits down noisily, displays a pen that looks expensive enough to have paid for several witnesses to have flown in from the USA and does not turn round as Sid Nicholson, settling in behind him, calls, 'Morning, Richard.'

'Morning, Sid,' says Rampton, who is now fiddling loudly with his laptop computer which will flash up the steno-graphers' recordings of every word spoken in court that day. Sidney Nicholson is a McDonald's UK vice-president and looks the part. He has thirty-one years' police experience in the Met and South Africa, rising to chief superintendent. He used to run McDonald's' security in the UK, and was also in charge of personnel, and is now in court most days. Today the florid-complexioned ex-cop is sitting with a wry smile and a thin-faced American corporate lawyer.

Next to them is Patti Brinley-Codd, McDonald's' senior solicitor. She is jangling with gold, cheerful and voluble. She brings her own drama to the Royal Courts theatre. Today she is flamboyantly rigged to look like the pilot of a supertanker about to negotiate thick fog and treacherous waters. There, too, is Timothy Atkinson, Rampton's junior counsel, who works in the same chambers. He wears his wig rakishly, does Timothy.

The court arises and in a moment Sir Rodger enters magisterially. He is greeted with warm and suitably deferential 'm'luds' by 'm'learned friends' from McDonald's on his right and curt nods from Morris and Steel on the other side. He briskly starts the day's proceedings. Where the McDonald's team tend to sport Armani and Savile Row, and Steel and Morris's friends wear jeans and T-shirts, Mr Justice Bell is the very image of British sartorial justice – white ermine half-sleeves, red (McDonald's' red) sash over his shoulder, full wig, gold glasses, white tie and black gown. The court, having arisen, is seated.

Today Ray Cesca, from Head Office in Illinois, will be in the witness-box all day. He is lean, relaxed, his hands thrust deep into his trousers. Steel cross-examines him first. She is intuitive, sharp, and she picks off her points, firing a series of quick questions. She will try to steer him this way and that, lasso him with detail. Sometimes there will be considerable pauses between questions and answers and at one point a painful three-minute silence until it emerges that Cesca has misunderstood Steel's London accent and does not realize that he has been asked a question. At other times the cross-examination will flow gently, like a river on flat ground, until it peters out, the inexperienced defendant bogged down. After lunch it will be Morris's turn to cross-examine him. Where Steel is subtle, he works more off the cuff, working from rough notes and seeking always to make broader political points. She is more methodical, prepares more. They've tended to split up the issues between them. She leads on areas like advertising and animal welfare. He is more at home with traditional workplace conflicts. The two complement each other like spin and speed bowling in a cricket match. It's a nice Jeff and Mutt routine.

Rampton will not question the witness today but, trained to be alert to a judge's every whim and nuance, the legal heavyweight will be on guard at all points. Now he fiddles with a ruler and appears mighty bored, now he pores over maps of Costa Rica. It is theatre: in an instant he will be alive, and the mouth, normally set like one half of the McDonald's arches, will be mobile, flashing his professional appreciation of Mr Justice Bell or his disapproval of the style, the manner, the substance or the direction of the defendants' questions. Constitutionally unable to remain quiet for long, he will emit frequent titanic harrumphs, interject under his breath and at one point will give an astonishingly loud, 'TUT!' It will be a masterly performance from someone not involved in the questioning – all jowl-shaking, mock irascibility and gamesmanship.

And Mr Justice Bell will lean forward, paternally, and try to help the defence with the legal points, play legal tutor. Steel and Morris at times struggle with a system, code, structure and form of thinking that is totally alien to them. Bell must devote time to helping them formulate their legal arguments, guide them through the thickets of libel law. To complicate matters they have very different temperaments and respond differently to his advice.

At times the proceedings are tortuous—

Bell: 'I thought you had grasped that yesterday . . .'

'I said this in the note I gave you which was designed to help you over a year ago . . .'

'Just please listen . . . I'm trying to help you . . .'

'Shush a moment. I'm trying to clarify . . .'

'This is a genuine attempt to try to help you.'

—with the judge trying to simplify, condense and synthesize their arguments:

Bell: 'What I think you are trying to say is . . .'

'The note I would make for your benefit . . .'

'What I've put down is that McDonald's . . .'

'I understand your point and I will take it into consideration in trying to work out what I think you mean . . .'

Steel and Morris take notes of his points. But law students as they are without grants, it's like a university tutorial gone mad:

Bell: 'Let me see if I can get you started here . . .'

'You would say that this decision is only worsened by them . . .'

'I'm very keen to see what you have to say about . . .'

'No, not that law book, this one . . .'

'Can I give you an example from this case . . .'

And just as Bell tries to teach Morris and Steel to be good lawyers, so they will try to teach him to be a good anarchist:

Morris: 'This is where the hunger comes in . . .'

Bell: 'I see . . .'

Steel: 'McDonald's is just one part of capitalism . . .'

Bell: 'And . . .?'

Morris: 'So the result of their activity is equivalent to a colonial invasion . . .'

Bell: 'Yes . . .?'

Morris: 'Yes.'

The strain of the case is now telling on all the characters. Everyone thinks it has gone on absurdly long, but because its terms of reference are so broad there is no fair or feasible way to shorten it. Steel now works two nights a week until 3.30 a.m. in a West End bar not just to earn enough to live on, but to get away from the case.

It has, too, become personal; a modern legal soap opera. All parties claim that they have no personal feelings for the others in the courtroom, but it is clear from the way they talk – or do not even acknowledge each other – that there are deep divisions. Steel has nightmares, she says, of Rampton, whose gauntlets she cannot resist picking up and regretting it; she is sick, too, of not having a life outside. Meanwhile Morris resents the fact that the case is damaging his relationship with his son, Charlie. Rampton seems horrified by the proceedings and unable at times to disguise his personal distaste.

For Morris and Steel it can be slow torture, too. Both have given up a private life for three years. The stress has been terrible, say both. The media likes to paint them as the only people able to challenge the corporation, since they have no real assets and therefore 'nothing to lose', yet they stand to be made bankrupt, to go to prison, to lose everything they have and may ever have.

After twenty months in Court 35 the case has bedded down into an almost existential dialogue about truth, image, the nature of subversion and honesty. On one level Steel and Morris are defending themselves on charges of libel. They are trying to prove that the details of the Factsheet which it is alleged they distributed when they were supporters of a small group called London Greenpeace (which predates and is nothing to do with the global environmental group) are legally accurate. The judge will have to decide on matters never before raised in the British courts about environmental resources in the widest sense – the treatment of nature and people. The case includes human rights, animal welfare, diet and disease, rainforests, food safety and the effects of advertising on children. Already there have been sections on the working conditions of teenagers, corporate attitudes to trade unions and plastic and cardboard packaging.

Just below the nitty-gritty of these often scientific questions is another layer of questions which examines the business conduct of McDonald's and of massive corporations that can wield more financial clout and political power than countries. All the linen of a global corporation is being inspected – how it thinks, acts and treats the world. Below this are more political and moral levels of the case: the issues of censorship and freedom of speech on both sides. Should people who offer a genuine critique of corporations be liable to lose everything? Should everyone have proper legal representation for libel? Should corporations have the right to sue individuals? What responsibility do pressure groups or indeed corporations have to tell the truth? Is justice only available to the rich?

And down near the core of the case are questions of image and of rights: moral, legal and human. Right at the centre is the million-dollar question that Steel and Morris always want to address: if two alternative worlds are here on show, what kind of society do people really want? At times McLibel – as the case has widely become known – is like a humdrum industrial tribunal; sometimes it broadens into a public inquiry; occasionally it floods its banks and is allowed to question how we all conduct our lives.

McDonald's says, metaphorically, 'Whoaaaa. Hold on, mister.' Just as the corporation now wants to put a cordon sanitaire around what is going on in Court 35 and would like to keep it a little local English affair, so, too, it does not want to discuss any of the issues that the trial raises until the case is over and – it appears pretty confident that it is going well – the verdicts are given.

Sometimes it's hard being McDonald's, but the corporation, like its clown Ronald McDonald, puts on a smile. By Day 222 of the case, without any fear of an unpredictable jury responding emotionally, they say it is going 'overwhelmingly' in their favour. The flak-catchers argue that the case is not political in any way. It's about protecting the corporation's reputation and about having to stand up against what it believes are foul allegations. It wants to keep the case carefully defined. The chief of communications says: 'We believe that we have a trust placed in us. A lot of people trust McDonald's. The allegations challenge that trust and if we don't stand up then it would be seen that there is some truth in the allegations.'

The case, it argues, is simple enough. These two Londoners have made statements that damage the good name of the corporation, and having spent years building up a strong image and trust with its customers it now has no option but to make Steel and Morris prove them, apologize or pay for them. It knows that Morris and Steel have no assets so what it wants is legal judgements against them. Once it has got the verdicts in these areas – which it believes will be to their favour – it can use them to advantage. It's a high-risk strategy but with the legal odds stacked in its favour, it can take the view that £5 million – or £10 million, or whatever it takes – to pay for Mr Rampton and his team will be worth it.

McLibel is tortuous, bizarre and unwieldy. It has its own momentum, logic, characters, pace, lore and references. It is often mind-bogglingly dull, sometimes riveting, often revelatory and usually surreal – as befits a case where American corporatism, Western materialism and the British Establishment are closeted with two people who describe themselves as anarchists and who propose a different society. There are echoes of First and Third Worlds, the sight of vast wealth being daily pitted against absurd poverty, of one set of values crashing against another.

Above all, though, McLibel is a battle of image, an appeal by both sides for the hearts and minds of the public. McDonald's' slick, clean, focused image is bought with a $1,800 million a year television and marketing budget. Steel and Morris's support campaign has spent perhaps $8,500 printing leaflets in the past four years and twice that sending letters, e-mails and faxes to their supporters around the world. And, to McDonald's dismay, a massive Website on the Internet called McSpotlight has been opened. It contains 1,500 files, twenty-five megabytes of information, millions of critical words. In its first week the site has been accessed 174,000 times.

Normally a plaintiff would be able to limit what comes out in an English libel case. The party who has been allegedly damaged can effectively sit back and say, 'Well, you claimed this, now you prove it.' But in a deft legal move following a leaflet put out by McDonald's, Steel and Morris have counter-sued the corporation for accusing them of lying over the same sixteen charges levelled at them. This means that McDonald's is in the dock with them. Both parties now have the onus to prove that in law the other side has wronged them.

The stakes get higher by the day for McDonald's. The popular interpretation at this stage is that big US business has drawn the legal sword thinking that everyone would bow before it. It is, says Mark Stephens, a legal commentator and senior partner of Stephens Innocent (a London firm of solicitors), a miscalculation on several counts: 'The multinational culture lacks an understanding of individual countries' characteristics.'

For all that British culture may be progressively being dominated by America, big US business is still seen as something alien here. There is still a fierce defence of the underdog, a sense of fair play. However much people are told by politicians, football managers, the press or business leaders that the only important thing in any contest is to win, there is a proud delight in Britain as elsewhere of seeing giants felled, bullies getting their come-uppance, the amateur beating the professional and the underdog having a day.

Did McDonald's underestimate the dogged mentality that Steel and Morris represent? The stubbornness of people who stand up for what they believe is right and refuse to back down against the odds is a powerful British self-image. Moreover civil disobedience in pursuit of a liberal cause or high principles is socially justified, even respected in the courts. Stephens is adamant: 'This case is big US business, the multinational culture, showing an appalling lack of understanding of British individuals.' McDonald's, he believes, was clearly worried enough to want to squash these people who were fundamentally not a problem. 'Now they can't get out and many people believe that they have turned a flea-bite on their big toe into a pustulating boil all over the body corporate.'

We are near the end of Day 222. Ray Cesca has been in the witness-box all day. He has parried Steel, held off Morris, been deferential to the judge, appealed to Rampton, fallen back on corporation-speak. He has painted the corporation as a boon, told how McDonald's is now involved in re-forestation projects, how communities everywhere welcome McDonald's and how the corporation invests large sums of money when its comes in to countries for the first time.

You can almost hear Morris gag.

Morris: '. . . because you want the publicity to counter the adverse publicity you have been getting about the effects of cattle ranching . . .?'

Cesca: 'That is untrue . . . you are speaking without knowledge of our company and the culture . . . it started with Ray Kroc [the corporation's founder] when he opened his first store in 1955.'

Morris: 'But you were not there then.'

Cesca: 'But that does not mean it did not start.'

Morris: 'But you do not know?'

Cesca: 'Yes, I do.'

Morris: 'But Ray Kroc might have hated the environment, for all you know?'

Morris and Steel have well ruffled the smooth-suited executive, but it's Cesca's opening, the moment he has been waiting for all day. The corporation man can now tell the judge just what McDonald's stands for, what McDonald's really is. The vice-president of the largest restaurant chain in the world tells how when the militias were out on the streets and the Noriega regime was collapsing in Panama McDonald's was there feeding the poor and looking after the children; how it was McDonald's that was the first one feeding and distributing and helping the families when the earthquake hit Kobe in Japan; and how when the Mississippi River burst its banks and flooded St Louis, McDonald's was there first, too.

You can hear a pin drop. Rampton looks up. Steel stares

hard at the corporation man justifying his world. The judge looks impassively down, but Ray Cesca has not finished. He goes on to tell how McDonald's 'engenders community spirit', and how people 'who participate in McDonald's think so much of the restaurants that they would think of involving a McDonald's restaurant in the protection of their own home and how common that is . . .' He pauses, sincerely. Morris leans back, smiling, as if he has heard it before.

Cesca: 'I know you are smiling, I am sorry you are doing that . . .'

It is a faint hallooo over the cultural and political canyons that separate the two sides, blips from Mars picked up on Venus. But there is no real recognition. Cesca has suggested a thought process, belief system, philosophy and purpose utterly alien to that of Morris and Steel. There can be no meeting. Each side believes utterly what it says. Both corporation and critics are possessed by their own vision of wanting to do good. Where McDonald's represents to Steel and Morris a system of unaccountable authority, globalism and the mass-industrial culture, they represent to the corporation a damned nuisance. And if for Cesca the world can be brought together with profits and efficiency, with money, control and organiz-ation, for Morris and Steel what the world really needs is more humanity. Their worlds are based on different values. But for a moment in Court 35 the two stand in perfect opposition to each other.

Mr Justice Bell clears his throat discreetly. This patient man will shortly declare Day 222 over. Cesca will step down, and return to the corporate folds in Illinois; Rampton and the judge will head to their families. Steel will take the rush-hour Underground back to her Tottenham flat and try to prepare for the next day, while Morris will pick up Charlie from his after-school club, make him a meal and read him a story.

Chapter Two

Da Do Ron, Ron . . .

'We sold them a dream and paid them as little as possible.'

– Ray Kroc.

Tottenham, London N17, 23 August 1996: Ronald McDonald's white Cadillac sweeps through down-at-heel North London. It's pouring with rain as the car goes through the metal park gates and up the drive to the Tower Gardens Play Scheme Centre. It is met by a group of quiet, overawed children clutching their parents' hands.

Ronald, an advertising spokesman for the world's largest hamburger company, has been invited to the annual Fun Day. The summer event is one of the highlights of the year for the group, which is subsidized by the council and attracts more than a hundred four-to-eight-year-olds a week. Parents have made sandwiches and teas and more than two hundred people are expected to come. The council has closed off the public park for the day to show how important they consider the event and there's a marquee, balloons and jellies. Pickles the clown has been quietly twisting balloons into sausage dogs and amusing the children before Ronald arrives. She will not try to compete.

When the best-known clown in the world gets out of the chauffeur-held door you see he is six feet tall, has red hair, bright red-and-yellow clothes, a white face and yellowing teeth. The rain has streaked his chalky cheeks, making Ronald look desolate behind the smiles and showbiz. He holds out his hand, pats the children on the head, and winks at the grown-ups. He asks people how they are. Two children attach themselves to his left leg, one to his right. He is loved. He has his arm round another and by the time he is in the corridor of the building there are screams of excitement. In minutes he has sixty children sitting on the floor in front of him or in chairs. Ronald starts his act.

'Hello, my little fries,' he says. 'I'm Ronald. Hands up those of you who have seen me before.' There's an instant forest of hands. The younger children are unsure what to make of the figure in front of them. Ronald, who does several shows a day, tells them he will do magic for them. His audience is spellbound.

Meanwhile nine or ten smart, clean-cut men and women in blue uniforms and spiffy white shirts stand at the back of the hall. The men are mostly bull-necked, buttoned-down and quiet. Some look as ill at ease in their suits as they seem out of place amongst the bouncy castle inflatables, and the hand-written signs saying 'NO FIGHTING', 'NO SWEARING', 'NO RACISM', 'NO BULLYING' and 'NO HIDING IN THE BUSHES'. Some have their arms folded. When asked, they tell no one their names, except that they work for McDonald's. A woman with tightly tied hair talks into a mobile phone. She smiles to anyone she thinks is a parent.

She speaks not for herself but for the corporation. 'We're so delighted to be here,' she gushes. 'The effect Ronald has on the children is just wonderful. It's worth it just to see their smiles. This is fantastic. We heard about this place and we thought we just had to help. We've got this community fund, you know . . .'

McDonald's has brought twelve people to the play scheme.

They have promised a £500 donation, advertised the show in the local restaurants, taken over the advertisements in the local paper, brought their balloons and orange squash and promotional materials. For a cash-strapped playgroup which has seen its grant fall and expenses spiral, it's a godsend.

But not for all the parents. Suna Mohamed, and at least six other women in Tower Gardens today, are furious with the corporation. What began in goodwill as a play scheme's Fun Day has, she says, become a McDonald's promotion. Many parents and residents who read the publicity thought the event had been organized by McDonald's and not them. Besides, she says, half the money, far from being an outright donation to the group, goes to pay for a marquee which McDonald's staff have taken over.

As Ronald McDonald gets into one act another is taking place at the back of the hall. Tower Gardens Play Centre is where Dave Morris's son, Charlie, goes to.

Large man (to Morris): 'Who are you?'

Morris: 'Who are *you*?'

Large man: 'It doesn't matter what my name is.'

Morris: 'Why are you here?'

Large man: 'I'm following orders.'

Morris: 'Who from?'

(Enter Large Man Two)

Large man two: 'OK, what is the problem?'

Morris: 'Where are you from?'

Large man two: 'Have you had an invitation?'

Morris: 'This is my son's play scheme.'

Man two: 'Can someone call the police?'

Morris: 'What's your name?'

Man two: 'It doesn't matter.'

At the front of the hall, Ronald McDonald is doing his patter. 'OK, my little fries, let's get on with the show. And who are you?'

Stephanie: 'I'm Stephanie.'
Ronald: 'How old are you?'
Stephanie: 'I'm six.'
Ronald: 'Have you got a boyfriend, Stephanie?'
Stephanie: (silence)
Ronald: 'Would you like a boyfriend?'
(All laugh.)

A policeman arrives and, flanked by McDonald's men, asks Morris for a word. Morris says no, he intends to watch the show with his son, thank you. He sits in the middle of the children.

Ronald: 'Have we said hello to the policeman, children?'

For twenty minutes the children gawp and cheer and the McDonald's men stand around. Suna thinks it's all a shame. 'I feel physically sick. These children cannot protect themselves. It's just a way for McDonald's to sell more products.'

The show ends with Ronald half-suggesting that the children might like to eat at his place. There are cheers. At this point, the Deputy Mayor of the London Borough of Haringey calls in. He is wearing his chain of office and calls for respect for different cultures. But Suna is still furious. 'The only culture on offer to our children here is the opportunity to purchase a burger. It's degrading,' she says. Outside, in the marquee, corporation men make up the faces of the children.

Quite when McDonald's identified children as one of the main arteries of its operation is not clear, but the corporation's growth has long been associated with little people. Ray Kroc, the founder of the empire, who in 1954 saw through the golden arches of the McDonald brothers to unparalleled wealth, immediately recognized the power of the young to influence adults, and that McDonald's' food appealed to the unsophisticated child's palate. The bright red and yellow of the sign, the strong simple tastes, the fun factor of eating unselfconsciously in public, the bright lights, even the speed and the quick, undemanding encounter between staff and customer, were all attractive to the young.

Not that Kroc was personally overfond of teenagers. He allowed no jukeboxes and cigarette machines, and at first even female staff because he said they tended to 'attract' teenage males. Teenagers were better off working than staying in school, he wrote in his autobiography. He was proud of not valuing traditional education too highly. His famous business motto, borrowed from Colonel Sanders, was 'KISS' – Keep It Simple, Stupid. Kroc had no high-school diploma, no great qualifications beyond his proven ability as a salesman. 'There are too many baccalaureates and not enough butchers,' he said. Now 66 per cent of McDonald's' 1.5 million staff worldwide are under twenty-one.

But Kroc knew how to get through to children. His first national advertising campaign ended with 10 million children responding. A great deal of study, he wrote, went into creating the appearance and personality of Ronald McDonald, right down to the colour and texture of the wig. Kroc loved Ronald as a way to advertise his burgers. Importantly, it was the kids who decided where to eat out in three out of four families. Kroc offered them other characters from McDonaldland – like the Hamburglar, Mayor McCheese, the Fry Kids and the Happy Meal Guys. But Ronald was always the favourite. In 1986, the corporation claimed that 96 per cent of children polled could identify Ronald. Only Santa Claus did better.

The appeal to youth has been intense. What began with Ronald McDonald in 1963 moved on to students in Wisconsin. Those with As on their report cards were offered free hamburgers.

Some television ads were aimed at young children, others at young adults. Some were pitched at grandparents who might be tempted to take children to McDonald's, and others at parents. The concept of linking the name of the corporation with youth moved quickly into setting up restaurants on campuses, offering to provide school meals, sponsoring child achievement competitions and funding children's hospitals. Today McDonald's ties its products to films, to sports, environmental issues – the faithful fellow-travellers of Western under-twenty-year-olds.

But above all, Kroc wanted McDonald's to be seen as a good corporate citizen, helping the young and needy. The first 'Ronald McDonald House' opened in 1974. These are built next to hospitals and provide accommodation for families of children with serious illnesses. There are now 166 worldwide, including three in Britain. Much of McDonald's' community involvement revolves around children – child welfare, education, youth-related social issues and environment, says the *McDonald's Fact Book*. The figures are impressive: Ronald McDonald Children's Charities had given by 1996 grants of more than $100 million since it started in 1984. In that time the corporation made approximately $9 billion net profit on a turnover of more than $120 billion. Put another way, for every $12 that McDonald's turned over in the period it donated 1 cent to children, which is about 0.167 per cent; or for every 90 cents profit that it banked, it gave 1 cent, or about 1.112 per cent. Depending on the country it was operating in and the tax regimes, much of the giving could be set against tax. Other corporations give far less or nothing at all.

Kroc, billionaire creator of the empire, only had one child, who died young. In other ways, too, Kroc's life can seem sad. He was not a man, you might think, to be pitied, but the story of his early years is of relentless struggle, someone pinched by big businesses, pinioned by punitive financial deals, always facing an ugly struggle against poverty and debts. Here was the archetypal little man fighting for survival in harsh conditions but showing a steely refusal to be crushed: 'I was an overnight success all right, but thirty years is a long, long night,' he said.

He was fifty-two when he first saw the McDonald brothers' arches, in San Bernardino, and he had diabetes – the diabetes which was later to limit his own intake of burgers – and the beginnings of arthritis. He had lost his gall bladder and most of his thyroid gland. He says he had 'rather wiry hair' and (here was a man whose self-image was low) a 'moustache which grew right down into my mouth. It was a horrible brownish-red colour'. In short, Kroc makes himself seem so crocked it's unlikely he would have got a job in one of his restaurants these days.

He was born in Chicago in 1902 to Eastern European parents who had fled oppression. His father was with the Post Office. When he was four, a phrenologist predicted that he would become a chef or at least work with food. At school, he set up a lemonade stand. He left at fifteen and sold coffee beans door to door. The First World War was starting, and lying about his age in his enthusiasm to get in he enlisted to drive an ambulance in France. In his company was another teenager who had also lied about his age, and who would grow up to be, if anything, more influential even than McDonald's on the psyches of the world's children . . . a loner who preferred doodling comic characters to hanging out with the boys. Walt Disney.

To Kroc's disappointment, the Armistice was signed just before his unit left for Europe. He returned to Chicago, where according to his biography he became a successful jazz pianist, working for various outfits including a radio station, a brothel and a speakeasy called the Silent Night. He describes coming home with his fingers swollen and almost bleeding, feeling exploited and complaining of 'getting a dirty deal'. This was Prohibition time in Chicago. One night, Revenue agents stormed the speakeasy that Kroc was working in. He ended up in prison. 'We were only there three hours but it was one of the most uncomfortable 180 minutes of my life.'

At twenty-three he took his wife and baby daughter to Florida, to work for one of the biggest property companies as a salesman. He was selling land that couldn't actually be built on: 'The property was underwater,' he admitted, 'but there was a solid bed of coral beneath.' He moved on to selling paper cups just when paper cups were big. Always, though, he saw himself as a victim of 'the System'. Finally, he found a product he thought he could promote for himself: a 'Multi-mixer' for making milk shakes. But the company he was working for demanded a crippling buy-out clause. His boss 'made a bargain with me that the devil himself would have been proud of . . . This was the first phase of grinding it out . . . building my personal monument to capitalism. I paid tribute in the feudal sense for many years before I was able to rise with McDonald's on the foundation I had laid.' He borrowed $85,000, was broke and on Mortgage Hill. Kroc, like America, was gripped in a passion for wealth. Free enterprise was the American way and everyone was dreaming big.

The assembly line, the Model-T Ford, the rise of bureaucracy, centralized thinking, technology and scientific management were all encouraging a desire for homogeneity at the same time as they were providing the means to create sameness. Army rations in Europe had been the staple diet of American troops and were the forerunner of fast food. Mass production of everything from armaments to agricultural machinery had been in place for years and was known as the 'American System'. 'The US led the world in exploiting the advantages of systematic mass production,' says Angus Buchanan, Professor of History of Technology at Bath University.

And then came the stock market crash which ushered in

the Great Depression. It killed Kroc's father, who was 'crushed beneath a pile of deeds he could not sell' and died of a cerebral haemorrhage in 1930. He had 'worried himself to death', said his son. The Depression hardened Kroc's drive to succeed. The 1930s were awful for the poor. Two in three people earned no more than the minimum to survive. Millions of acres of farmland were left to dry up and blow away as hundreds of thousands of small farmers fled the land; industrial work was hard and badly rewarded, if there was any to be found. Over and again Kroc had to fight for his economic life; very occasionally he was on easy street but mostly the man who seemed only able to sell was an entrepreneur in search of a niche.

Fifty years on, it is tempting to see that it was the harsh underside of life in Thatcher's Britain which produced a similar determination in Steel and Morris. In one sense, they have an inverse affinity with the founder of the empire which they have done more than anyone else to challenge. The 1980s in Britain saw a rapidly widening gap between rich and poor, thousands of young people homeless, the sale of state enterprises for a song and the deeply unpopular poll tax which sought to make the poorest pay the same as the richest for local authority services. It saw organized labour effectively shackled, and the mining industry crushed. Nor was there much hope in party politics: the opposition was neutered. The left wing was crumbling.

But where Steel and Morris, who see themselves (like Kroc) as allied to the ordinary person, fought 'the System' and all that it represented, Kroc became its epitome, even calling the McDonald's production method 'the System'. In Kroc's case, the bullied and exploited 'little man' yearned to be a winner and top dog. Steel and Morris, rather, threw themselves into a struggle to change a system which they believe forced the majority to be losers and the bullied became not bullies in turn but allies of other victims.

1954, London, England. Morris, David, is born.
1954, San Bernardino, USA. Kroc, Ray, is born again.

The small town of San Bernardino on the edge of the California desert is an unlikely place for a burger bar to be ringing up $250,000 per year. Ray Kroc has gone there to sell his Multimixers. As he watches the two McDonald brothers and their helpers in 'spiffy white shirts and white paper hats, bustling around like ants at a picnic ... and a steady procession of customers lockstepping up to the windows', he has a vision of riches. He likes what he sees. He likes the set of arches with neon tubes lighting the underside, but mostly he likes the idea of the place. Here is a restaurant stripped down to the basics, in terms of service and in choice. Everything is prepared on the assembly line basis ... speed, volume, low price. It is the food equivalent of the Model-T Ford. He stays to admire. He tells the brothers he 'wants in'.

Kroc also liked the name. McDonald's, it seemed, harked back to a nursery rhyme and old barnyard songs. The name, an unofficial biography of the company would say, 'appealed to the six-year-old mind, just as the food appealed to the six-year-old palate'. 'I had a feeling that it would be one of those promotable names that would catch the public fancy,' Kroc wrote. But the brothers McDonald were by all accounts both fussy and thrifty, whittling away anything wasteful in their food conveyor belt. They were cautious but happy with the fat profits they were making. And they weren't that enthusiastic about Kroc's involvement.

Kroc was tenacious. He did a deal with the brothers that he could have rights to give licences to other people to copy the 'McDonald's' operation across the USA. This wasn't a new idea. 'Franchising' had been promoted by the Singer Sewing Machine company after the American Civil War and had been taken up by many retail businesses and even restaurants since. The agreement specified that Kroc could not alter anything in their plans for the units unless the changes were spelled out in writing, signed by both brothers and posted to Kroc registered mail. It put the Chicago man in an impossible legal stranglehold. He could not even add a basement or an oven to the original plans.

Kroc wanted all rights, copyrights, formulas, trade marks, the Golden Arches and the name. He offered $500,000. He ended up paying $2.7 million which he didn't have. At the last, if only to rub salt in the open wound of Kroc's bank balance, the McDonald brothers insisted on keeping the original store. It 'forced me into grinding it out, grunting and sweating like a galley slave for every inch of progress'. Kroc's response, in the end, was to open his own McDonald's right across the street from the original McDonald's and run the brothers out of business. Kroc moved back to Chicago and founded the McDonald's Corporation in March 1955. On 15 April the McDonald's empire began to grow, with Kroc opening his first new restaurant at Des Plaines, just outside Chicago.

It coincided, almost to the week, with the first significant expansion of another radical Chicago operation. On the opposite side of town from McDonald's, the Chicago School of Economics was gaining intellectual ground for its espousal of free-market economic policies and a radical, dissenting, anti-Establishment culture that was starting to prove deeply attractive to the political Right and the corporate world.

In June 1955, four Chicago economics professors arrived in Santiago, Chile's capital, to launch a US government funded research programme at the new centre for economic research at the Catholic University. The professors were to teach crusading Chicago School economic theory to the middle- and upper-class sons of the Chilean Right and there began a major exchange programme between the two university economics departments backed by scholarships and postgraduate studies.

Chile was then a democratic Socialist state. The 'Chicago boys' – as the American-trained students began to be known – 'shared a conservative religious background, a total rejection of Socialism and a deep contempt for Chile's freewheeling mass democracy' according to political scientist Arturo Valensuela. Where Keynesianism in the West and central planning in the Communist world were still voguish, they were urged by their mentors to tear down trade barriers, liberate the market and revolutionize the relationship between the people and the state. The advantage would, it was said, pass to corporations whose wealth would benefit all.

Amongst others, three future Nobel Prize-winning Chicago School economists, Theodore Schulz, Milton Friedman and George Stigler, helped teach the Chileans their market theories. Within a few years of the link being established between the two universities, eight 'Chicago boys' had been commissioned by senior members of the Chilean armed forces and American industries to draft a massive economic plan to be put in place when and if the Communist President Salvador Allende was toppled.

While the Chicago professors were training a generation of students to develop and influence the global economy to favour the likes of McDonald's, Kroc was laying down the cornerstones of his financial empire. One empire was to radically change the diet of hundreds of millions of people, the other would intellectually colonize every country in the world. Kroc's dog-eat-dog, rat-eat-rat business philosophy and the economists' worship of the market would spread around the world, each complementing the other. The era of

control passing from government to corporations was beginning and Kroc was to become the epitome of the economic
system that the university men preached.

Ray Kroc was obsessed with efficiency. He had a highly
developed sense of order and control, spearheading the principles of rationalization and uniformity that would later
become the dominant characteristic of the age. His first
Operations Manual, in 1958, spelt out how the franchises
should be run. It was control run amok: operators were told
precisely how to grill or fry. Exact cooking times and temperatures were stated. Portions were fixed down to quarter-ounces
of onions and thirty-two slices per pound of cheese. The basic
hamburger patty was to weigh 1.6 ounces and measure 3.785
inches in diameter, containing no more than 17–20.5 per cent
fat. 'Grill men' had to move left to right, put out six rows of
burgers, flip the third row first, then the fourth, fifth and sixth
before the first and second. The hamburger appealed because
there was only one way to prepare it. It was a simple product.
Kroc wanted a standardized menu, one-sized portions, same
prices, same quality everywhere.

The first McDonald's *Operations Manual* had seventy-five
pages. Since then it has become a fast-food bible, a six-
hundred-page 'McWorld' where everything that takes in a
McDonald's store has a reason, everything must be uniform,
predictable and homogeneous. Just as Henry Ford's principles
were that workers' movements were to be reduced to a
minimum and that parts were to travel the least possible
distance, so Kroc emphasized the calculable, the quantifiable,
the controllable. This, said sociologist George Ritzer, author
of the classic *McDonaldization of Society*, led inevitably to
the conclusion that quality equated with size.

The formula worked, and McDonald's grew fatter each
year, even though Kroc's profits didn't. By 1959, he had sold

over a hundred franchises with no risk to himself whatever and was turning over millions of dollars a year, but his income, he complained, was still being ploughed back or paid in fees to the brothers McDonald. Real financial success only came when the company went down the real-estate road. It was to be the one thing that marked McDonald's out from all the other wannabe big franchisers. The McDonald's empire, which would in time help to determine global agriculture, knew that its control had to extend even to the land itself.

Back at the start, all Kroc's franchisees either leased their own properties directly from a landlord or bought the land themselves. They put up their own buildings based on their ability to finance them. McDonald's saw that it needed more than just percentage profits. The idea was daring; it would require the franchisee to lease their premises to the corporation, which would then sublease the property back, so giving the corporation absolute control over the property and the business practices of the franchisee. All new franchises were to be run like this.

It was a neat business. Having got control over the franchisee, Kroc started charging a 6 per cent rent of gross sales on top of the royalty due under the franchise agreement. Richard Frankel, who was Vice-President of the McDonald's Operators' Association (MOA), a collection of established but concerned McDonald's franchisees, says that in simple economic terms Kroc 'was able to increase his income by 300 per cent without investing a nickel, without giving any service to the franchisee ... McDonald's was not paying a dime for advertising, or exploiting its trade mark and trade name. All of that was paid for by the franchisee.'

It got better and better. The next step in quite legal empire building was to use the franchisee's dollars to buy land and construct buildings that McDonald's would own and to insist that the corporation could throw people out when their lease had expired. After this, McDonald's' success snowballed. By 1962 total sales soared to over $76 million. In 1963, the five hundredth restaurant opened. The five hundredth student graduated from the Corporation's training centre, called Hamburger University, and Ronald McDonald, icon of Americana, and controversial star of Tottenham play centres, made his debut. By the 1970s the McDonald's Corporation might have been said to be as much a real-estate company as a hamburger business.

But the price of massive expansion, and becoming a cash machine which was pushing his franchisees to what seemed the limit, was open revolt – the first in the corporation's history. MOA members felt that the ground rules were loaded against them. By 1975 they had started lobbying Congress and then going to court to try to limit Kroc's right to terminate their licences. Some challenged the company over its real-estate policy. Kroc responded robustly to this collective pressure, seemingly giving way, then coming back with proposals for licences that were interpreted as even more objectionable. The franchisees collected $100,000 to prepare for litigation. The corporation for once caved in.

But nothing would stop the ketchup flowing. From the mid-1960s McDonald's was experiencing rise after rise of popularity. In 1965, just ten years after the first Kroc restaurant, the corporation went public. A year later it was listed on the New York Stock Exchange. In 1967, the first McDonald's restaurants opened outside the USA, in Canada and Puerto Rico. By 1974, sales surpassed $1 billion and the three thousandth McDonald's restaurant opened in Woolwich, South-East London, the first in the UK. Within four years, the five thousandth restaurant opened in Kanagawa in Japan. The Chicago boy had changed the eating patterns of a continent and was taking on the world.

*

Meanwhile the other Chicago experiment was reaching its first peak. Many of the Chilean 'Chicago boys' had moved into influential positions in corporations, academe and government. In 1973 the right wing, with significant help from the US government, murdered Allende and threw out his democratically elected government in a particularly bloody coup. Within hours, the generals had a copy of the Chicago School inspired economic master plan and within months the Chilean 'economic miracle' had begun. Following a visit by Milton Friedman to the country in 1977, Chicago-influenced ministers of the economy and finance were appointed. As Joseph Collins and John Lear have shown in *The Ecologist* magazine, there began a repression of all labour movements, the right to strike was outlawed and the right to organize labour was severely curtailed. Public assets were sold off at bargain, subsidized prices, millions of people were made unemployed, health care was cut back severely and a draconian shock treatment was unleashed to control inflation. The Chilean 'miracle' gave economic growth but it slashed the welfare state, made official unemployment rise to 30 per cent and has encouraged the plunder of the country's forest and fishing resources. The financial advantage went uniformly to the few.

Within two years Milton Friedman had been given the Nobel Prize for Economics and Margaret Thatcher had been elected Prime Minister of Britain. She soon approached Friedman to advise her. Under his and others' guidance she began to impose similar free-market economic policies. Meanwhile that other Ronald – Ronald Reagan – was to follow and the foundations of a ruthless Western corporate globalism were laid down in an open challenge to Socialism and welfarism.

America was changing, too. In 1977 the Bureau of Labor Statistics had reported that the average family was spending more money on transport than on food, but that the amount spent on cheap meals in restaurants was soaring. 'A family of four can save Mother two hours in the kitchen, eat and drink for about $5 and get back into their station wagon in fifteen minutes flat', wrote Jonathan Steele, the *Guardian*'s America correspondent. Even as he was writing, 200 high-school children were walking out in protest at the Board of Education trying to provide a salad as well as burgers for the annual picnic: 'We don't want to be pawns of a nutrition chess game,' said one child who called the new salad menu 'extreme'. 'Convenience foods are creating so much a cult of their own taste that the trend may be irreversible,' Jonathan Steele added perceptively.

Burger culture had been born and it carried with it all the trappings of a developing belief system. McDonald's was to become like a religion to many people who worked for it, with Kroc's 'disciples' described as 'revering' his principles. Kroc wrote that 'the French fry would become almost sacrosanct' for him, its preparation 'a ritual to be followed religiously'. A Big Mac has been described as the communion wafer of the consumer society and Kroc, not a church man, wrote of 'faith in McDonald's as if it were a religion . . . I've often said that I believe in God, family, and McDonald's . . . and in the office, that order is reversed'.

The commonality of this quasi-religious feeling was crucial to the corporation in its hiring and firing of personnel. Image was vital. People in contact with customers had to be seen as 'All-American boys', 'McDonald's men'. 'They must display such desirable traits as sincerity, enthusiasm, confidence and a sense of humour.' Image was and is all, and image must be single, homogeneous; one face, one smile, one man. As the one-time dean of Hamburger University – where McDonald's trains its managerial staff – put it: 'It gets so your blood turns to ketchup.'

The ketchup professors continue Kroc's mission, aiming, they say, to give their 'initiates' the feeling of belonging to a club, a select few who understand the system and will profit from its proven success. Every year McDonald's puts more than 400,000 fifteen-to-nineteen-year-olds through its basic on-the-job training, taking over from the US Army as America's largest job training organization. The training is on one level about how to prepare food; on another it is about 'standards', one of its managers told the *Wall Street Journal* in 1996. 'We're father, minister, rabbi, counsellor, big brother and boss.' A senior vice-president of the corporation said that McDonald's plays the same kind of 'crucial role' for young people as the army used to in teaching discipline, teamwork and routine.

The drill for hamburger people is compulsory enthusiasm and politeness – rudimentary skills for American adulthood – and a sense of belonging to a (successful) system that would transpose onto family values those of a corporation. One in ten Americans are now believed to have got their first job at a McDonald's. It has employed more than 10 million people.

The system may also be said to breed a fierce competitiveness and suspicion of opposition. Fred Turner, Kroc's successor, has been described as taking the *Insights* internal communications manual of McDonald's Corporation home with him every night in case someone read it who shouldn't. Kroc wrote: 'Fortunately we don't have too many begrudgers in the McDonald's organization. Their style doesn't suit ours, and they don't stay around long. But I have had people with us who seriously proposed that we plant spies in the operations of our competition. Can you imagine? Next thing we'd learn that Ronald McDonald is a double agent! My response to that kind of claptrap has always been that you can learn all you ever need to know about the competition's operation by looking in his garbage cans. I am not above that, let me assure

you, and more than once at two o'clock in the morning I have
sorted through a competitor's garbage.'

It's a tacky image – the one and only Hamburger King
prying through the bin bags of his competitors – and usually
as a corporation McDonald's tries harder to put its best face
forward. Image was all, and anyone tarnishing it met a fierce
response. Kroc: 'I get mad as hell and cuss when someone
takes cheap shots at McDonald's or me in print.'

Kroc must have cussed a lot in his later years. The more
McDonald's outgrew its beginnings, the more contentious its
cultural presence became and the more the detractors took
vitriolic shots at the corporation. In New York, an upmarket
anti-McDonald's campaign presented 11,000 signatures to the
mayor. It was backed by the *New York Times* Food Editor
who described a McDonald's burger as 'irredeemably horrid
. . . it is ground, kneaded and extruded by heavy machinery
that compacts it so that the texture is like that of a baloney
sausage . . . once cooked the burger is insulated in a soggy
bun, topped with pickle slices that seem recycled . . . or
shredded lettuce that is like wet confetti and one or another
of the disgusting sauces . . .' Kroc was incensed: 'Our development in New York City . . . was characterized by snobbish
writers as some sort of sinister plot. Here was Daddy War-
bucks dressed up like Ronald McDonald setting out to milk
money from an unsuspecting populace. What these fanatics
actually opposed was the capitalist system.'

The 'fanatics' were inside and outside. It's a feature of the
company that it has consistently paid its crew members – the
majority of its workers – at or near the legal minimum; and
the more that it has developed a system where everything is
minutely organized, the less the corporation has encouraged
its workers to organize themselves.

There were more than 400 attempts to set up unions in

McDonald's restaurants in the 1970s and Kroc resisted them all. The man who was paid to keep them out said bluntly that 'unions were inimical to what McDonald's stood for and how they operated'. Likewise McDonald's franchisees were among hundreds of businessmen who lobbied for an exemption to minimum wage laws so they could pay students less.

Outside, the public perception of the corporation was changing, too. There was an early Black protest against McDonald's. Before 1969, there were reportedly just five Black franchisees. Late that year, there were riots in Cleveland, and mass demonstrations and boycotting of McDonald's' stands in Black neighbourhoods. Kroc was to comment: 'We responded to the social changes of the late 1960s by increasing minority hiring. We've been a leader in advancing Black capitalism.'

Mostly, the allegations against McDonald's were as similar and predictable as the burgers themselves. McDonald's allegedly destroyed the character of a community; when the restaurants came local food outlets were driven out of business, and the specific local cuisine was made homogeneous and bland. Anti-McDonald's campaigns began on American student campuses, with posters illustrating Ronald McDonald holding a sign that read 'Boycott McDonald's'. One of the strongest criticisms was that the workers received the lowest wages on offer. Kroc was unapologetic: 'We sold them a dream and paid them as little as possible,' he said of the early company employees in his autobiography.

One of the fiercest struggles was in San Francisco, which had a strong history of unions and workers' protection. McDonald's was stalled for a year by the mayor, community groups and unions. McDonald's threw all its influence and legal and financial resources to defend the non-union shop but in the end not even San Francisco's united front could withstand Big Mac. Much came out – McDonald's managers were using lie detectors and crew members testified that they had been grilled about union sympathies – but after nearly a year and a half of litigation, pressure and appeals, McDonald's was finally issued a permit.

Quickly, all the things that has made McDonald's successful – its predictability, its uniformity and controls – were perceived by many liberal critics as mass produced and lacking individuality. Kroc's publicist saw the corporation being tagged 'part of the plastic society'. No longer could the corporation pretend to be apolitical, either. Kroc was found to have given Nixon $250,000 in 1972. It was linked by the press to Watergate and particularly to the corporation's trying to use political donations to seek governmental protection for raised prices and reduced wages.

And as it moved international, McDonald's became the butt of translators' jokes: a Big Mac in France became Gros Mec. The name was abandoned when it filtered back that 'gros mec' was French slang for 'big pimp'. Likewise when in a publicity stunt McDonald's sent a hamburger to the Mayor of Hamburg, he was, of course, to say, 'Hamburger? Hamburger? Ich bin ein hamburger!'

But far more dramatic things happened in Sweden. Bombs placed by left-wingers in protest at what they termed 'creeping American culturalism' exploded in Stockholm in 1975. Kroc once wrote, with a vivid blindness worthy of Nelson: 'People everywhere – from Japan to Sweden – are welcoming the Golden Arches.' Irony without intent.

Protest against McDonald's came from many sources, and McDonald's responses were often both defensive and aggressive. When *Fortune* magazine published an article criticizing the McDonald's arches for spoiling views, the company's secretary-treasurer riposted: 'Uninterrupted scenery, too, can get pretty monotonous.' Sometimes the corporation appeared at best insensitive. When it opened in Japan, with the memories of the Second World War very much alive, McDonald's chose to be in Hiroshima, close to where the first atom bomb exploded. The symbolism and the significance were not missed but the President of McDonald's' Japanese operations, Den Fujita, gave the relationship a further twist, stating: 'The reason Japanese people are so short and have yellow skins is because they have eaten nothing but fish and rice for two thousand years. If we eat McDonald's hamburgers and potatoes for a thousand years, we will become taller, our skin will become white and our hair will be blonde.'

World conquest is on the cards. The corporation now claims to be feeding 35 million people a day and is massively and aggressively expanding. Its 21,000 restaurants in 101 countries are just the start: it intends to add between 2,500 and 3,200 restaurants a year – one every three hours. Two-thirds of the new openings are from now on to be outside the USA, where the corporation sees wide open spaces where they can 'gain first-move advantage' over rivals like Burger King. In 1996 they moved into their hundredth country and, for the first time, earned more from their overseas restaurants than they did from McDonald's America, where business is stagnating: operating profits are expected to grow at more than 20 per cent a year over the next five years. Targeted areas include Eastern Europe, where they will have more than 350 restaurants by the end of 1997, Germany, where they intend to have 1,100 restaurants serving 2 million people a day within three years, and the Far East. In 1995 they moved into ten new countries. Why? Jim Cantalupo, President of the corporation's International Operation, says that countries are queuing up for McDonald's 'as a symbol of something – an economic maturity'.

McDonald's abroad does far more than provide food. Such quick service meals are uniquely American. The diet that McDonald's exports is alien to most cultures. McDonald's learned that globalization did not mean having to diversify or take account of indigenous foods or tastes and that through television and strong marketing they could 'teach' people, especially the young, that the diet they were promoting was good.

The effect the arches can have on communities is dramatic. The thought of them conjures something between loyalty and adoration from those people who see this sort of culture as a 'release' from their own political or personal oppression. The arrival of the Arches can mark a nation's place in the world economy, or be little short of the revolutionary in places which pride themselves on ways of life developed over centuries. If Kroc saw the arches first as a way out of his own grinding poverty, and secondly as a symbol of empire as powerful as any national flag, they have become for others a symbol of cultural colonialism, of uniformity, lack of choice, homogeneity – in short the Zeitgeist changing for the worse.

In India, where nationalists have targeted US corporations as culturally dangerous, McDonald's' presence is being challenged for ecological and animal welfare reasons. The corporation argues that it is effectively local, 'sourcing 98 per cent of its products from local companies', while politicians, and academics like Professor Vandana Shiva, have accused it and other fast-food chains of 'violating the right to cultural diversity, and the ecological rights of all citizens'. But it takes the point that in a land where the majority hold the cow sacred, it should not try to offer burgers made of beef. Meanwhile orthodox Jews have been picketing Israeli stores, arguing that it offends the country's identity. McDonald's argues that the religious parties are opposing it because they want to prove that they have the power to enforce their beliefs on other people's behaviour.

Meanwhile it is moving into China, Russia and all points once Red, slipstreaming in on a post-Communist whirlwind of automobiles, televisions and Hollywood as the global corporations start to colonize potential new markets. The corporation is now cross-fertilizing its culture with that of the main players in the global league, doing deals with petrol companies (Shell, Chevron, Amoco, BP, etc.) to open in garages, linking up with film companies (such as Disney), and having found a way to slash opening costs with production-line buildings it is planning to move in on airports, hospitals, schools and military bases. In short, the American giant is expanding its market, becoming as ubiquitous as Coke and as culturally pervasive as credit cards, cars and aspirin.

Already the statistics are gross. At random: profits more than $1.8 billion a year; 35 million people served a day; 100 billion burgers served since the start; the restaurants capture one in seven of all restaurant visits in the US; one spud in every twelve that is grown in America is bought by the corporation; it is the largest retail property owner, beef user and chicken buyer. In Britain they now take some part from 8 per cent of all the cattle slaughtered (255,000 a year), and need 3,765 pigs a week and millions on millions of chickens annually.

Customer love cannot always be measured in terms of size, though. The corporation conducted a survey in Britain in 1991 only to find that its own customers characterized the company as being 'loud', 'brash', 'American', 'successful', 'complacent', 'uncaring', 'insensitive', 'disciplinarian', 'insincere', 'suspicious' and 'arrogant'. It didn't stop McDonald's writing to Mrs Mary Blair.

Mrs Mary Blair has a small shop in Fenny Stratford, in Buckinghamshire, England. She does a good line in sandwiches but sells no burgers or French fries. In 1996 she commissioned a sign to be put outside. She liked the word 'Munchies' and thought that because she was Scottish she would add 'Mc' to give her shop a touch of Scotland. Her sign was to be the national flag of Scotland – a blue cross on a white background. It did not occur to her that she could offend anyone.

In September 1996 she got a letter from McDonald's. She read it with growing amazement. Unless she took down her sign within fourteen days, it said, the McDonald's Corporation of Chicago (turnover $30 billion a year) would sue her. McDonald's, it transpired, is touchy about the word Mc (which means 'son of' in Gaelic) and has the trade mark on it. Effectively anyone who uses 'Mc' for a food establishment runs the risk of getting a letter from the corporation.

Mrs Blair was furious. How could anyone stop her using 'Mc'? Did that mean that the corporation owned half the names in Scotland? Did it mean that anyone with a Mc surname could not use it without the corporation's consent? 'Do they really imagine that I am a threat to their business?' she asked. Far from acknowledging Mrs Blair's point that the corporation had, perhaps, lost its perspective and that her sandwich bar was not much of a threat, McDonald's insisted that the sign must go.

The corporation stated that it 'had made significant investment over the years to build up its reputation of restaurant services and food items associated with this trade mark', and therefore: 'If anyone either deliberately or unintentionally uses the corporation's trade marks in their own food or restaurant-related businesses, they are effectively using something that does not belong to them,' said the corporation spokesman. 'We request that unauthorized users of the trade mark cease to do so.'

When it comes to restaurants, McDonald's effectively owns 'Mc', it owns 'McDonald's', it owns the arches, it even has a say on the colours red and yellow when they are associated with restaurants; it owns colourable imitations of itself, logos and anything that is distinctive of McDonald's restaurants. In the US McDonald's and its affiliates have at least seventy protected names, designs, logos, slogans, numbers and combinations of letters that no one else may use. They include 'Royal', 'You', 'McFamily', 'McKids', 'McNuggets', 'You Deserve A Break Today', 'Great Breaks', 'Extra Value Meal', 'Super Size', 'Lift Kids To A Better Tomorrow', 'Happy Meal', 'What's on your plate', 'McRecycle USA', 'You're the One', 'McDonald's Means Opportunity', 'Good Jobs For Good People' and the very long 'Twoallbeefpattiesspecial-saucelettucecheesepicklesonionsonasesameseedbun'.

Mrs Blair belongs to a big club of people who have received stirring letters from McDonald's. In 1995 the corporation began proceedings to sue the operators of a restaurant called McDonald's in Kingston, Jamaica, which has been running for twenty-six years. The big McDonald's wanted to set up in Jamaica and argued that the little McDonald's was infringing all manner of trade marks and was taking advantage of the $1.5 billion that the big corporation spends a year advertising its name. Mr Chang, the defendant, argued back that more people in Jamaica knew about his restaurant than they did about the chain of big ones. And rather than trade on its good name, as alleged, he argues that the corporation is potentially bringing his own restaurant into disrepute. The case goes on and at one point the American McDonald's was ordered not to use the name McDonald's in Jamaica until the case is decided.

Meanwhile there is a growing list of people who have had to apologize to McDonald's for criticizing it. Hundreds of individuals and organizations have offended it and have apologized. In the four years before it served writs on Morris and Steel, at least fifty national, regional and local newspapers, student magazines and other publications in Britain alone, as well as trade unions, Green groups and even a Scottish youth theatre group, received letters from the corporation threatening to sue them if they did not apologize or retract statements. They included the *Guardian*, *Today*, Channel 4, the *Sunday Times Magazine*, *Time Out* and *Spitting Image*. The fear of expensive and time-consuming litigation is an increasingly real factor for the media in considering a response to powerful corporations. The cost of court action is fearsome, and many would argue this fear frightens people into apologies. At least one organization, the Youth Section of the Vegetarian Society, now says on the record that it published an apology 'because there was not the money to fight the case'.

Kroc died in 1984. He had been a no-nonsense small businessman who got lucky. He'd spent too long at the bottom of the pile to countenance anything that might stop him getting to the top. He was patriotic, blunt, proud to be part of the corporate Establishment. He saw his success as America's and vice versa, and anyone who opposed him opposed the whole system that had made him rich and had kept so many people poor: 'I feel sorry for people who have such a small and wretched view of the system that made this country great,' he would say.

And just as Kroc's corporate empire grew, so did the schools of political, economic and intellectual thought that justified how the corporation operated. Chicago was to collect another seven economics and business Nobel prizes for free-market inspired work. Within ten years there would only be one or two countries fully resisting the globalism and market economics that were being formulated in Chicago as Kroc set up. By 1997 McDonald's would be in 101 countries and contemplating going into another dozen. Unfettered market economics would have swept through world bodies, banks, corporations, institutions and governments. The world would be mostly 'free' of Socialism and Communism. McDonald's would be feeding 33 million people a day but the International Labour Organization would report that more than 1,000 million people were unemployed or in part-time, insecure work and the Food and Agriculture Organization would be warning of future famines and environmental catastrophe. And corporations would never have been so powerful or so unaccountable.

Milton Friedman: 'I stand for the values of freedom . . . even if free-market economics was not the most efficient system, I'd still be in favour of it, because of the human values it represents of choice, challenge and risk.'

Ray Kroc: 'The only way we can advance is by going forward . . . we must take risks involved in our free enterprise system. This is the only way in the world to economic freedom. There is no other way.'

Margaret Thatcher: 'There is no turning back.'

Dave Morris: 'It's lucky they only sell fucking hamburgers.'

Chapter Three

Street Legal

The first rule of business is – do other men, for they would
do you.

— Charles Dickens

19 January 1985. How fares the land? The miners' strike –
one of the most bitter disputes in British labour history – is
about to go into its forty-seventh week and most newspapers
this Saturday morning are full of the Labour Party's efforts to
avoid discussing it in parliament. Bob Geldof is just back from
a trip to Ethiopia where millions of pounds raised by Band
Aid is said to be countering the effects of famine. Graham
Fowler and Mike Gatting have cheered armchair cricketers by
scoring a double century each in Madras against a weak India.
England has a deep frost so there will be next to no football
this afternoon.

Meanwhile Prime Minister Mrs Margaret Thatcher will
be forced to explain to a defence committee why she gave the
orders to sink the Argentinian cruiser *General Belgrano*
during the Falklands War – a command which resulted in
hundreds of deaths on board the ship, that was torpedoed in
international waters. A government report says that Stone-
henge should be put under a perspex dome. The West End
theatre district of London is 'shamefully' full of adaptations

of classic novels like *Great Expectations*, says theatre critic Michael Billington. One in five Londoners is reported to be unable to read or write by the age of eight.

But the children going into the McDonald's restaurant right by Trafalgar Square are well able to recognize the pictures of Big Macs and milk shakes above the counter. Hand in parent's hand, they must pass half a dozen people who are standing outside stamping their feet and rubbing their gloves. Duffel-coated arms and gloved hands stretch out to offer a sheet of A4 printed on both sides. Some are declined, some are stuffed in pockets and some just add to the litter outside. A few people stop for a chat and at least one person remarks that more people than usual seem to be interested in this leaflet.

An earlier leaflet advertising this, the first day of action against McDonald's, had been a happily abusive rant against all fast food. 'The American fast-food nightmare has invaded our streets. Fast food for fast people who're rushing about all over the place like nutters and who haven't got the time to even think what they're eating,' it shouts. It claims that thirteen chemicals are used on lettuces, that millions of cattle are being slaughtered, rainforests ('beautiful beyond belief') are being felled for cattle ranches and it concludes that 'The Whole Thing Stinks'. What can anyone do? 'Like everything else in this moronic profit-oriented society we seem to have little choice. Well, in that case, choose a different society run by people themselves ... IT'S OUR WORLD – LET'S TAKE IT BACK,' it exhorts readers.

One of the people handing out leaflets on the Strand is well aware that publishing or possessing 'or even thinking' about certain leaflets could be dangerous. Some ten years earlier Albert Beale and others had leafleted British soldiers in Northern Ireland telling them how they could leave the army. It had been a pacifist campaign, mostly organized by the

British Withdrawal from Northern Ireland Campaign. Several people were arrested and charged with conspiring to contravene the Incitement to Disaffection Act. It was a cause célèbre: Beale defended himself in Britain's premier criminal court, the Old Bailey. He and his co-defendants were acquitted on all counts.

Beale now jokingly calls himself a 'freelance agitator'. He co-edits *Peace News* and works beneath the radical bookshop Housmans in King's Cross, and is, he thinks, known to the police, who drop in to keep themselves up to date with the radical world. On this particular day, he is leafleting not because the McDonald's Corporation has been singled out by London Greenpeace as the worst in the world or anything dramatic but just because it seems to symbolize a lot, he says. McDonald's has a very high profile and is spending a fortune promoting its image.

But in 1985 not even Beale thinks that criticizing McDonald's will be anything more than a pinprick: 'No one,' he says, 'has even considered what the corporation's reaction might be.' The group has done similar actions against Unilever and others. They consider this 'day of action' not civil disobedience so much as 'educational protest'.

The campaign is a relative success but it takes off the following year when London Greenpeace produce a more detailed Factsheet for the 16 October 'World Day of Action against McDonald's'. A few months later an A5 version is produced, and because the group, as ever, is next to broke, they cannot afford to print out and give away the full 'Factsheet' just on spec, so they invite anyone wanting more information to write in for a copy. People are then sent six sides of A5 called 'What's Wrong with McDonald's' – prophetically subtitled '*Everything they don't want you to know*'. It features a leering cartoon American capitalist hiding behind a Ronald McDonald mask. Its contents are no more than what numerous environmental and social justice groups are saying, but no one can remember quite who wrote it.

Nevertheless, it contains along its top edge satirical graphics of the McDonald's Arches with the words: 'McTorture', 'McCancer', 'McMurder', 'McGreedy', 'McDollars' and 'McProfits', none of which have been trade marked by McDonald's but all of which the corporation will find offensive enough to leave it, they will later say, 'no option' but to wield the legal sword. This is the essence of McDonald's' complaint, the use of words which the defendants will have to establish later if they are to win. In the meantime the London Greenpeace people think the leaflet 'dynamite' but they can barely afford to print more than a few hundred copies.

London Greenpeace was the first Greenpeace group in Europe and one of the first anywhere to campaign against nuclear energy. It was founded in 1971 specifically to protest against French atom bomb testing but it was never constituted and refused to be part of the formal International Greenpeace organization that was later set up from Vancouver, Canada. London Greenpeace's philosophy was anarchistic, anti-militaristic and anti-being-told-what-to-think-or-do-by-anyone. It originally evolved around a pacifist newsletter, got popular slightly against its will, but always resisted having a membership, and at one point printed a leaflet saying 'Don't join us'. 'The whole point,' says Beale, 'is not paying someone else to do your politics.' If people lived close by, they were encouraged to join, but if they did not, they were encouraged to set up their own group. Its campaigns ranged from water and chemical pollution to pesticides to cadmium in toys, from the Falklands War (it was against both sides), arms trading and animal rights to the very existence of national borders.

But for its distinguished history, London Greenpeace could have been any one of the 557 varieties of minuscule Green/ Left groups active in Britain at the time, all jealous of their autonomy, all manically opposing something or everything and all joining federations of similar groups when they could overcome the painful negotiations needed for collective decision-making. The informal open collective met weekly on Wednesday or Thursday evenings for many years at the headquarters of the Peace Pledge Union. Mostly they were humdrum working sessions; sometimes speakers would be invited. There was no chair or anyone telling anyone what to do. The group was never large – anything between two and thirty people.

Morris, people remember, was upfront, full-on and in-yer-face. He came to the group for the first time in 1979 with a long history of working in trade unions and in community groups. He wanted, he said, to be part of a group that had a global perspective to balance his campaigning for local issues in North London where he lived. Beale, one of London Greenpeace's earliest members, remembers him as 'brusque', 'bloody-minded', 'totally dedicated' and 'committed'. 'Dave was always one of the loudest voices in meetings. He would launch forth on philosophy. There's something outwardly belligerent about his manner. That's the way he is.' Beale adds, says Morris, that he was also 'very optimistic', 'good at organizing things', 'always keen to involve any new people'.

The mid-1980s were an active if politically depressing time for the leftist grass roots. Margaret Thatcher's great experiment in privatization and liberalization was – with the help of the Chicago School of Economics, Milton Friedman and the gurus of free-market economics – massively redistributing state wealth, tearing, it seemed, the guts out of the common-wealth with harsh laissez-faire monetarist policies. There was much liberal talk of a North–South 'divided nation'; this was the age of the yuppie, of state-endorsed greed and of privatization. It was also the age of spiralling house prices, escalating personal wealth and easy money for some, and at the other end the tax burdens falling on the worse off, with services for the old, the young and the needy cut.

In an age of rampant individualism, Thatcher herself could deny that there was such a thing as society. Britain, she said, was being ruthlessly 'rationalized' and 'modernized' and great swaths were up for sale. Water, electricity, telephones, gas and other state-owned utilities were sold off at give-away prices and snapped up by small investors, most of whom took an immediate profit and sold on to corporations. There was still gloom following the Conservative Party's re-election after the Falklands War, and after a surge of activism in the early years of the decade there were few sparks of hope for the Left. Meanwhile the full scale of the environment crisis was becoming clear, and swaths of public order and anti-union legislation were being prepared by the government.

Helen Steel had come to London in 1982 and got involved in political activity around various environmental and social issues, but it wasn't until 1987 that she first went along to London Greenpeace, to join protests against the re-enactment of the First Fleet sailing to Australia, in support of Aboriginal land rights. She decided she liked the group because 'it was about people taking action for themselves rather than writing off to politicians and asking them to take action for us', and from 1988 attended meetings regularly. Steel was twenty-two, not very confident at speaking in meetings and, others remember, self-effacing, although she clearly had strong beliefs and a determined character. Her main interest then was the International Monetary Fund and the World Bank. Another reason she liked the group was that 'you did not have to join in or agree with every campaign run under the umbrella of the group. Whereas with a lot of political groups you have to agree with all their aims and principles, at London Greenpeace you could just get as involved as you wanted to with each campaign.'

Morris and Steel got to know each other at a demonstration called 'Stop The City'. In a gesture of defiance, London Greenpeace and thousands of others tried to blockade the City of London, the financial heart, they reasoned, of the world's problems. There were arrests and Morris helped organize a meeting for those charged. Steel was squatting a house that had been empty for years and had a large room. The meeting somehow ended up there.

But the first time they spent any time together was at a small active local group called Haringey Community Action. The group raised money for the striking miners and once Steel and Morris hitch-hiked up to Warsop, on the Nottinghamshire border with Derbyshire, to stay with miners' families. Steel says: 'It was good being there with him, because I was less confident about speaking to people. If I'd gone on my own, I probably wouldn't have learnt much. But Dave will always chat to anyone, although I think he tends to avoid company directors.' Steel and Morris lived together with others in a shared house for a while and worked an allotment. And no, they both say, before you ask, there was never anything between them except respect and friendship. 'I think it's quite encouraging that we can have been so close together for so long without there being any sex angle,' says Morris.

Steel spent her early childhood in Preston and then at six her family lived in Newcastle. They went back to Preston, then later south to Surrey. Her father was a maths teacher and branch secretary of his union; her mother did office and shop work. Both she and Morris are complex characters, wary, and keen to make statements about the world rather than reveal themselves. This is Steel:

'Why do you hate being personal?'

'Because it's not important . . .'

'When you were a child did you have role models?'

'No.'

'Or people you most admired?'

'No.'

'Did you have people you despised?'

'No.'

'No one?'

'No, no.'

'Are you being difficult?'

She laughs. 'No, I'm not. I never had anyone I idolized, never had pictures of pop stars on my walls, or anyone I thought, "Wow, this person's the best thing in the world." I don't know why not, I just didn't. I was obviously a natural-born anarchist,' she jokes. 'No idols. Although I didn't know what an anarchist was. I'd had the anarchist politics without the label.'

She will, though, talk of her childhood in terms of her first political activities. Since she was quite young, she says, she was interested in environmental and other issues. She would raise money for large organizations, doing sponsored walks for Help the Aged or the Worldwide Fund for Nature. 'I think, looking back, I always had empathy with people and animals that are suffering and not wanted that suffering to carry on.'

While she was at comprehensive school she had what she calls an 'unreal dream' about having a bit of land and being a farmer. She and a friend had to fight to get on an agriculture course. 'We had to find boys to swap with us and do home economics instead. Towards the end we visited slaughter-houses and really what I saw there was so horrific that I decided I wanted to become a vegetarian. I didn't want to be involved in the death of animals. I still thought at that time that I could do dairy farming, or eggs, but as I became more knowledgeable, I discovered the cruelty involved in the battery egg system.' Then she saw the connection between the meat and dairy trade, and was put off both. She went to sixth-form college and worked weekends in a supermarket where her views were further shaped. 'We were told to stay late without any notice and weren't paid for the extra hours. The management just said, "If you don't like it, there are plenty of people on the dole who want a job." Big companies treat workers as bits of machinery rather than human beings. They don't treat you as though you had any feelings or deserved any respect.' She stayed a year at college, turned vegan and at seventeen left home and moved to London with six O-levels.

If the one side of Steel is compassionate, empathetic, playful and teasing, the other is marked by an absolute stubbornness and refusal to be cowed. Her mother tells her it's always been like that: 'When I was quite young there was a boy at the end of the street who used to bully everyone and everyone used to go crying to their mums and dads saying, "He's being really horrible, he hit me," and things like that. Eventually Mum got fed up with it and said, "Well, hit him back." So I did.'

Then when she moved south there were a couple of really 'obnoxious' girls at school: 'I think they were looking for someone to pick on and because I was the new girl and had a bit of a strange accent they were picking on me. One of them stuck her pencil in my leg and they didn't back off until one day they said they wanted a fight after school.' Pause; she laughs.

'I didn't want that at all, but as I was in a situation where they wanted to beat me up, the only option was to fight back. As soon as I hit back, they went off. I had learnt from the first incident that the only way to deal with bullies is to stand up to them. If people are trying to intimidate you into doing something you don't want to do, you have to stand up and fight back, and call their bluff to make them back off.'

She worked as a London gardener. Sometimes she was unemployed but busy on her allotment or doing voluntary work. She worked, both paid and unpaid, as a minibus driver, taking kids and pensioners around London. Later she did secretarial training.

Morris followed an altogether different route to London Greenpeace. His parents are London East Enders by birth, but his family is originally pure East Europe. And here, though it would be foolish to follow them too far, there are parallels with Ray Kroc of McDonald's and his family. All four of Morris's grandparents were Jewish émigrés from the Ukraine and Poland (Kroc's family came from down the road, Bohemia). Kroc's father worked for the Post Office, as did Morris's in his later years. Kroc sold everything from land to milk shake mixers. Morris's father was a door-to-door sales-man – a 'retail credit draper' – for most of his life. Both families fled from persecution and oppression. 'There's always two sides to a family,' says Morris. 'Like with any immigrant background, there's the side of the family which became well off in business. Our side didn't. There's always that feeling of insecurity.'

It was a stable, close enough family. He grew up in a terraced house in Perivale, West London. His parents were active Labour Party supporters, and, he says, encouraged him to be 'humanitarian'. He describes his childhood as 'Socialis-tic', and doesn't feel he had any particularly strong role models, though there were shadowy figures in the extended family, whose politics he viewed 'with interest': 'I had an uncle who was a Communist and an activist jailed for two years in a British Army mutiny in Burma.' He knows little more about him.

The family had a television but Morris and his elder brother were rarely allowed to watch ITV because his parents hated the advertisements. Was he interested in them? Did he peek? He says not. He applauds the decision: 'It showed me that you didn't have to just swallow the things that are forced on you,' but he cannot help himself pronouncing on this; he follows a fine tradition of British 'ranters' in the old sense of the word: 'Advertisements are sermons of the modern religion which is consumerism. Advertising is the propaganda of the worship of money.'

When he was about eleven his parents moved across London to the more salubrious suburb of Finchley where – horror – Margaret Thatcher was their MP and McDonald's was to set up its UK HQ and Thatcher, indeed, would open it. Morris remembers his parents' reaction to her. He laughs and speaks in capitals here – 'She was the Absolute Total Epitome of Everything My Parents Hated Deep Down In Their Soul. Not only was she the rising star of the Tory Party but her voice, her disciplinarian middle-class voice . . .' He trails off in recollected alarm.

Thatcher and Morris almost met. Morris was about fifteen when Thatcher, as the unpopular Education Minister, came to open an annual fete at his school. She had recently abolished the children's free milk handouts and was being called 'Milk Snatcher Thatcher'. Morris had recently been to Italy on a school trip and had brought back a bunch of firecrackers, which were illegal in Britain. He intended to introduce them to his object of hate: 'So I was going to chuck them at her from a window, but I was restrained by other pupils. Probably just as well,' he says.

But the Finchley move was also 'going up in the world', a

move to what he calls another class. Morris says that he felt he was being pushed into his parents' vision of how he should 'get on'. One root of his revolutionary anarchism, he says, developed in the Finchley home: 'I think being brought up to question things was most important. I would later ask questions like: "Do we need money at all? Or government at all? How can we stop wars?"' But where Mr and Mrs Morris and his school wanted him to go to university like his elder brother, he says: 'I rejected that. I didn't want to go up to the middle class.'

But the questioning that his parents encouraged ended up distancing him from them. 'They did pretty well with me,' he says, 'but they always felt I wasn't succeeding in what they wanted. Some people want to elevate their children so that it can be better for them than it was for themselves, but I didn't see why anyone should have privilege over somebody else, and my aim was if things should be better it's because they should be better for everyone.' Again, he broadens out his own situation to the general and political: 'It's more than personal circumstances, it's about everybody; it's about hunger, about pollution, everything. You can't just say everyone should be well off, it's a question of more fundamental things.'

So what have you got against the middle classes?

'The middle-class view is elitist and based on privilege. Considering the state of the world how can anyone have privilege and status as an ambition? To me it was a question of choice and I chose to stay with my roots. I didn't know what I was doing very clearly.'

He did well at school but from fifteen onwards he started arguing with his teachers. He didn't think much of what they were teaching him and rebelled – or as he says now, he became a 'dissident'. He liked music but when he was thirteen he refused to take lessons because his piano teacher wanted him to learn 'great' music and he wanted to play what he enjoyed. He saw this, too, as all part of a move to join the middle classes, into the professions and 'their way of thinking'. History and English – the canon of so-called 'great literature' – he thought elitist and subjective. He largely stopped reading because he wanted 'to be active' and the only reason he did maths (he got two A levels in it) was because he thought it 'less damaging' because it was more objective.

So what did he want?

'I don't know, really,' he says, 'I just wanted people to be free.' The turning point came when he went to the first Glastonbury rock festival, then utopian and small. It was free in every sense for the sixteen-year-old. He remembers thinking that if 5,000 people could create a free festival, 'then let's go for the whole world'. 'Couldn't see any problem at all. After that my aim was to change the world. No doubt about it. Virtually everything – and this may sound extreme – that I have done since has been directed towards that end and it may sound extreme and heavy, but it's true.'

He embraced the politicized wing of 1960s youth counter-culture. It was a time of international protest and strikes. Student and other uprisings in Paris, Czechoslovakia, China and Mexico still reverberated and the American universities were still in turmoil with Vietnam. In Britain, the old Establishment politics were completely useless, he felt. Instinctively he supported the Labour Party, but when he handed out leaflets for it in the 1970 election he found them 'garbage'. 'It was about pensions. Vote Labour and get a £10 Christmas bonus. It was just bribery. When you start thinking deeper than that, you think of what you can create as part of a movement with others – about real change, and real participation in society.'

He left school at eighteen, did voluntary work in Sweden, Turkey and the USA. He remembers eating at a McDonald's:

'I remember having a bit of a taste for their thick shakes, but when I discovered that they had the equivalent of eleven teaspoons of sugar in them, I started going off them.' Six years later he travelled round Europe and was in Poland as Lech Wałesa and the Polish shipyard workers started rocking the Communist world with Solidarity. In Britain in the 1970s he had been active with the anti-nuclear, labour and squatting movements.

Like Kroc's dad, and his own, he got a job in the Post Office. It was 'crappily paid', but he thought it useful. 'Postal workers have a great deal of power and have international contacts. I felt this was a good base to be challenging the set-up.' There he skirmished with the National Front (a Fascist group which had members in the Post Office at the time), and was elected union branch secretary. 'This anarchistic guy was chair, and we said, "We're not running the union, because the union is the members not the officials." But because the union is part of the system, you couldn't really do anything in that formal framework, so we both resigned ... both of us together.'

Steel says her politics come from within. Asked what her political influences are, she answers, 'Life,' and laughs at herself. She denies that she is influenced by political parties or figures. What she sees in a slaughterhouse or on a picket line may have more effect than any textbook or world leader; pollution motivates her more than fine words. 'If I see oppression it's just like a gut feeling that I want to do something to challenge it and change it and end it and it's not because I have been sitting around reading some textbook about the way things should be.' Rather than learn from books or theories, she says she prefers learning from people. 'I would chat to people on demonstrations, meetings, and in the street. I don't automatically accept what people say, but if someone says something and I think, "Hmmm, that makes sense," then I'll adopt that as my view as well. Really my influences are other ordinary people and their ideas, views and experiences.'

Like most of her generation she barely knows the order of British prime ministers before Mrs Thatcher. She's far more interested in Latin American tribes, and grass-roots revolts around the world. Party politics are irrelevant and out of touch with her concerns. Her knowledge of the World Bank or the International Monetary Fund is impressive. It is a conceptual world informed by what she feels are the forces most affecting the people she relates to. Like Morris, she is not and never has been interested in money or material possessions.

Her politics are utopian, environmentally based – 'wanting to see a society based on cooperation and sharing of resources, where people work together for the good of the community'. She wants to see no one in a position of authority over anyone else. 'We're all on this planet as equals. The whole planet is here for all of us to use in a sensible way and to take care of and there's no reason why some people should own huge chunks of it and prevent others from making use of it and there's no reason why anyone should have any other form of power and authority over anyone else.' Like the line in the exasperated leaflet that London Greenpeace originally handed out, she adds, 'It's Just Generally A Bad Idea.'

She doesn't see herself in revolt against society at all. 'I think that most people are pretty caring and don't like seeing suffering or oppression or damage that is being caused to the planet, but they don't see what they can do about it; and they've got loads of problems of their own and they're trying to keep their lives running.'

Where Steel leans towards the language of the new environmentalists, Morris is more full of slogans and the now arch political jargon of the 1960s and 1970s. It sounds quaint: 'Both of us are committed to the revolutionary transformation of our society to something better.' He talks of 'struggles', 'the Establishment', 'dissidents' and the 'organization of society'. Steel, too, can sound as pat as US Vice-President Al Gore: 'We're all on this planet as equals.' 'The whole planet is here for all of us to use in a sensible way and to take care of.'

But where they distrust middle-class ideals, they happily draw on the research of middle-class Establishment environmentalists, the analysis of human rights workers or the ideals of emerging new democracy groups around the world. Morris says he is not hooked on any words, slogans, or organizations. Nevertheless he wants to identify with groups that he says are opposing what he calls 'the System', and sees himself as a standard-bearer for a new society. He wants his analysis to be seen as representing the alternative to the world that McDonald's represents. No group would necessarily share all his analysis.

Where McDonald's might be portrayed as a monopolistic world, Morris' vision is dualistic, a battle to the end between the forces of light and darkness. 'There are two distinct tendencies in society,' he says. 'One is towards greater power where money rules ever greater parts of our lives; the other is a grass-roots urge for freedom, for self-organization, for mutual aid.'

Steel and Morris both say that they are anarchists but fitting them in to this political pantheon is not easy. There are as many types of anarchism as there are anarchists. There are anarcho-Communists, anarcho-syndicalists, pacifist anarchists, individualist anarchists, Christian ones, Green ones and mutual ones. The list goes on and the history is disputed: Pierre Joseph Proudhon (1809–65) was the first person to call himself an anarchist, but historians often start with the ancient

Greeks. It was Zeno who proposed that society should be based on natural law, with no police, no armies, temples, schools, money or marriage. And no law courts, either.

More recently anarchist traditions have been upheld through the Diggers and Levellers and through to Victorian times and William Morris, with huge anarchist-influenced labour movements in Europe in the first half of this century. But the label is likely to provoke misunderstanding today, and Steel and Morris are shy of labelling themselves. Why the shyness? Largely because anarchists have, they say, been misrepresented. 'If you don't mention the word "anarchist", most people agree with most of what you're saying,' says Steel.

Why use it, then?

'I generally don't. It's been so misused by politicians and the media and people who are desperate to cling to their positions of power and want society to keep being run in the same way. If you introduce yourself to someone and say you're an anarchist and then tell them your ideas, they generally won't bother listening. But if you explain your ideas first, they'll listen and think, "Oh yes, quite sensible."'

The cliché of the anarchist is the cloaked, masked figure in a broad-brimmed hat, bomb under arm, running along some mist-shrouded street. A century ago, a few nihilist anarchists, exponents of a philosophy called 'Propaganda of the Deed', did live up to this, willing to resort to violence – including the assassination of heads of states – but overwhelmingly the majority of anarchists are opposed to such violence. Many anarchists developed their politics out of the modern peace movement. Plus, as more than one anarchist likes to remark, it is states, not anarchists, who throw bombs. It is states, not anarchists, who commit themselves to violence in wars.

It is often in opposition to wars, particularly unjust ones, that people have adopted anarchist philosophies. The American Henry Thoreau (part of the anarchist tradition without ever technically calling himself an anarchist), considered the US war in Mexico of 1846–8 to be imperialist and wrong, so he took the path of civil disobedience, refusing to pay his poll tax in protest. Peter Kropotkin in Russia (1872–1917), reacted against the militarism of his times, supporting neither right nor left, but seeing the totalitarian dictatorships of both sides equally insufferable, and advocating instead a system of cooperation and community. In the UK, the Aldermaston marches and direct action in protest against the bomb were a great influence on promoting anarchism. So, too, the Vietnam war influenced the growing anarchist sympathies of Noam Chomsky. More recently Greens and the women's liberation movement, international solidarity campaigns, the organized occupations of empty property by squatters, open-air free festivals and animal-liberation activity have influenced anarchist thinking.

If a mistaken cliché of 'the anarchist' is the cloaked assassin, so there is a mistaken cliché of the meaning of 'anarchy' itself. As Morris – Dave, not William – points out: 'Anarchy is continually portrayed as chaos. But chaos is the complete opposite of what it's about.' The original meaning of 'anarchy', far from 'chaos' or 'furious destruction', was 'without rulers' and therefore 'self-governing'. Says Steel: 'Sometimes it's portrayed that anarchists are trying to destroy society, but that's not what it's about. It's not trying to destroy everyone else, it's trying to create a more equal society and get rid of the power structures and just run things differently.'

Steel says she has reached her politics intuitively, based on her own experiences and her own reaction. Her anarchism is similarly a way of life, at once moral and practical; what you eat, how you grow your food. If she wasn't in Court 35, or on her allotment, she says she would probably join the leaderless actions of the proliferating anti-roads protests. She has taken part in the land reform campaigns of The Land Is Ours – a group which is very conscious of its historical affiliations to the Diggers. She says: 'At the time when there were a lot of protests about Aboriginal land rights I began thinking that a lot of what applied in Australia, about dispossession leading to despair, alcoholism, etc., also applied here. It's not so obvious, but a lot of the problems we have now stem from the fact that a minority owns and controls the vast majority of land. When people have no access to land they have no real control over their lives. They are dependent on industry or others to "provide" them with jobs to make an income in order to buy what they need to survive. And when that "provision" isn't met people often despair and lose hope.'

The anti-McDonald's leafleting campaign, beginning that freezing day on the Strand in central London, became, as Morris says, 'London Greenpeace's most successful campaign by far. It just hit a chord with the public.' Steel says, 'Lots of letters came in asking for information about McDonald's. People were fed up with litter all over their streets and fed up with their friends and themselves going to low-paid, dead-end jobs. The campaign went international and changed over time to being run by local groups all over the world.'

But Steel and Morris say neither was actively involved in organizing the anti-McDonald's campaign, preferring to concentrate on other 'issues'. Both worked on campaigning against global financial institutions and for miners and the print workers made redundant when Rupert Murdoch took the *Sunday Times*, the *Times*, the *News of the World* and the *Sun* overnight to Wapping in East London. 'Helen and I used to go to the picket lines two or three times a week. Standing on a picket line for hours in the middle of the night gave us a lot of time to explore what we believe in. It solidified the friendship.'

Both, too, were involved in local community campaigns for housing and the unemployed. They helped set up an 'Unwaged' centre. Morris became less and less involved with London Greenpeace; he was now involved in organizing resistance to the poll tax, becoming Secretary of the London Federation of Anti-poll-tax Groups. 'I think the most important struggle that I've ever been involved with was the anti-poll-tax movement, because it was mass defiance of the law, the courts, the media, the political parties and because 18 million people refused to cooperate with that unjust law.' Steel too was active in her local anti-poll-tax group.

As Morris was being drawn away from London Greenpeace, so Steel became more involved in it. In 1988, when she was going to meetings regularly, McDonald's was not a major concern of hers. 'I supported the McDonald's campaign, but I didn't have a big grudge against the company. At the time, I was more involved in a campaign against the World Bank.' She went to Berlin to join protests against the IMF.

If London Greenpeace had initiated the McDonald's campaign, the follow-through was really done by a campaigning group called Veggies in Nottingham. They reprinted and became the main distributors of the 'What's Wrong With McDonald's' Factsheet and leaflets, printing them in bulk and sending them out to groups around the country. In 1987 Veggies was threatened by the McDonald's Corporation with legal reprisals over the Factsheet. McDonald's demanded an apology over the rainforest section and the heading 'In what way are McDonald's responsible for the Torture and Murder of Animals?'. The corporation made no complaint about any other part of the Factsheet. Veggies changed the words 'Torture' and 'Murder' to 'slaughter' and 'butchery' and amended the rainforest section to refer to the burger industry in general. This was accepted by McDonald's' legal department and Veggies have carried on distributing the Factsheet ever since.

McDonald's never wrote to London Greenpeace about the Factsheet before serving writs in 1990. Morris and Albert Beale remember only one letter coming from McDonald's and that, they say, was about a previous, completely different leaflet. Beale: 'When the letter came from McDonald's to ask London Greenpeace to stop leafleting, it was addressed "Dear Sir or Sirs". We refused to even discuss the letter because of that, because they were ignoring half of the people in the meeting – the women' and a letter was sent informing McDonald's of this.

But from October 1989 to spring 1991, funny things began to happen at London Greenpeace. Steel says: 'This guy turned up at the meetings who didn't quite seem to fit in. He just made me suspicious. The first meeting I remember seeing him at, I thought, "Hang about." It was partly his manner, the way he carried himself, the way he expressed himself. He didn't seem to have any political background. He didn't really say that much about what his politics were, what his particular interests were, although he did say that he was against fast food.'

Albert Beale says Steel is 'pretty sensitive'. She noticed what he didn't. Only with hindsight did he see she was right in suspecting an infiltrator. 'One looked back and thought, "Yes, they were a bit odd."' Morris, who was hardly involved in the group by this time, knew that Steel and others suspected that there were some kind of infiltrators in the group: 'I said, "Don't be stupid, that's something which you only read about in books," but they were proved absolutely right.'

Then it became clear there was more than one infiltrator. Things began to go awry. After an occupation of the World

Bank offices, some photographs of the protest went missing. Steel asked someone who would later be exposed as a private investigator whether he had taken them. He denied it, but pointed the finger at another member of the group, Alan.

It would transpire in court, some five years later, that this 'Alan' had indeed taken the pictures away and was also a private investigator, though this was not known to either the first 'spy' or to Steel.

One of the spies followed them home after meetings to find out their addresses. One, John, had twigged that he was being followed. He phoned Steel to ask if she had been. 'I didn't know. I wouldn't take any notice, I don't look behind me while I'm walking along.' But the next week, she took her camera along to the meeting as a precaution. Again, they saw the man who had followed John. After the meeting, Steel, John and another campaigner, Paul, left, and went to the tube. They were followed. They came up out of the tube and were followed out. Paul peeled off home. John and Steel kept walking. The spy kept walking after them.

'We deliberately didn't go back to John's and just kept walking, and we walked to this estate and he was still following us and' – she breaks off and laughs at the cartoon-escapade atmosphere of it all – 'we got to this estate, and we ran up an external flight of stairs to the top and we hid up there, and we could hear him looking for us, opening doors and looking around. Then it went quiet and so we came down and he was standing there—' she breaks off again, and chortles with laughter. 'It was really chronic.' Steel and John carry on walking. 'And he *still* carried on following us – it was quite incredible. You would have thought he would have twigged that we obviously knew that he was following us.' So Steel and John went up another set of external stairs, and hid. As the spy came past the building, Steel leant over with her camera and took a photograph of him. She says, 'We then walked in front of him trying to get photographs, and he was putting his hand across his face and going, "Leeeeavemeealonel'mdrunk." He wasn't. He was just trying to pretend he wasn't following us.' In another episode Steel turned the tables on the spies and followed one of them after he left the meeting. Again she laughs: 'I was wearing a wig – it was quite funny. But he just *vanished* in the tube station.'

'Beyond following spies to try to find out who they were, we never really did anything about them. It was difficult. You can't go up and confront somebody unless you've got some concrete reason for it. And a group can't work if it's continually suspicious about everybody who's coming to meetings. We hadn't got anything to hide, anyway – it wasn't like we were planning any secret protests or illegal action.'

The group didn't suspect all the spies. One woman, Fran, who infiltrated the group 'just seemed like an all-right person', Steel says. Then one day she introduced a woman using the name 'Shelley' (her real name was Michelle). Steel's emotional antennae were sensitive. She remembers thinking: 'This woman just gives me an air of being a policewoman.' It was, she says, a strong feeling, but she tried to ignore it, knowing that Fran – whom 'she thought was OK' – had brought her. Again, Steel argued, 'We're not talking about anything dodgy, so why worry?'

Shelley, Steel remembers, was very enthusiastic about doing all sorts of campaigns. But, she says, her instincts were right: it turned out later that Shelley was an ex-policewoman. 'She came on the picket of Scotland Yard,' says Steel, 'in support of all the people being arrested for the anti-poll-tax demonstrations. It was just after the Trafalgar Square demonstration, and loads of people were getting their houses raided and smashed up, and there was a day of protest against this and against the heavy-handedness of the police.' 'Shelley came on this picket, and was holding a banner saying *No Police No Poll Tax* – and she was an ex-policewoman.'

Shelley helped organize meetings and pickets, says Steel, and she regularly attended pickets of McDonald's and distributed anti-McDonald's leaflets, including at the picket of the McDonald's Head Office. But Shelley got involved in the group, in more ways than one. 'She had a relationship with somebody in the group, which is just completely disgusting,' says Steel bluntly. 'The spies totally abused people's trust and the open nature of London Greenpeace. It was really sinister.'

But no one knew who they were.

Chapter Four

M'Lud on their Boots

People who go voluntarily to law, or are taken forcibly there
for the first time, may be allowed to labour under some
temporary irritation and anxiety.

– Charles Dickens, *The Pickwick Papers*

On the evening of 20 September 1990 Helen Steel had been
given a lift to a friend's house. Just as she was getting out of
the van a man stepped out in front of her and said, 'Helen?'
She didn't say anything because she had no idea who he was.
He threw something down on the pavement in front of her,
turned and left quickly.

It was an envelope addressed to her. She and her friend
went into the house, where they opened it. Inside was a writ
and a fat document called a 'Statement of Claim' from
McDonald's' solicitors. Her first reaction was anger. Here she
was at a friend's house, some way from where she lived.
Someone must have followed her there on at least one
occasion to have met her as she got out of the van. Someone
knew a lot about her.

Her next reaction was incomprehension. What was she
meant to do? The accompanying solicitors' letter stated that
that there would be a court case unless she apologized. But
apologize for what? The letter talked of libel. She knew

nothing about libel. The McDonald's Factsheet had been written before she joined the London Greenpeace group and she'd never been involved in running the campaign. What had she done? Above all, she asked herself, why should she apologize?

Meanwhile Morris had received a writ, too. He was in no state of mind to take it seriously as he was nursing full time his sixteen-month-old baby son and his partner, who was ill. He'd dropped out of London Greenpeace some time before, and any spare time now was spent with his local anti-poll-tax group. Like Steel, he was outraged that the corporation should want an apology, but he was in no mood to fight.

Elsewhere three other members of London Greenpeace, Paul Gravett, Andrew Clarke and Jonathan O'Farrell, had also received writs. None of the five knew why they and not others had been sent them. They contacted each other and discussed their options. They needed legal advice so they went to a solicitor at Birnbergs in Borough, South London.

The good news was that they got two hours' free advice under a legal aid scheme. But this, they were told, was all they would get, and the advice boiled down to three words: Get Out Fast. Libel, it emerged, was one of the most complex areas of English law. Cases are not heard at magistrate's or even county court level, but go straight to the High Court. It seemed that it was next to impossible for anybody to conduct a case as complicated as libel without some form of legal assistance. Legal aid is usually available for people on low incomes but not for defamation cases – a rule made, it was said, to stop clogging up the courts with minor claims.

The more that the five heard, the more it seemed that if they chose to fight McDonald's it would not be an uphill struggle so much as a possible two- or three-year yomp under fire across a mountain range that nobody with their meagre resources had climbed before: the onus would be on them to prove everything stated in the Factsheet.

McDonald's was throwing the legal book at London Greenpeace. The statement of claim argued that everything in the Factsheet was libellous, down to statements linking diet with ill health. Responding would be a nightmare. It would not be possible to rely on newspaper reports, books, films or academic literature in defence. To prove a libel case in Britain you have to have 'primary sources'. This meant finding witnesses, collecting first-hand accounts and official documents. They would have no help and not much time and be swamped by paperwork.

It was worse, explained their sympathetic lawyer. Even if they assembled a half-decent case they were on a hiding to nothing. The pre-trial procedures for civil libel cases in Britain are notoriously long-winded and complex and the chances were that without any legal aid they'd get something wrong. So there was a real likelihood that they would slip up somewhere along the line and lose on a technicality before the case ever got to a courtroom. They would then still be liable for tens of thousands of pounds' worth of costs – they were already liable for several thousand, it seemed – which, they were told, could click up by £500 or more every time McDonald's' solicitors so much as wrote to them. The nightmare scenario was that they could be bankrupted without even getting to the courts, their assets could be frozen and all their future earnings be given to McDonald's.

The five got the message: don't bang your heads against a brick wall, be pragmatic, just say sorry. No one will think that you really mean it, you will save yourselves time, energy and money and be able to get on with campaigning elsewhere. You can comfort yourself with the fact that a trial would hardly be fair if you defended yourselves. Leave while you can.

The five also went to see Keir Starmer, a young barrister at Doughty Street Chambers who was making a name for himself in cases that involved the public interest. The secretary of the Haldane Society of Socialist Lawyers was realistic about their chances but, crucially, said he was prepared to help them on a 'pro bono' – or free – basis where he could, *if* they decided to fight. The case, as he read it, had great legal and censorship implications that stretched beyond the immediate questions of whether Steel, Morris et al. had or had not libelled McDonald's. In his view it raised questions about who had access to the law, how people who have genuine criticisms of society but few resources can stand up against the powerful and whether the libel laws should be reformed.

One of the problems with the libel laws as they now stood in Britain, he explained, was that it was not a battle for the truth in court, so much as a battle of the purse. Libel was there for the richest to take advantage of: 'If you have the money you can hire a good legal team and you can hope for victory. If you have no money you can't hire a legal team and you run huge risks because if you lose you could pay the costs of the person that's suing you,' he said.

There was, moreover, a built-in incentive for those who could afford it to pay lawyers to suppress information and the opinions of those poorer than themselves. Many people, he said, withdrew from libel cases or settled cases before they came to court simply because they feared the costs, which for the simplest case often came to £50,000. He didn't put a figure on it but he knew that if the five instructed lawyers to work for them on such a potentially broad case as this, it could cost somewhere near £1 million. By contrast, he said, other countries had far less oppressive libel laws. In the US McDonald's would not have been able to stop the five expressing their opinions, where it would be seen as a violation of constitutional rights. Moreover, the onus would be on a corporation to show that its critics knew that their allegations were false. The more they learned about libel, the more they felt the law was being used to suppress free speech, especially in written and broadcast material.

They thought about it. No one doubted the others' commitment and no one was about to blame anyone for caving in. McDonald's' solicitors had set a deadline for an apology and each of the five in turn was asked what they proposed to do. Gravett, Clarke and O'Farrell pulled out, feeling that there was no point in fighting against such odds. It was the only realistic option for them and it seemed pointless to go on, especially as they had such little chance of even getting to court.

Morris said that he would go along with everyone else. His line was that if they all felt that apologizing was the only option, then he would, too, given his personal circumstances. But Steel held out. 'It was really offensive. It really stuck in my throat to apologize for something that didn't deserve an apology, and I just thought, "Well, I'm going to fight this case come what may, whether or not I comply with all the legal obligations and actually get as far as a trial,"' she said.

That was all Morris needed. 'If she was going to go for it,' he decided, 'then so was I.' The rest of his life needed sorting out, but so did politics, he was to say: 'Politics is not a luxury. It's an essential. It doesn't matter what else is happening in your life, you've got to do what you've got to do. You've still got to go to the toilet, you've still got to eat and you've still got to fight the system.'

An apology on behalf of the three was read out in court. They were upset, but Gravett remembers that they consoled themselves that it was just a piece of paper and they had even less respect for the corporation now. Moreover, they had every intention of continuing to campaign in many areas. This was not a defeat, they reasoned, so much as a pragmatic retreat in the face of overwhelming odds. They later issued a statement condemning the libel laws as protecting the interests of the wealthy and powerful, rather than protecting the truth – and backing Steel and Morris. A support campaign was launched.

Steel and Morris had little or no idea what being a 'litigant in person' – someone who legally represents themselves – involved. Had they known that it would be practically a full-time job, would take four years to get to court, involve twenty-eight pre-trial hearings, applications to European courts, Appeal Courts and even the House of Lords, with more paperwork than either could imagine, they might have been daunted. As it was they spent the next eighteen months gathering what information they could on the corporation and 'exchanging pleadings'.

The pre-trial stages of a British libel case are somewhere between a courtly dance, a sword fight and two football teams checking each other out before the match. On them the whole course of the case may depend, with each party using legal arguments to soften up the other or to weaken or destroy their case. The first stages of a libel case are conducted with a cloak of medieval formality and courtesy hiding vicious tactics. Parts of it depend on trust and the propriety of the lawyers who are theoretically firstly responsible to the court, then to their clients.

Libel cases start with what are called the formal 'pleadings' for information by each party. Both sides try to find out more details of the other side's case and must reply when asked. As McDonald's had made the first move, delivering the 'statement of claim' with the writ, Steel and Morris had to respond with an outline defence of the leaflet, drawing up a long, formal document laid out with proper title and in a certain manner which refuted each of the sixteen points that McDonald's said were libellous.

There then follow formal requests for 'further and better' particulars. Here each side seeks more information about the allegations, requesting the other to lay out in greater detail what they mean. This goes backwards and forwards, gets deeply convoluted and eventually leads to 'interrogatories' where specific questions are asked and each party is bound to answer on oath. Effectively each side cross-examines the other before they even come to court.

But this is just the start of the tortuous process. When these 'pleadings' are over, each side asks the other to disclose all the documents that it has which might be relevant. Normally each party's lawyers would offer the other a list from which, on request, they can pick what they want. In this case it was to prove a nightmare for Steel and Morris because they found time and again that the corporation claimed to have very little documentation or none at all in certain areas. Steel and Morris described it as a 'cover-up'. It was to prove a quarrel which would run throughout the next three and a half years as the defendants applied continuously for more documents. Indeed McDonald's was still being ordered to hand over documents in the closing stages of the trial.

There is far more to the pre-trial process. The next stage involves the exchange of witness statements. Here both sides must collect signed statements from each of their witnesses which are then exchanged with the other side. All the way through the process there are legal disputes, deadlines to meet and 'directions', automatic or otherwise, from judges. Add in frequent appeals and 'hearings' and requests to knock out bits of evidence or amend pleadings and requests for 'further and better particulars of further and better particulars' and you get a notion of the complexity of what was clearly going to be a mammoth case if it ever reached the trial stage. If a lawyer well-versed in English law finds it excruciatingly long-winded and narrow, anyone else considers it arcane. Not surprisingly, there are only a few legal chambers that handle libel.

With background help from Starmer, they hacked their way up the lower slopes and through the first thickets of legal niceties with enthusiasm if not trepidation. Both found they had an aptitude for detail. For a long while there was a leisurely exchange of pleadings. Steel had gone to live on an organic farm in Yorkshire in December 1991, thinking that a trial was probably not going to happen and that if it did, it would last only a few weeks. Morris had time to put his personal life back together.

McDonald's' strategy until the end of 1992 seemed to be to try to wear down the defendants with legal points, drag out the proceedings and exhaust their meagre resources. In June, Steel and Morris summonsed McDonald's to try to force it to hand over details of their alleged involvement in the leaflet. They had already learned that the corporation's case was not that they had written or printed the Factsheet themselves, but that they had handed it out on two occasions. Now the mystery of the infiltrators was partly cleared up. Pleadings they were given indicated that it was McDonald's, not the police, which had employed private investigators to spy on the London Greenpeace collective.

By August 1992 they had appeared in only five pre-trial hearings. It had been ominously quiet. Just as Steel and Morris thought that the corporation had lost the taste for a fight, the first legal storm began to blow up. In December, McDonald's served interrogatories on the defendants and took out a summons for 'directions' (a hearing to set down the schedule leading up to the trial). Mr Justice Drake ordered both sides to serve lists of the documents in their possession within twenty-eight days, and exchange witness statements and experts' reports within ninety-eight days.

The time-span for exchange of witness statements was

longer than usual because it was recognized that with such a wide range of issues it would be a time-consuming process to read and digest the documents, pass them to the relevant witnesses and get statements. Steel and Morris argued it would be particularly difficult for them to do all this with no experience in taking statements. After a mutually agreed extension because neither side was ready in time, the lists of documents were exchanged on 11 March 1993.

Steel and Morris couldn't believe what they got. McDonald's had not served a complete list. It admitted this, saying that it would be applying for an order to limit discovery and that further discovery was 'not necessary for disposing fairly of this action or saving costs'. They also said the list did not include any documents whatever relating to employment issues. So Steel and Morris took out a summons for an order that McDonald's provide a full list of documents and also that exchange of witness statements be delayed until two months after the inspection of those documents.

The hearing took place on 6 April in front of Mr Justice Drake. McDonald's may not have served a full list of documents, but Drake criticized Steel and Morris because they had not prepared an affidavit to support their application. They had no idea that they could or should have prepared an affidavit, since no one had ever told them about this.

Says Steel: 'He told us off for having underestimated the length of the hearing (despite our having no experience in how long such hearings would take), and he then adjourned our application until *after* the service of witness statements – thereby reversing the normal order of discovery before statements. It seemed that he had accepted without question Thomas Shields' argument [for McDonald's] that our case was "based on press cuttings" and that we were on a "fishing expedition" to get documents from McDonald's to prove our case because we didn't have any of our own evidence.'

Steel and Morris were learning fast about DIY law and how the professionals worked. They were amazed, for instance, to receive 'Document 45', which not only post-dated the alleged libel but included sixty-eight pages on the history and geography of Ebbw Vale. So far, with the clock ticking fast, McDonald's had disclosed twelve pages on the whole rainforest issue and nothing whatever on employment. They prepared an affidavit stating that McDonald's' list was defective because it was full of useless information, didn't list relevant documents and so on.

This time the hearing was in front of a different judge and this time the application had slightly more success – McDonald's was told to provide a list of the employment documents in its possession but the judge said he could not go back on Drake's decision and witness statements would have to be exchanged before 7 June as originally ordered. Effectively they had a month to assess McDonald's' documents and prepare their witness statements.

Meanwhile they were having to fight hard just to be heard. Barristers, QCs, solicitors and litigants in person all have designated seats in court. Litigants in person usually have to sit at a table at the front of the court, whilst barristers and QCs sit further back in rows of benches which are raised from the floor and are closer to the judge's eye level (the judge's bench being the highest in the courtroom). At one particular hearing Steel and Morris were right at the front, at floor level, and couldn't even see the judge over the top of his bench unless they were standing up.

Steel remembers: 'He spoke really quietly and we could barely hear him. At one point I couldn't hear a word that was being said, so I stood up, hoping I might be able to make out what he was saying. I didn't say a word, but the judge shouted at me to sit down and stop interrupting. I said: "If I could just say we can't . . ." but was cut off in midflow and told again to sit down. Eventually I actually had to shout over the judge to finish the sentence and let him know that we couldn't hear what was being said.'

What no one had told them was that court procedure deems that you signal your desire to interrupt or correct the other side (or address the judge) by standing up. 'How were we to know?' asks Steel. 'What are you supposed to do when you can't hear what's going on – just wait until you get asked for your comments and then tell the judge you haven't heard a word of what's been said? We felt this was pretty indicative of the way litigants in person are treated, as an irrelevance or obstacle to the proceedings rather than a party with the right to be heard and participate.'

Steel realized that the case was going to take up much more time than she or anyone had thought and so came back to live in London. The 7 June deadline for exchange of witness statements arrived and they were not ready, but neither was McDonald's. A new hearing was set for 7 July. The paperwork was getting out of hand. They still hadn't got their witness statements, partly because they did not know how they should be written or what needed to be included. Meanwhile they were being swamped with other pre-trial procedures, making them answer even more requests for details of their case. 'Sorting and photocopying around 2,500 pages of documents which we had to serve on McDonald's, reading all the documents they had served on us to determine what was useful and what was missing ... it was almost impossible,' says Steel. 'Dave had full-time responsibilities looking after Charlie, and I was looking for a flat and trying to sort out gas, electric and telephone, then moving everything down from Yorkshire. It was a complete nightmare.'

She developed stress-related eczema and insomnia. To make it worse they were then told by Mr Justice Drake to serve the witness statements within three weeks. Again they appealed for more time, but were refused. One of the grounds for appeal was that after the 7 July hearing, when the court usher had handed back their papers, in amongst them was a 'skeleton argument' on behalf of McDonald's, which had been handed up to the judge.

Steel and Morris knew something was wrong. They should have been given a copy. Whether this was deliberate or an oversight was never resolved. The Appeal Court ruled that the skeleton argument hadn't made any difference to the judge's ruling. But this didn't square since he'd read out, virtually word for word, large chunks of it. 'Other barristers we mentioned this to were shocked by the fact we hadn't been given a copy at the hearing – they considered that since it's much harder for litigants in person to follow all the legal arguments, it would be particularly important for them to get copies of any skeleton handed in,' says Steel.

She was close to desperation: 'It really felt at this point like we were banging our heads against a brick wall with the judicial system. This was the first time I ever seriously considered pulling out. I couldn't see the point in putting ourselves through all this stress (and jeopardizing my health) just to be treated with such utter contempt by the courts. It's odd how even when you don't have a lot of faith in the courts you still go in hoping they'll be fair, and it felt like a real slap in the face every time they weren't. I would never have apologized to McDonald's, but if we decided not to continue fighting the case, effectively McDonald's would have got an injunction without a trial and could then have had us jailed if we handed out leaflets or repeated the criticisms. At the time I felt like that couldn't be nearly as stressful as the huge amounts of legal work and court procedures we were having to endure. Anyway, Dave persuaded me to hang on in there.'

It was a real crisis. They had three weeks. Morris took the lead, and with some help from their friends they went back to all the campaigning groups and people they could think of who might help. The task was enormous. Not only did they have to find ex-employees and people with first-hand experience of working in the corporation and persuade them to give evidence on their behalf, they had to find experts in every area from nutrition to diet, disease, employment, the rainforests, animal welfare, even advertising techniques and child psychology. Morris was on the phone for twenty days solid. 'I said to people, "Just write down your experiences and opinions . . . put it in a letter and post it to me today . . . please."'

The response was tremendous. Researchers, trade unionists, environmentalists, nutritionists, McDonald's workers and others contributed. In three weeks they had collected sixty-five witness statements from a dozen countries. There were gaps in some of the international issues where it was particularly hard finding people to respond at such short notice, but the bundle they exchanged with McDonald's' solicitors on the day of the deadline was the basis of a case against the corporation in all areas covered by the Factsheet. 'It was a mountain to climb, but people climb mountains,' said Morris.

Morris and Steel say that the McDonald's lawyer in the court seemed visibly surprised that they could get the signed statements together on time, having previously told the judge that the defence case was 'just based on press cuttings'. Recalls Morris, 'he was chewing the pink ribbons that bind up legal documents'. Instead of it being a legal walkover, as the corporation might have expected, it was becoming clear that there would now be a full fight. 'We began to be taken seriously,' says Morris.

If they now saw the scale of what they were up against, it was also clear that the case had broader implications than they might have supposed. Steel and Morris were being made by McDonald's to substantiate absolutely everything in the Factsheet, including what they saw as the glaringly obvious (like, for example, McDonald's workers being 'low paid') or the common sense (some of its packaging ending up as 'litter'). They were, too, being forced to substantiate with facts and detailed arguments a lot of statements that many other organizations and social change movements around the world had been arguing for years. In a sense they were being asked to justify many others' words.

The further the defendants climbed up the legal mountain, the more the questions of freedom of speech and censorship – issues that no judge or jury were to be asked to rule on but which would possibly contribute to future law reforms – came fully into view. Starmer had expressed the way the imbalance in the libel laws between those who had money and those who didn't created 'a real risk ... that criticism would be stifled, purely and simply because those without money could not afford to stand up and try to prove what they say is true'.

The whole idea of multinationals suing individuals for libel seemed to Steel and Morris increasingly offensive, too; to them the principle fundamentally violated the rights of people to express opinions. A multinational was not constitutionally like an individual. It did not have feelings which could be hurt. It was not a person that had a reputation in the sense that people would think greater or lesser of it. It was a business entity, well able to express its views and counter criticism. Yet here was one of the most powerful corporations in the world suing two people for what it claimed was the lowering of its reputation, without having to prove or show that it had lost the sale of a single hamburger as a result of the leaflet being distributed.

Starmer told them that the British courts had recently ruled that government departments and local authorities could no longer sue for libel on the grounds that it would stifle free speech. The reasoning was that it was in the public interest that bodies like these be subject to unfettered scrutiny because of their role in society. The importance of free speech, indeed, was seen to outweigh the right of these bodies to protect their reputation. The same arguments – that it was important to be able to criticize local authorities – surely applied equally to multinationals. Could not these corporations, which often wielded more financial clout than whole countries, be seen to have a similar legal standing as local governments or departments? Did they genuinely need to use the British courts as a forum for getting their arguments across?

Meanwhile McDonald's seemed to hold all the trump cards. Early on Steel and Morris had applied for legal aid knowing that their application would be automatically turned down because no aid was available for defamation cases. With this ruling and the help of Liberty (the National Council for Civil Liberties), Britain's leading civil rights group, they took the British government to the European Commission of Human Rights in December 1992, saying that two unwaged people could not properly defend themselves against the almost unlimited resources of a (then) $20 billion a year corporation. They claimed that it was a denial of their rights to a fair trial and made free expression impossible. In March 1993 the Commission dismissed their case.

The European Court made what seemed to Steel and Morris the most illogical judgement yet: 'It boiled down to them saying that we were not being denied access to justice because we were putting up such a spirited defence. It was completely ridiculous. Perhaps if we had crumbled and said, "Oh dear, please have pity on us because we just can't cope," they might have said it's unfair. But as soon as you try and put up a fight then everything is fair and fine,' says Steel. 'If we collapse under stress then we will lose the case. If we don't collapse they will say the libel laws are fair. It's Catch-22. You have to be a victim to get sympathy, but the victim gets nowhere.'

How seriously McDonald's was now taking the case quickly became clear. In 1993 the corporation considered the weight of evidence assembled by Steel and Morris and raised the stakes. Thomas Shields, the barrister who had been handling the McDonald's case since the start, left, and in came Richard Rampton, one of Britain's most formidable libel QCs.

Rampton was a legal heavyweight, who had had more experience of this branch of law than almost anyone else. The successful defender of the *Sunday Times* editor Andrew Neil when he was libelled by Peregrine Worsthorne, the man who fought for Count Nickolai Tolstoy against Lord Aldington, was the co-editor of one of the most authoritative textbooks on defamation. His involvement in McDonald's vs. Steel and Morris was fundamental to everything else that happened.

Normally people of Rampton's calibre are not brought in at the pre-trial stages of a libel case, but are reserved for the full trial if only because of their cost. McDonald's was taking no chances. The case had been brought not just by McDonald's Restaurants (UK) but the parent company, the McDonald's Corporation, based in Oakbrook, Illinois. Money was no object. This was hardball and the corporation was about to assemble one of the strongest libel teams possible.

Rampton had come into the case at almost the same time as Mr Justice Drake handed over to Mr Justice Bell. In late 1993 the QC went for the jugular and applied to have a non-jury trial. McDonald's' whole case against Steel and Morris could be thrown out by a contrary British jury. The lottery of libel was well known. Here was one of the world's largest corporations – and a foreign one at that – taking on two people who had evident courage but few resources. A jury is always unpredictable, and might identify with Steel and

Morris and regard a stream of heavyweight executives as alien or distasteful.

The application was heard on 21 December 1993 and Rampton was on top form. His team had prepared their legal arguments well and he argued impressively. The most important issue in the case, he said, was whether McDonald's' food was linked to disease and worse. Rampton led with his ace: both sides, he said, would be presenting epidemiological arguments that both in their detail and methodology might be too complex for a jury.

Mr Justice Bell countered that a jury should be well able to deal with any complexities. Rampton flattered his trade: 'I would not feel confident of it in the way that I would with a judge ... a judge can immediately stop an expert and say, "Look, I am not following this ... explain again," and so on and so forth. A jury cannot ... a judge can do what he can, trying to anticipate the difficulties a jury might have. Of course he can. There is not the same dialogue.'

Then he raised the stakes, building up the importance of the judgement for McDonald's: 'It would be catastrophic for us if that issue went wrong because a majority of the jury did not understand the evidence properly ...'

Bell countered that this case did not just concern McDonald's.

Rampton was not deterred. His tactic seemed to be part psychological – to flatter the judge – and part professional – to persuade him with deft legal points. 'This can be avoided with a judge ... who understands properly the ... refined criticisms a jury cannot ...' Having caught him, he would not let go ... 'you get a reduced chance of a wrong decision and a reasoned judgement at the end ...'

Then, abruptly, he switched tack, arguing that a 'judge alone' trial would not just be good for the plaintiff but it would be in the interests of justice itself, good for the law and the public indeed, to have a reasoned decision (on which there could be an appeal), rather than a simple verdict one way or another. It would, he said, even help in the event of an appeal.

Bell again tested him. Nutrition was only one issue, he argued. Were not the environment, animals, packaging and waste, advertising, pay and work conditions of public interest, too? Rampton agreed (it is the first law of advocacy never to disagree with a judge) but none, he argued, was quite so important as the food issue.

He then threw in telling subsidiary arguments which in time would come to haunt him: the case, he said, was getting longer by the day. He said that he had made a mistake, that where he had said before that the case would last six weeks for a jury trial, now it was looking a bit longer . . .

But how long? For five minutes he built up the argument for saving time, and therefore money.

Rampton: '. . . and your lordship knows what happens in a judge-alone case. Just take the opening. If this is a jury case I am likely to have to open the case for maybe three days . . . with a judge I can do it in half a day . . . A jury does not get the reading time . . . and very often, as your lordship knows, when an expert is in the witness-box, if it is the judge alone, the jury does not have to sit back and grin and bear it while the counsel try and elucidate the matter and they are fumbling away for the benefit of the jury. He just leaps in and asks the question himself . . .'

He revised downwards the weeks he had thought it would take for a judge alone – 'It is more likely three than four . . .' and he revised upwards the number of weeks he thought it would take with a jury: 'more likely six or seven with a jury. I am not trying to exaggerate . . . but that it is how it seems to me at the moment . . .'

Even then Bell was not convinced.

Bell: 'Just about everything could be more conveniently tried by a judge alone.'

Rampton: 'It is not a case of sufficient public importance to sway the thing back again, away from a judge alone towards jury. Even if it were in one sense because the issues are emotive . . . in fact the interests are much better served by a careful hearing before a judge alone and above all by a reasoned judgement given in open court.'

Now it was Steel's turn to fight for a jury. The series of hearings and two years' immersion in legal arguments had well prepared her. First she dealt with the question of public interest.

Steel: 'Here we have a multimillion-dollar company which has taken out full-page advertisements on various of these issues. They have been matters of comment in newspapers . . . it is quite obvious that it is a matter of public importance . . . therefore it ought to be tried by the public, or representatives of the public.' She quoted Lord Denning saying that length and complexity were no bar to a jury; she quoted Lord Lawton saying that one of the benefits of a trial by jury was that everyone had to keep the issues few and simple. 'If the case is too complicated for a jury to understand, it is very likely it is going to be too complicated for us to understand and therefore it is not going to be possible for us to have a fair trial.' She argued that it was their absolute right to have a jury to try the charge that they had criticized the great and the powerful on a matter of huge public interest. She returned to Lord Lawton's arguments via Denning, passionately arguing that 'it would be wrong to get rid of a mode of trial which had become identified in the minds of many with constitutional rights and liberties . . . our reputation is as much at stake as McDonald's' is'.

When Bell gave his ruling he was persuaded on all counts that the scientific issues were too complex. He thought, yes, a judge would have advantages over a jury, yes, it would take longer with a jury and it would be more expensive. But the most important issue, he said, *bearing in mind the plaintiff's business*, was the scientific issue. There would be no jury.

Having secured the judgement Rampton moved straight on to other matters. Bell asked Morris his opinion on them.

Morris: 'The position is, and if you could put this on the tape, that I am suffering from shock from the decisions you have just made . . . So it does not – I am just suffering from shock, because if I may take the liberty of expressing an opinion on your judgement—'

Bell: 'It is not appropriate. You know what your remedies are if you are not satisfied with any decision which I make.'

Morris: 'Bearing in mind . . . that the issue of having a jury or not having a jury is in itself probably the most fundamental issue of public importance in the entire criminal and civil system, I would ask you to give us leave to appeal.'

Bell: 'No.'

Steel and Morris were devastated. They had not thought it possible that a jury would be denied them. They thought McDonald's was trying it on. Juries, in the very ordinary public world that they inhabited, were as fundamental as air or water and the right to be tried in front of one seemed to be the one right that everyone had. They had expected Mr Justice Bell to throw Rampton's arguments out. After all, who could be more ordinary than a gardener and a postman both without scientific or legal training. If they were deemed capable of grasping the science well enough to defend themselves and present a reasoned case to a judge over issues which everyone agreed were of interest to the public, then why could not their peers follow their arguments?

It was a defining moment of the case. Nothing confirmed their view of the system working against the 'ordinary' person so much as this. Any confidence they might have had in the legal system was swept away. Nothing, they said, gave them so much sense of being on their own and isolated by the power of money and privilege as this.

Both Steel and Morris were politically outraged, arguing vehemently out of court that this was an insult to the public (of which they were members) and that the British legal Establishment was protecting a $24 billion a year US corporation at the expense of the rights of members of the public. The prospect of presenting a case to a judge was not nearly so appealing. Here, it seemed, was a member of the Establishment who, they thought, was already showing himself to be on the side of their opponents. The decision seemed to be entirely consistent. The whole point of people distributing leaflets was to make the public aware of what they felt were important issues. Now they were being denied the right to even put those opinions to representatives of the public in a court case that could adversely affect the rest of their lives and the public's access to information.

They immediately appealed to the Court of Appeal. The hearing took place in March 1994. The case had been taken up by Liberty, which provided a barrister for their appeal. Patrick Milmo QC, acting without a fee and instructed by solicitors Michael Skrein and Sallie Spilsbury, argued Steel and Morris's case.

The stakes were high. Liberty argued that the case now raised issues of great importance, notably the right to the freedom of speech and the fundamental question of access to justice. Philip Leach, Liberty's Legal Officer, said: 'As has been previously said by the Court of Appeal, where the issues in a case are likely to affect the public to a great extent, "the opinions of twelve jurors may reflect the public's view more accurately than the assessment of any judge".' Again they were refused a jury. The legal profession raised its eyebrows.

Marcel Berlins, *Guardian* columnist and leading legal commentator, remarked: 'I cannot think of a case in which the legal cards have been so spectacularly stacked against one party.'

Milmo had argued strongly, but there was to be no jury despite a further application for leave to appeal made to the only court left in Britain, the House of Lords, the upper chamber of parliament. Steel by that time was sanguine: 'It was probably just as well they refused because if they'd allowed it the next stage was to stump up £18,000 security before you can go ahead; so it would have been worse if we'd lost it after putting up so much money which we didn't have anyway.'

But Milmo was arguing not just about the right to have a jury. At the same time that Rampton had argued so strongly against a jury trial, he had claimed that Steel and Morris had not got enough primary evidence to defend parts of the Factsheet and had applied to have whole chunks of their case about rainforests and McDonald's' international employment practices thrown out of court, potentially reducing their case. Mr Justice Bell had agreed and it seemed as if the defence case was falling apart. This time Milmo won the point and Mr Justice Bell's ruling was overturned. Steel and Morris's defence was restored and it was ruled that they were entitled to rely on future discovery of McDonald's' documents, and evidence that they might reasonably be expected to discover 'by interrogation, subpoena and in cross-examination of witnesses'.

It was a landmark legal decision which Skrein described as having 'a particular importance to media defendants and investigative journalism. It may well serve as a bulwark of free speech'. Andrew Puddephatt, General Secretary of Liberty, interpreted it to mean that those who wished to sue for libel could no longer keep documents which might be valuable to the defence from the court.

It was their first legal victory. It was March 1994, more than three years since the writs were received; it looked certain that it would reach a full trial. They were encouraged and exhausted.

McDonald's entered 1994 in good financial shape. The corporation was expanding in Britain and now had almost 500 restaurants. The plan was to double the number within ten years, Michael Quinlan, Chair and Chief Executive of the worldwide chain told the Institute of Directors in April. And in his first annual review of the company, UK President Paul Preston stated that 'we are aware that many people know little more about us than the fact that we have a restaurant in their town . . .' The corporation, he said, was making real progress on the health front, 'looking at ways to reduce the sugar and salt content of our products'.

It was also looking for ways to stop the tactics that Steel and Morris's supporters were employing. The McLibel Support Campaign (MSC), set up after the writs were served to increase pressure on McDonald's, had as the trial approached taken off in a dozen countries with coordinated 'days of action', including London marches of 500 people each time, and mass leafleting (coordinated by MSC and Veggies of Nottingham). Meanwhile the support campaign was linking with resident groups, and starting to target new McDonald's stores. Offers of help came in from legal volunteers. Money began to trickle in, with small amounts from many individuals, group fund-raisers and collections at trade union conferences.

The act of taking two people to court was having the exact opposite of the desired effect, it seemed. Instead of stopping McDonald's' critics, it was exacerbating the situation. Instead of just a few people from London Greenpeace leafleting its stores, the corporation now had hundreds of people to contend with. By April 1994, the McLibel Support Campaign was claiming that more than half a million 'What's Wrong With McDonald's?' leaflets had been handed out since the writs were served.

Rhian, from Manchester, was typical of so many who had been part of the campaign since its earliest days. Firstly in Northamptonshire, later in Manchester, she and groups of people would go out with Reggie the Veggie, a mock Ronald McDonald with a green wig and a pantomime cow. It was simple good-natured, cheeky agitprop street theatre. Once they planted a tree in a McDonald's drive-through. Occasionally they would collect the litter around the restaurants and return it. They were once locked into a restaurant by an irate manager while he called the police. Always they handed out the leaflets.

And then, in April 1994, just as the trial was about to start and the chest-beating on both sides was getting louder, McDonald's started distributing its own leaflets about the case. More than a quarter of a million started appearing in its restaurants. Titled 'Why McDonald's is going to court' they stated that the action against Steel and Morris was 'not about freedom of speech; it is about the right to stop people telling lies'. They issued a press release and attacked London Greenpeace, inviting leaflet readers to contact Mike Love, Director of Communications for McDonald's UK (and previously Conservative Party constituency manager for Margaret Thatcher when she was Prime Minister) for more information.

The leafleting wars hotted up. Rhian and others in Manchester went down to the McDonald's in Market Street. As they handed out their leaflets to customers, a McDonald's man would come out and hand out his. 'We were quite happy to let people hear both sides of the story,' says Rhian. 'It was all quite jolly, really, at least on our side. People seemed really interested by the issues, more than when we started. They seem more aware.'

Meanwhile Steel, Morris and their legal help pounced. To be called 'liars' by their adversaries on the eve of the trial was legal good fortune. They immediately counter-claimed for libel against McDonald's. Suddenly the trial was to be put on another footing. The counter-claim was most important, said Starmer: 'It turned the tables and changed the focus of the case. Until the McDonald's leaflet came along, the company were able to sit back and cast Steel and Morris in the role of the people in the wrong, who had to defend themselves and show that they were telling the truth.'

With the counter-claim, McDonald's would now have to prove why it was saying that the original Factsheet was lies, indeed to prove that its business practices were not as described in the Factsheet, and produce evidence to that effect. This appeared important in several ways. With the focus of the verdict now less on Steel and Morris, McDonald's would run a real risk that the public would be more likely to see it as the wrongdoer. Effectively McDonald's was on trial and Mr Justice Bell would have a doubly hard task, eventually having to rule not on sixteen but thirty-two charges.

Morris was ebullient: 'Now they are under the same burden of proof. They will have to *prove* that the ideas of their critics are actually untrue, that they do *not* pay low pay, that they do *not* target children in their advertising and so on. Effectively a multinational corporation is in the dock on trial for its business practices. It's probably never happened before.'

It also meant that Steel and Morris would have to go through all the rigmarole of the pleadings and the discovery again. This time, though, they had already had many months' court experience, and could use the legal system to their advantage. Where McDonald's had made the running at the beginning, it was now the defendants' turn to attack. They had long argued in hearings that it was 'implausible' that McDonald's could provide so few documents, especially about its beef sources in Brazil and Central America and international labour disputes. Now they argued in court that there had to be more. Mr Justice Bell ordered three US McDonald's vice-presidents to swear further affidavits about the existence of company documents.

The stakes were high on both sides. 'It would be the kiss of death for McDonald's if the public should come to the conclusion as a result of the verdict that the plaintiff's food is apt to give them cancer of the bowel or breast . . .', Rampton had said in an appeal court hearing only a few months before. 'If McDonald's succeed it will give the green light to corporations everywhere to use the UK libel laws to silence their critics,' said Steel.

The full trial was finally due to start on 28 June and was scheduled to run three months. First in the witness-box was to be McDonald's UK's President, Paul Preston, an American who joined the corporation at sixteen and had been twenty years in Britain. He was recently quoted as saying, 'McDonald's isn't a job, it's a life.'

Steel and Morris were beginning to understand what he meant.

Chapter Five

Action, Lights

Clerk of Court: 'Court rise.'

Enter Mr Justice Bell.

Mr Justice Bell: 'Yes, Mr Rampton?'

Rampton: 'My lord, in this action I appear with my learned friend Mr Timothy Atkinson for the plaintiffs who are the McDonald's Corporation, an American company which has achieved some renown throughout the world for the sale of fast food including, in particular, hamburgers and what in this country we call chips but which, in the context of this case, I shall call French fries.

'My lord, there may well be people ... not too many ... who do not like McDonald's' food, whether because it is made from meat or because they do not like the taste of it, or whatever other reason. Such people may wish to add expression to their views about McDonald's' food sometimes in strong terms. So far as McDonald's are concerned, anybody is free to express his criticism in whatever terms he wishes. McDonald's may not like it, but they would never try to prevent it. They cannot and do not object to fair and reasonable and honest criticism of their business or their products.

'What, however, they will always seek to prevent ... always have sought to prevent ... is dissemination of false factual information about the company, its business and its products.

'[The Factsheet] is, your lordship may conclude at the end of the case, a wholesale attack on almost every aspect of the plaintiffs' business which, if it were accepted as being true, would necessarily cause McDonald's an enormous amount of damage. . . . It is, on the plaintiffs' case, completely false in every material respect.'

COURT 35. 29 JUNE 1994.

Mr Justice Bell: 'Yes, Ms Steel?'

Steel: 'We feel there is one word that can sum up what this case is about, and that word is "censorship". McDonald's are using the libel laws of this country to censor and silence their critics. During this trial we intend to show that the public face of McDonald's is a fraud; that the truth that lies behind their image is far from savoury.

'As Mr Rampton has admitted, their aim in taking this case to its conclusion is to gain a legal seal of approval for their business practices. This is a show trial against unwaged, unrepresented defendants. McDonald's hope that because of our lack of resources and legal experience they will gain an easy victory and a detailed judgement in their favour which they can then use to say to all their critics that they have proven, to the satisfaction of the court, they are squeaky clean.

'I am not ashamed of wanting a society where people are equal, where animals and the environment are respected and treated well. We do not want to change society for the sake of it. There are probably a hundred and one things I would rather be doing than campaigning and fighting this court case, for example, climbing mountains, walking through forests, gardening, just to name a few.

'The fact that I want to live in a more caring, equal society does not mean that I would deliberately tell lies about a company. There is enough that is bad about McDonald's without inventing false allegations.'

Mr Justice Bell: 'Yes, Mr Morris?'

Morris: 'We believe it is not only the public's right but also their duty to criticize those with wealth and power in society . . .

'We do believe that the Factsheet is true and is fair comment. I do not like bullies, I do not like exploitation and I do not like propaganda in order to make profits . . . The more sophisticated the deceit or propaganda, the more concerned I am to question and challenge it.

'We are facing a well-paid, well-versed and rehearsed team with all the resources and backing they could possibly need. We are unpaid, unrehearsed, inexperienced, we have little time to prepare, extremely nervous and probably what might happen – it is possible – is that Mr Rampton might wipe the floor with us . . .'

By the time the trial started, Rampton's 'three to four weeks' estimate for the proceedings had been abandoned and the hearing was scheduled to last twelve weeks. Over 170 witnesses from both sides were lined up, including many of McDonald's' directors and executives, department heads, advisers and consultants from the UK and the US. Steel and Morris were to rely on researchers, former employees and academics. Each would be questioned first by their own side and then would be cross-examined by the other side. They could all be re-examined.

The plaintiff's witnesses are usually called first, to be

followed by the defendants', but because the case covered so many areas both sides agreed it would be easier to divide the trial up into 'issues' and take them one at a time. Everyone agreed it would make the case smoother. Perhaps even shorter.

That was the plan . . .

Chapter Six

A Diet of Words

COURT 35. 28 JUNE 1994.

Mr Rampton (reading extracts from the Factsheet published by London Greenpeace): 'One reads the text on the [third] page: "McDonald's try to show in their 'Nutrition Guide' that mass-produced hamburgers, chips, colas, milk shakes, etc., are a useful and nutritious part of any diet. What they do not make clear is that a diet high in fat, sugar, animal products and salt (sodium), and low in fibre, vitamins and minerals – which describes an average McDonald's meal" – and your lordship will notice I emphasize the words "diet" and "meal" – "is linked with cancers of the breast and bowel, and heart disease. This is accepted medical fact," says the leaflet, "not a cranky theory. Every year in Britain, heart disease alone causes about 180,000 deaths."

'My lord, if the implication of that passage is that the person who eats a McDonald's meal is running a significant risk or, indeed, any risk at all of giving himself cancer or heart disease or, as the defendants additionally allege now, diabetes, then, my lord, it is an entirely false statement.

'Next heading: "Fast = junk. Even if they like eating them, most people recognize that processed burgers and synthetic chips, served up in paper and plastic containers" – my lord, in passing, McDonald's chips are not synthetic. They are made from ordinary potatoes – like other chips people cook in their own houses.

' "Paying for the habit" is the next heading: "Chewing is essential for good health, as it promotes the flow of digestive juices which break down the food and send nutrients into the blood. McDonald's food is so lacking in bulk it is hardly possible to chew it. Even their own figures show that a 'quarter-pounder' is 48 per cent water." If that is meant to suggest McDonald's add water to their meat, again it is 100 per cent false.

'Nothing is added to the beef which goes to make the hamburgers.

' "This sort of fake food" – my lord, perhaps there one finds the confirmation that the defendants in this leaflet are alleging water is added to the quarter-pounder – "encourages overeating, and the high sugar and sodium content can make people develop a kind of addiction – a 'craving'. That means more profit for McDonald's, but constipation, clogged arteries and heart attacks for many customers." Once again, my lord, if this is meant to mean something more than that, there are quite a lot of people in the world who rather like to eat McDonald's' food, then again it is completely false.

'Your Lordship may not find it difficult to see why it is that the plaintiffs brought this action. It is a wholesale attack on almost every aspect of the plaintiffs' business which, if it were accepted as being true, would necessarily cause McDonald's an enormous amount of damage.'

*

Nutrition was the single most important section of the whole libel case for McDonald's. The Factsheet's allegations about this issue struck at the heart of the corporation's business. If a court of law ruled that McDonald's' food was unhealthy, found, too, that McDonald's knew it was unhealthy and furthermore found that the company was deceiving its customers, the effect on business worldwide might be catastrophic.

But it was always going to be tricky for McDonald's, given the virile debate on food in the public domain and the passionate but varying views expressed by scientists. The defendants rejected Rampton's interpretation of the Factsheet, calling it extreme and arguing that people would not read satirical banner headlines and cartoons in such a literal way. They believed that it expressed little more than established scientific opinion about the links between diet and ill health.

But McDonald's' strategy was to require Steel and Morris to prove every word in the Factsheet. The corporation had analysed in advance the defendants' expert witness statements and knew pretty well how they and their witnesses would argue. They aimed to pressurize the two legal amateurs to come up with primary evidence, to prove in particular terms what many respected dietary and food organizations were saying in general terms about diet. The onus was on Steel and Morris to provide conclusive proof of cause and effect between particular elements of the diet and particular diseases, instead of the broad general statement about the link between a high-fat/low-fibre diet and heart disease and cancer. Any argument, scientific or cultural, that was legally incomplete, contradictory, inadmissible or given by someone whom McDonald's considered to be unqualified would be mercilessly dismissed by Rampton.

Steel and Morris would also have liked to have argued culturally. Their objection to McDonald's was as much to do

with the role the company had played in changing centuries-
old ways of eating that they considered important. Most
people, they said, throughout history had eaten the best
quality food possible, usually cooked in the home and eaten
communally. Now they saw an industrial structure beginning
to dominate neighbourhoods and people's lives – 'undermin-
ing' food habits as people knew them. In their eyes, mass-
produced, processed food has gradually replaced fresh food.
McDonald's was only a small reason for this, but its influence
was enormous.

Steel and Morris had decided that their best tactic would
be to try to force admissions from McDonald's' witnesses,
many of whom were company men and who, they believed,
would be vulnerable. In this section, however, they had to nail
down some elusive facts.

Statistics about food can be notoriously contradictory and
open to interpretation. Each side's witnesses tried to summarize the state of medical and scientific opinion. Steel and Morris
argued that in the main there was a consensus about the link
beween diet and ill health backed by such authorities as the
World Health Organisation and the UK Health Education
Authority. McDonald's countered that if any contradictory
evidence existed at all then the claims about a link were false.

Nevertheless, it seemed the defendants had a dream start.
Very early in the trial, McDonald's produced its star witness
on the connections between diet and cancers. Dr Sydney
Arnott was an undoubted authority, a consultant in radio-
therapy and oncology at St Bartholomew's Hospital in
London for ten years. Morris quoted him a McDonald's
pamphlet that had been distributed by the corporation in
1985 to health workers. It read: 'There is a considerable
amount of evidence to suggest that many of the diseases which
are more common in the Western, affluent world – diseases
such as obesity, diabetes, high blood pressure, heart disease,

stroke, and some forms of cancer – are related to diet. The typical Western diet is relatively low in dietary fibre (rough-age) and high in fat, salt and sugar.'

Morris: 'Do you agree with this?'

Arnott: 'Yes.'

The trap was set. Morris then read him another, milder statement: 'A diet high in fat, sugar, animal products and salt and low in fibre, vitamins and minerals is linked with cancers of the breast and bowel, and heart disease.' Arnott was asked what he thought of this. He paused and replied: 'If it is being directed to the public then I would say it is a very reasonable thing to say.'

Morris then revealed that it was a direct quotation from the Factsheet. Rampton was horrified. He had cited this section of the leaflet in one of the pre-trial hearings as being the most 'defamatory' adding that, if proven, it would be the 'kiss of death' for a fast-food company like McDonald's.

Steel and Morris were elated. The fact that McDonald's' own expert had agreed with this statement from the leaflet seemed to mean that they had won hands down on the issue of nutrition. The words that McDonald's complained about were thought to be reasonable by the corporation's star witness. What more could a judge or an absent jury have wanted? What they felt was their advantage was only con-firmed when Robert Beavers, a senior vice-president of the corporation and member of the board of directors, came to the witness-box. He was challenged with the two quotes, and stated: 'I cannot spot any difference.'

Of course it was not to prove that easy. McDonald's made a deft legal move: it won an application to change its 'Statement of Claim', which forms the base of the plaintiff's case and is McDonald's' interpretation of the alleged libel against it. The original claim had read: 'McDonald's "are deliberately misleading the public as to the nutritional value of the goods they sell, when they know full well that the contents of an average McDonald's meal are linked with cancers of the breast and bowel and heart disease" and that this is untrue and damaging to McDonald's' reputation.'

It now read: 'McDonald's "1. Sell meals which cause cancer of the breast and bowel and heart disease in their customers. 2. despite knowing that this is an accepted medical fact, deliberately and dishonestly conceal that fact from the public by publishing nutritional guides which (a) suppress that fact and (b) falsely claim that their meals are a useful and nutritional part of any diet" and that this is untrue and damaging to the reputation of McDonald's.'

The crucial change was from using the word 'link' to using the word 'cause'. Steel and Morris had taken it as their starting point. It immediately became harder.

Steel and Morris had prepared their case and sought statements from their witnesses on the basis of the first claim. All McDonald's' witnesses had been cross-examined on that basis. What's more, the defendants argued that this new claim strengthened what was in their view the interpretation that it was the meals themselves, that is the burgers and buns, which caused disease rather than the nutritional content of this type of meal. Rampton here relied on the satirical elements of the leaflet – the cartoon and the arches containing the words 'McCancer' and 'McDisease', arguing that it was this context rather than the text which enabled this interpretation. The judge allowed McDonald's' changes to the claim and a trip to the Court of Appeal failed to make a difference. This bitter dispute over meaning simmered throughout the trial. Whatever one may think of either side's arguments, the heart of a libel case is always the publication of remarks made and what the plaintiff alleges these mean. The judge's final ruling on meaning was that the leaflet, for better or for worse, meant that those who eat a significant amount of

McDonald's' food run the very real risk of suffering degenerative diseases.

Steel and Morris had intended to expose the way the corporation worked at every point, but where they sought to broaden the arguments McDonald's fought always to refine their argument down and down; by offering slim but strong presentations of information it argued from the most particular angle, rather than the impossibly general angle forced on Morris and Steel. As far as nutrition went, McDonald's was to cut back the argument to this: statistics of who ate what in McDonald's at various ages would suggest that over the course of a lifetime the consumption of McDonald's' food by even its heaviest users would have non-existent effects on health.

McDonald's' expert witness, Professor Verner Wheelock, a consultant employed by McDonald's since 1991, initially tried to play down the links between diet and ill health. But when confronted with an article he had written a couple of years earlier he agreed that there was a considerable body of evidence that medical conditions like obesity, diabetes, high blood pressure, heart disease (which he had said was the 'number one health problem of the nation'), strokes and some forms of cancer were related to a diet high in fat, saturated fat, salt and sugar, and low in dietary fibre. The article had continued: 'We have now reached the point where we can be very confident that diet is the primary factor in the development of most of the degenerative diseases [including cancer] in many industrialized countries'. Wheelock confirmed this view from the witness-box. He also agreed with government dietary recommendations based on such views. A typical McDonald's meal he said, was high in fat, saturated fat and sodium (salt). Paul Preston, McDonald's UK's President, had earlier said that McDonald's' products were low in fibre and would not come within dietary recommendations. Wheelock further said that it was 'not sensible' to encourage the eating of foods high in fat, saturated fat, sugar and sodium and low in fibre. He accepted that people were attracted to high levels of sugar and salt and found it hard to give up the taste.

Wheelock tried to keep McDonald's' foods in perspective. There was, he said, an assumption that they made up a large part of people's diets. But if you ate one McDonald's meal a week it showed that it was quite possible to achieve the dietary recommendations for total fat, saturated fat and sugar, even though an individual meal did not conform to the guidelines. Besides, he said, people exercised their powers of choice in deciding to eat at McDonald's.

Professor Wheelock continued: 'It is the responsibility of individuals to determine what exactly they are going to eat. If they are to construct a healthy diet, then it is absolutely essential that they know what is in the food . . . I would say there has been a complete transformation in the attitude of the British government towards diet and health in the last fifteen years or so. When I first came into that field there was very little interest at all. The attitude taken from the government at that time was: "It is not our job to tell people what to eat . . ."' He said that McDonald's was highly responsible: 'They have been producing literature since about 1984 or 1985 which gives information on the main dietary constituents in the different McDonald's products that people are likely to be interested in and concerned about.'

Geoffrey Cannon, Chair of the National Food Alliance of consumer organizations and Scientific Director of the World Cancer Research Fund, was then called by Steel and Morris as an expert on public health policy. He said that the US government, the European Union and the World Health Organisation all recommended reducing consumption of fatty foods and increasing consumption of fruit, vegetables and other foods containing fibre in order to prevent a significant proportion of the large number of deaths each year from heart disease (200,000 in the UK) and cancer (160,000 in the UK). The 1990 World Health Organisation Report stated: 'dietary factors are now known to influence the development of ... heart disease, various cancers, hypertension ... and diabetes. These conditions are the commonest cause of premature death in developed countries ... The "affluent" type of diet that often accompanies economic development is energy dense. People consuming these diets characteristically have a high intake of fat (especially saturated fat) and free sugars and a relatively low intake of complex carbohydrates (from starchy, fibre-containing foods).' The defendants repeatedly referred to this report: if authorities such as the World Health Organisation could say these things, then why couldn't they? Why did they need to call experts to prove them?

Cannon agreed that for those seeking to improve the population's health, it was 'not sensible or responsible to encourage people to eat foods nutritionally worse than the dietary guidelines'. Such food could 'be reasonably considered as being unhealthy' and a 'negative contribution' to the diet.

McDonald's was not conceding legal points. Dr Neal Barnard, President of the US Physicians' Committee for Responsible Medicine, appearing for Steel and Morris, told how 'many products sold at McDonald's are high in fat and cholesterol, and low in fibre and certain vitamins' and as a result these products 'contribute to heart disease, certain forms of cancer and other diseases' (including obesity, diabetes and hypertension). The links between diet and these now epidemic diseases were, he said, 'established beyond any reasonable doubt', and were causal in nature. During Dr Barnard's evidence, Richard Rampton conceded that 'we would all agree' that there is a link – note that word, 'link' not 'cause' – between a high-fat, low-fibre diet and cancer of the breast and colon.

Dr Barnard pointed out that 'McDonald's' products clearly contain significantly more fat than government guidelines and health authorities recommend'. Evidence had shown that 'fatty foods tend to be habituating' and 'increase the likelihood of continued high fat intake'. McDonald's, he suggested, remained part of the problem, rather than part of the solution.

The type of questions which were posed might seem on the one hand impossibly broad – what does 'nutritious' mean? – or, on the other hand, impossibly obvious – does a diet high in fats contribute to coronary heart disease? However, in reaching his conclusions about such questions, the judge could, by law, only take account of the evidence with which he was presented during the trial itself; he had, as it were, to make himself an intellectual 'tabula rasa' – 'forgetting' what he might have understood about these matters from the wider world or learned during the course of his whole life, and giving judgement solely on the evidence presented in Court 35.

Before the trial began McDonald's had made what is known as a 'formal admission', the point of which is to prevent the need for either side presenting evidence at trial on the specific admission. It had stated: 'there is a considerable amount of evidence of a relationship between a diet high in saturated fat and sodium, and obesity, high blood pressure and heart disease'. Making this admission, McDonald's made one notable omission, that of a 'relationship' between diet and cancer.

Barnard stated that he had 'outlined several health hazards linked to McDonald's' products and similar foods. In response, the plaintiffs have submitted statements attempting to dispute some, although not all, of these links . . . it must be noted that there are some who claim that, in spite of an enormous number of well-controlled research studies, it is impossible to draw any conclusions about the role of food in the causation of illness.'

The judge ruled that: 'although Dr Barnard used words such as "links", "connections" and "association" in relation to high-fat diets and foods and heart disease, hypertension, certain cancers, gall-bladder disease and diabetes, it is clear that he was saying that such links, connections and associations were causative'.

Barnard was strong on the causative links between diet and cancer. He said that there were well-known biological effects of meat consumption that offered plausible mechanisms for the causation of cancer and encouraged its progression. He said: 'The issue at hand is whether products sold at McDonald's pose a potential risk. Overwhelming evidence is that they do.'

McDonald's came back equally strongly, stressing the inability of science to prove a causative link between diet and cancer, which was its interpretation of the leaflet. This, of course, is where it became ever more apparent that its alteration of 'link' to 'cause' was crucial. For if scientists themselves had been unable to prove 'cause' though they could demonstrate 'links', how on earth could Steel and Morris hope to?

Dr Arnott now dealt at length with the aetiology or causation of certain cancers, particularly cancer of the breast and colon. He was prepared to accept that one could say that consumption of saturated fat or total fat was related to breast cancer but he denied that a cause and effect relationship was established. Much the same, he said, applied to cancer of the colon. Under cross-examination, Steel tried to find out how far Arnott had during his career concentrated on treatment of cancers rather than research into causes. He said that he recommended a low-fat/high-fibre diet to his cancer patients. This, he said, was 'prudent'.

A succession of witnesses took the stand, often questioned at length – sometimes painful length – by both sides. The defendants called Professor Colin Campbell from the USA, Chair of the Dietary Prevention of Cancer Worldwide, a highly distinguished international committee of scientists. He was convinced that 'a high-fat, low-fibre diet is causal in the development of a wide range of cancers and cardiovascular disease'. Most importantly he considered that these serious diseases are largely preventable by dietary means. Professor Michael Crawford, an expert on dietary fats and their relation to human health, and a consultant to the World Health Organisation, also gave evidence for the defendants. He emphasized the association between a high-fat diet and increased risk of cancers of the breast, colon and prostate. This, he maintained, was particularly evident from 'population studies' of different countries with varied diets and disease rates, from 'migration' studies (showing that immigrant populations soon adopted the diet and disease rates of the country of settlement) and from the large increase of heart disease and cancer in countries such as Japan where the modern Western diet is fast replacing traditional, healthier diets. He stated that 'not only are McDonald's encouraging the use of a style of food which is closely associated with risk of cancer and heart disease whilst health professionals are trying to reduce the risks to Western populations, but they are actively promoting the same in cultures where at present these diseases are not a problem'.

If one of the crucial issues of this part of the trial concerned the relationships between diet and disease, the other issue was whether or not the leaflet meant that McDonald's was misleading the public about the nutritiousness of its products.

Peter Cox, a former marketing consultant giving evidence for the defendants, said that the effect of the company's efforts to promote its products as 'good, nutritious food' over the years was 'to debase the concept of "healthy eating" to no more than a cynical sales promotional ploy'. He went on to say that the company's claim to be concerned about healthy eating was not borne out by the products it sold. Even their salads had a 'ludicrously high' fat content (over 50 per cent calories from fat).

Steel and Morris cross-examined a succession of McDonald's' witnesses about what the company meant when it described its products as 'nutritious'. They referred to the company's nutritional guide for customers which said that 'every time you eat at McDonald's, you will be eating good, nutritious food'. What, they asked, did this mean? All McDonald's' witnesses basically agreed that it meant (in the words of Edward Oakley, a vice-president) 'foods that contain nutrients'. When the man responsible for the 'nutrition guides' in McDonald's' stores was asked if there was any food he knew of that is not nutritious, he said, 'I do not know if you would call it food or not, but you could put up an argument for black coffee or black tea or mineral water.' Asked 'What about Coca-Cola?' he said, 'Coca-Cola has a good source of energy, no question of that.' He was then asked if he thought it was nutritious, to which he stated, 'Yes, it can be.'

David Green, Senior Vice-President of Marketing (USA), argued, similarly, that he thought Coca-Cola was nutritious, because it provided water, and that was part of a balanced diet. Even Professor Wheelock, McDonald's' consultant on nutrition, defined the word nutritious, similarly, to mean 'contains nutrients'. He accepted that all foods have nutrients. When asked to define 'junk food' he said it was 'whatever a person doesn't like' (in his case semolina). Richard Rampton intervened to say that McDonald's was not objecting to the description of its food as 'junk food'. Steel riposted that the word 'nutritious', if used in the way that McDonald's suggested, was effectively completely meaningless.

Dr Tim Lobstein, Co-director of the Food Commission, a consumer organization, gave evidence for the defence as an expert on food policy issues. On studying eight suggested typical McDonald's 'meal combinations', he concluded that they are 'generally imbalanced with regard to their nutrient content'. He said they are 'excessively fatty and salty', and correspondingly low in the 'nutrient density' of several essential nutrients such as vitamins and minerals. A Food Commission survey in 1987 had found that 31 per cent of people questioned at fast-food stores in Peckham in South London ate fast food every day, and that 9 per cent of the total sample ate burgers every day.

Dr Lobstein concluded that there were sections of the population eating a very unbalanced diet – this view was backed by reference to other surveys. He was particularly concerned by the diets of school children, and also by the expansion of McDonald's' promotions in schools and hospitals.

McDonald's' argument that its food could be eaten as part of a balanced diet was, according to Dr Lobstein, 'meaningless'. Rather than using the word 'balanced', he would suggest greater consumption of healthy foods.

When questioned by Rampton, Wheelock said that McDonald's adopted a very responsible attitude on providing information about their products. 'McDonald's in this country is one of the leading companies in helping to make changes that are in line with the dietary recommendations to their products.'

In her summing up of this part of the case, Steel reminded the court that Wheelock had agreed that it was not sensible to encourage people to eat foods which are high in fat, saturated fat, sugar, sodium and low in fibre; she continued, 'which is precisely what McDonald's are doing, they are continually marketing those very products and encouraging people to eat more and more of them. And at the same time, trying to promote them as if they were nutritious.' She continued: 'We heard that they do not have a nutrition department and that Mr Oakley, the Senior Vice-President of McDonald's UK, had said that it was not felt to be an important enough issue to have a separate nutritional department like McDonald's have marketing or communications departments. So we say their so-called support for 'Health of the Nation' dietary initiatives is basically just another PR stunt, and that any changes they are making are very slow, minimal and are only being done because of the huge amount of pressure that the company has come under from nutritionists.'

She would also tell the court of an internal company memo, which reported on a high-level meeting in the US in March 1986 with public relations advisers prior to a major advertising campaign. The memo stated: 'McDonald's should attempt to deflect the basic negative thrust of our critics ... How do we do this? By talking "moderation and balance". We can't really address or defend nutrition. We don't sell nutrition and people don't come to McDonald's for nutrition.'

Steel said that this was an admission from McDonald's that its use of the word nutritious was effectively deceptive. She said, 'It is as clear as day that they are well aware that their food is not nutritious and it is not viewed by the public as being nutritious, but they are then going to proceed to attempt to deceive the public in order to persuade them to eat more of the company's junk food.'

McDonald's' summing up of the case was lengthy and complex, an argument couched in the language of figures, percentages, charts, tables, acronyms, statistics, references, cross-references, headings, sub-headings, sub-sub-headings, appendices and asterisks. Where Steel and Morris had to prove the potentiality of harmful effects on health, McDonald's chose to argue the actuality of such effects. It focused on a real, typical meal, for a real, typical customer, and asked if that meal was problematic for health. A burger, fries and a beverage was a pretty standard meal. Rampton continued: 'If there is a danger to health' in respect of saturated fats, . . .' (which is by no means 100 per cent clear, on the evidence), then' most people 'should probably refrain from eating such a meal more than one [sic] a day'. But, he argued, in practice virtually no one did eat at McDonald's more than once a day, so this hypothesis was irrelevant.

He then asked, 'How often must one eat such a meal in order to give rise to any significant health risk? How often, in practice/reality, do people eat such meals?' In a lengthy breakdown of the so-called 'Heavy Users' and 'Super Heavy Users' – i.e., people who eat at McDonald's very frequently and incredibly frequently – he argued that the 'total number of customers who are "heavy users" is relatively small'. And 'of those, about 80 per cent eat at McDonald's once a week, but no more often than that. So one can forget them. Of the remaining 531,000 (merely), and now one is approaching statistical insignificance (531,000 = 2.4 per cent of all customers), a mere 55,000 (0.24 per cent)' eat there 'nearly every day'. Therefore, he said, 'Not very many people in the UK are using McDonald's' food as a "staple".'

Steel and Morris countered this barrage of figures with McDonald's' own figures, which had specifically measured and targeted customers considered to be 'heavy users', defined as those that ate at McDonald's an average of three times a week. These heavy users were those most likely to also eat at other fast-food outlets and the research to pinpoint these customers was aimed at cultivating a loyal clientele. McDonald's' summing up was at pains to draw on the sense of the customer's responsibility in choosing the whole diet. 'I am unwilling to concede the relevance of the consumer's choices of food from other sources: that is the consumer's responsibility,' said Rampton, continuing: 'The question at this stage is – "Is the food itself high in fat? Answer, by

Mr Richard Rampton QC: 'a great judger of judges and reader of juries and one of Britain's most formidable libel lawyers, he will have earned himself the better part of £1 million by the end'.

Helen and Dave, the defendants: 'at the centre of the trial is the million-dollar question that Steel and Morris always want to address: if two alternative worlds are here on show, what kind of society do people really want?'

Paul Preston, President of McDonald's UK: ' "McDonald's isn't a job, it's a life." '

Sid Nicholson: 'as Head of Security he employed spies to follow Steel and Morris'.

Dan Mills, who 'kept the
McLibel Support campaign
going for three years'.

Ronald McDonald at
a children's party.

An artist's impression of Court 35, the Royal Courts of Justice.

reference to the contribution which that meal makes to that day's fat intake, *NO*." With reference to what is defamatory, the statement, "Do not eat too much of the kind of food that McDonald's sells; YOU may well make your diet high in fat, etc., if you do (with adverse consequences for your health)" is not defamatory of McDonald's. Whereas, "Do not eat McDonald's' food: IT may well make your diet [etc., as above]" plainly is.'

Suppose, he said, that a customer 'eats the "typical" McDonald's meal ... for lunch twice a week: in itself, harmless (indeed, probably beneficial) ... But then suppose that he/she eats

– the McDonald's meal twice a week
– a similar Burger King meal twice a week
– a Kentucky Fried Chicken meal twice a week
– fish and chips twice a week
– pub sandwiches twice a week
– pizzas twice a week
– Berni Inn steaks twice a week

... such a person would, almost certainly, be overloading on Total Fats and Saturated Fats ... And if that were the pattern of his diet ... then it might fairly be said that his diet was "unhealthy".'

But, he said, in one of the keys to McDonald's' argument, 'what is it in that diet which has made it unhealthy? ... The obvious answer is: "Individually, none of them; – in combination, all of them." This means that no single food source can make a diet "unhealthy" ... unless it is, on its own, a very substantial – probably dominant ... element of the diet. Absent such "dominance" no single food source – be it McDonald's, Burger King, fish and chips, pub sandwiches or bacon and eggs – can logically, or fairly, be inculpated as the prime cause ("maker") of an "unhealthy" diet ... Each makes a contribution, and the extent to which each makes that contribution is the whole extent of its responsibility for the overall diet.'

McDonald's concentrated its summing up on four witnesses, Professors Naismith, Crawford and Campbell, and Dr Arnott, whom Rampton called 'proper' experts. He proceeded to rubbish most of the other witnesses for the defence. Barnard has 'none of the necessary qualifications (and anyway [is] wholly unbalanced in his presentation of the relevant material)'. Cox: 'no qualifications (if, indeed, he was giving evidence about nutrition at all)' . . . 'Cannon: ditto . . .'

It was to be a running theme of the trial, with Steel and Morris complaining that McDonald's' witnesses were in some way 'compromised' by an association with McDonald's or the food industry and McDonald's frequently dismissing the defendants' evidence as 'irrelevant', 'specious', or just plain 'wrong'. In a moment of literary flourish and irony combined, Rampton declared: '. . . the defendants' witnesses are all completely independent, having, as it were, descended from Olympus to explain to the court why McDonald's' food is so unhealthy.'

Actually, said McDonald's (although there was no evidence to this effect), the defence witnesses were all 'associates' of each other. 'Not that any of this is terribly sinister. Simply that it makes a nonsense of Morris's adulation of his witnesses' supposed "independence" (and of his silly, and offensive, assertion that the plaintiffs' witnesses are "tainted").'

Rampton twisted the knife, setting up a set of quasi-religious metaphors to present Steel and Morris and their witnesses as alarmist members of a clique, who relied on passion rather than logic, emotion rather than rational argument. Words like 'credo' and 'adulation' enter his arguments. Then he went for the kill: 'One has a suspicion, grounded both on their mutual associations and on the nature of their evidence, that the defendants' witnesses may be part of a dedicated "anti-animal-fat" clique or coterie (motivated in some cases – Cox, possibly Barnard – by a concern for animals rather than human health) which saw this trial as a convenient platform for the promulgation of its views. Which is not to say that their views are, for this reason alone, to be disregarded (they are wrong because the evidence shows them to be wrong); simply that their supposed status as wholly independent Olympians may not be entirely credible.' And later he said: 'What it does suggest is that the almost hysterical obsession with fat, and particularly animal fat, which may be seen in some quarters (Barnard, Cox, e.g.) is scientifically unjustified – and socially irresponsible: alarmist.' By contrast, continued the urbane tone, 'Much better [of course] the dispassionate balanced view of McDonald's' men.' Indeed.

Chapter Seven

Settling In

'For us it is all right if the talks succeed and it is all right if they fail.'

– Zhou Enlai

August 1994: The invitation from McDonald's came out of the blue in the form of a note. After six weeks in Court 35, when not much had been heard beyond Packaging and the opening shots on nutrition and labour, the corporation was, said one of the American board members, 'prepared to come to London to wrap up the case'. It would fly over a director at twenty-four hours' notice, meet Steel and Morris anywhere they liked.

The defendants were impressed. They must have hurt the corporation more than they imagined. 'Two of the most powerful people on the planet wanting to meet little old me and Helen. Well, we just thought, "Go along, see what they've got to say, and put our demands,"' says Morris.

So it was that Dave and Helen meet board members Dick Starmann and Shelby Yastrow, McDonald's' senior legal adviser and a senior executive, to negotiate a settlement to end the case. The venue is a solicitors' office, 'quite a dramatic setting, on the top floor of this office block, overlooking London', remembers Morris. McDonald's assumes it is confidential; Steel and Morris, however, say nothing and sign nothing to this effect. 'We did not agree to anything,' says Steel.

They remember Starmann and Yastrow saying: 'Look, we're all lumbered with this court case, but nobody really wants it, we don't want it, McDonald's don't want it, you don't want it, so now we have a window of opportunity – the summer's come, see what can be done.' 'Yastrow,' says Morris, 'was trying to be really friendly.' Starman was giving the impression he wanted to be somewhere else.

There were to be two meetings, late in August 1994.

Steel and Morris put their demands on the table. Firstly they wanted an undertaking from McDonald's that the company wouldn't sue anybody again for making similar criticisms to those made in the Factsheet. Second they wanted it to apologize to those who they believed may have 'been wrongly forced to apologize to the company in the past', and thirdly it should make a substantial payment to a third party in lieu of costs and damages (as recognition of being in the wrong).

Steel: 'I was most concerned about the first of these, I didn't want McDonald's to be able to pull out of this case and then sue someone else who'd either be forced to apologize or to go through five years of exhaustion and stress.'

The executives flew back to Chicago. The defendants were sent proposed details of settlements.

There was to be a statement of terms, some of which were to be read in open court. The material terms were that neither party would pay any money to any other party by way of compensation or costs. Neither party would be expected to apologize to any other party for the making of any allegedly libellous statement. Steel and Morris, thirdly, would undertake not to make any public statements about McDonald's in 'any form of communications other than private communications'. And, fourthly, McDonald's would equally undertake not to make any public statements about Morris and Steel. Fifthly, a certain sum of money (the exact amount was never negotiated) would be payable by McDonald's to a mutually agreeable third party. This last part was to be kept secret. There was more: 'The parties will at all times keep the terms set out in this Agreement confidential.' And, finally, in equally media-sensitive vein, the last agreement was that for 'a period of twenty-four hours only following the above statement in open court that in the event that any party receives any enquiries of any nature relevant to this action from any newspaper or from any other news media no reply will be made except in so far as the text of the reply has been agreed between the parties'.

An accompanying letter, from McDonald's' solicitors, Barlow, Lyde and Gilbert, to solicitors assisting Steel and Morris, Richards Butler, was to repeat these fears: 'We would ask you to remind the defendants that both parties agreed at the meeting that both the fact and the substance of the settlement negotiations and discussions are confidential and shall remain so at all times,' it said.

Steel and Morris are unimpressed; they cogitate hard and decide no. The proposed settlement, they feel, favours McDonald's and doesn't take in their major concerns. Steel faxes Yastrow.

They reiterate their wishes for any settlement agreement to include an undertaking by McDonald's not to sue others for libel for making statements like those made in the Fact-sheet, and some form of apology to be made by McDonald's to groups and individuals who had received libel threats in the past, 'particularly where McDonald's has lied or been deceptive in order to obtain apologies'. And they will not accept any agreement which infringes their freedom of speech.

Shelby Yastrow, just back from a vacation, picks up their fax. Within minutes he has faxed back a quick note – could they meet again as soon as possible? Twenty minutes later, he has read the fax in depth, and responds again. He is, he says, 'surprised and disappointed'. 'At our meeting, I very specifically said we would *not* agree not to sue others for libel in the future.' He goes on to say, 'You must trust that we will not go about frivolously suing people. As I told you when we met, if McDonald's loved being in court, we wouldn't have been sitting at a settlement meeting with you for two days last month.'

He is piqued by the line in Steel and Morris's fax concerning cases of libel threats. He responds: 'I would like to ask you just who – or what group – you had in mind. And if you have any evidence that anyone at McDonald's "has lied or been deceptive in order to obtain apologies", please advise me. I promise to reconsider your request if any such evidence exists.'

He tries to be more emollient: 'I acknowledge the dedication and resourcefulness with which you and Mr Morris have defended your position but to have an otherwise sensible – and mutually beneficial – resolution thwarted simply because of our past or future dealings with others simply makes no sense. The tail is wagging the dog.'

Finally, the fax reaches the critical point about 'freedom of speech'. By asking Morris and Steel to undertake not to repeat their criticisms of McDonald's, he says, he is not restricting their freedom of speech. They are welcome to say whatever they want, in private or personal conversations. He closes, asking to meet again.

Steel and Morris discuss the reply. And again the answer is no. Two days later Steel faxes back to Yastrow. She does not, she says, see why they should 'trust that McDonald's will not go about frivolously suing people'. That, she feels, is exactly what they have done, in the UK. 'The effect on freedom of speech has been chilling, with people afraid to criticize McDonald's for any reason.'

Moreover, she can put her hands on 'numerous' examples of times when she thinks she can demonstrate that McDonald's may have lied or been deceptive in order to gain apologies. 'Two examples are in letters to the BBC in May 1984 and to the *Bournemouth Advertiser* in February 1990. Copies of the letters from your solicitors to those organizations follow on.' But the part which really stuck in her throat concerned freedom of speech. 'Please do not insult our intelligence by suggesting that your proposal would not restrict our right to criticize McDonald's because "it does not prevent us from saying whatever we want about McDonald's in private or personal conversations". Freedom of speech is not about what you can say in private.'

Yastrow's argument was, she says later, 'a joke'. 'To point out how ridiculous it was we wrote back saying we would consider that point, if they agreed to cease all advertisements and promotions of McDonald's and its products, and we said, "Of course this agreement wouldn't prevent you from privately recommending McDonald's to your friends and neighbours." But they didn't reply to that one.

'The whole reason we were fighting the case was to defend the right to criticize them and other multinationals, so we're hardly going to agree to gag ourselves.'

Chapter Eight

Harum, Scarum

'The first law of dietetics seems to be: if it tastes good, it's
bad for you.'

— Isaac Asimov

COURT 35. 28 JUNE 1994.

Mr Rampton (reading extracts from the Factsheet published by
London Greenpeace): 'Another box with the heading: "What is
your poison? Meat is responsible for 70 per cent of all food-
poisoning incidents, with chicken and minced meats (as used
in burgers) being the worst offenders.

'"When animals are slaughtered, meat can be contaminated with gut contents, faeces and urine, leading to bacterial
infection. In an attempt to counteract infection in their
animals, farmers routinely inject them with doses of antibiotics. These, in addition to growth-promoting hormone drugs
and pesticide residues in their feed, build up in the animals'
tissues and can further damage the health of people on a
meat-based diet."

'My lord, if that implies or suggests that the person who
goes and eats a McDonald's' meal is likely to be poisoned by
some kind of organism such as *E. coli* or salmonella, or is

likely to be damaged by hormones or antibiotics in the meat, then again it is false.'

Six-year-old Joanna Nash from Hayes in Middlesex was rushed with kidney failure to the Great Ormond Street Hospital in September 1994. After five days on a dialysis machine her heart failed too. Doctors tried to revive her for five hours but without success. The case was undiagnosed at the time but blood tests concluded in 1996 that Joanna had ingested *E. coli* 0157, a virulent bacterium. Her parents said that they had been warned about salmonella and listeria poisoning in food, but nobody had ever told them about *E. coli* 0157.

E. coli 0157 comes from infected water, milk or meat. The bacterium, thought to be present in about 5 per cent of all cattle, cannot survive high temperatures. It has a predilection for children and frail old people. Its potential effect, say microbiologists, is more serious than most other food poisoning. There were more than a thousand cases of *E. coli* related poisoning involving up to a dozen deaths in Britain in 1995, but precise figures are not recorded. The Consumers Association says that between 1985 and 1994 the number of reported cases increased from fifty to 650.

The world's worst outbreak was in Canada in 1986 when nineteen people died in a nursing home, but the largest outbreak recorded in Britain was in Scotland in 1996 even as the McLibel trial was concluding. Eighteen people died from eating contaminated, undercooked meat and up to 400 more were taken ill.

Just weeks earlier, Mr and Mrs Nash had been given permission to take the McDonald's Corporation to court in the USA over Joanna's death. Their case for punitive damages will be based on what they will claim is the fact that while Joanna ate a variety of foods, the only burgers she ever ate were McDonald's'. Shortly before she fell ill, they say, Joanna and her family visited two McDonald's stores, one in Barcelona, the other at home in Hayes. One of these burgers, the Nash family's solicitor believes, must have been the origin of the *E. coli* 0157. Joanna, they say, only drank bottled water when in Spain and did not consume any unpasteurized milk. McDonald's will not comment on the case except to deny involvement vigorously.

But it, other food companies and even government departments may now face legal proceedings in Britain too. Following publicity about Joanna, other parents of young victims of *E. coli* approached the Nashes' solicitor. Three of them say that they had eaten at McDonald's. Arguing that *E. coli* was a growing problem and was not getting the attention it deserved from government or food companies, the parents have been given legal aid to take a 'class action' suit against the UK government's Departments of Health and Agriculture and McDonald's UK. All have denied involvement. Thirty families have now come forward claiming similar *E. coli* related food poisoning, including four deaths.

Although it is sometimes known as the 'burger bug' in the US, there has only been one known serious outbreak of *E. coli* 0157 in fast-food restaurants in Britain. In 1991, about fourteen people fell ill after eating burgers at McDonald's' Preston branch. Some were hospitalized. McDonald's made five out-of-court payments without admitting liability. Very little was known about the incident because the official Public Health Laboratory Service Report was never made public. Indeed, the company only admitted liability in the McLibel case after Steel and Morris served a witness statement from one of the affected people.

Food safety threaded its way through almost all sections of McLibel and was given piquancy when the BSE panic began in March 1996 and McDonald's – along with other main burger companies – took British beef off the menu for several months. BSE had been raised in the first week of the trial. Steel and Morris had challenged McDonald's UK's President Paul Preston over the threat that it posed to humans. The man responsible for buying at least a part of one cow in twelve reared in Britain said he knew about the disease but the corporation had never checked its UK beef supply sources for it. When asked if McDonald's UK would stop selling beef if it felt there was any risk to the public from eating beef slaughtered in the UK or anywhere where 'mad cow' beef was thought to be possibly present, he replied: 'If we thought BSE was a health hazard . . . we would not sell beef. We are not going to endanger our reputation with customers.' Mercifully for court time, Mr Justice Bell later ruled that BSE could not be brought into the trial except where it had welfare implications for cattle.

The basis of McDonald's' case against Steel and Morris was, said Rampton, that the leaflet had 'actually stated that McDonald's are trying to hide "the fact" that the food is "at worst poisonous",' he wrote in his summing up. Claiming that this was defamatory, he argued throughout that food safety was McDonald's' absolute number one priority. It would, after all, be commercial suicide for a food company to risk poisoning large numbers of people, and McDonald's spent vast sums of money and time on it, he said. The proof of the pudding, moreover, was that the corporation was serving 10 billion meals a year (a phenomenal 100 billion just since 1979) and there had been a 'statistically insignificant' number of cases of poisoning. Perspective, he would argue, was everything. The real risk of getting food poisoning was very, very small.

Indeed, he said, if the food had any significant risk of poisoning, one would expect to find that there had been hundreds of outbreaks of food poisoning and many thousands of individual cases. But 'the score' was one E. *coli* incident in America 1982 (when forty-seven customers were affected), and the Preston one in 1991. McDonald's didn't deny that these were serious, but Rampton said that quantitatively they were very, very small: 'This does not mean that there may not have been some cases particularly of salmonellosis [salmonella] which haven't come to light, but the fact remains that the flood of cases which one would expect from the consumption of such a vast quantity of food over so long a period, if the food were significantly unsafe, simply had not occurred.'

Steel and Morris continued with their 'public inquiry into McDonald's' approach. One of their witnesses was Dr Richard North, an environmental health officer specializing in food hygiene and safety. North had visited, on their behalf, McKeys Ltd. (McDonald's' beef and pork suppliers), Sun Valley Poultry Ltd. (its chicken supplier) and a McDonald's store. The high-volume, intensive Sun Valley production system, he said, produced chicken meat with a salmonella 'burden' of 25 per cent, magnified from 1 per cent in the live birds.

Campylobacter organisms were widely present in both chicken and red meat and could cause disease, even in small quantities, unless the meat was cooked at high enough temperatures, North told the court. He thought that the cooking systems in McDonald's stores had 'no defence in depth' and had to be maintained at all times to overcome defects in an inherently unhygienic and fragile business. The Preston incident was an example. 'The McDonald's chain in the UK continues to regard adherence to hygiene codes as more of a marketing tool than an issue of public safety,' he said.

But Rampton found a quote from a book that North had written with Teresa Gorman MP, in 1990, in which he had said '. . . we should keep in perspective the number of food poisoning cases as a percentage of the number of meals eaten . . .'

*

Rampton: 'Are you speaking there of food poisoning cases generally . . . or merely about salmonellosis?'
North: 'I think you can have application to both.'
Rampton: '[Your quote that] "It is so small as to be statistically insignificant and the number of deaths even more so". Does that hold good today?'
North: 'It still applies.'
And still on salmonellosis:
North: 'I do not think, frankly, salmonella poisoning from McDonald's is a major risk.'
Rampton: 'Would you agree that . . . the risk is insignificant?'
North: 'Would you be content with me saying I would not waste a lot of time on it?'
Rampton (in his closing submissions): 'Yes!'

The defence set out to show that the corporation was slapdash with hygiene and food safety. A former floor manager at the Bath store told how there was pressure to cut corners on food safety, and how meals were sometimes served undercooked. Similar charges were levelled by people who had worked in the Heathrow and Sutton stores. The court heard how sometimes raw meat kept over the recommended temperature of 4° Celsius was used to manufacture burgers, as was beef which had more than 10 million bacteria per gram – officially 'unsatisfactory' according to the plant that supplied McDonald's.

Marja Hovi, a vet at Alex Jarrett Ltd., an abattoir near Bristol that supplied McKey Foods, told how she found 'poor hygiene', 'improper inspection' and higher than recommended storage temperatures in the slaughterhouse. All, she said, could contribute to contamination and bacterial growth in McDonald's' burgers. She had been dismissed after she refused to sign export certificates verifying that the beef had come from herds free of BSE (as the EC required) without the necessary proof.

The defence had no luck, however, getting McDonald's to

hand over company documents showing the bacterial content of the beefburgers. After several months, Rampton told the court that they had been held for safe keeping by Group 4 Security and had inadvertently been destroyed by them.

As always, it was hard going. The defendants established that the company got between 1,500 and 2,750 complaints a year; and also several hundred complaints about 'foreign bodies' (mostly bits of plastic in the meat and bone in the chicken). On several occasions local authorities had taken action against the company for selling undercooked food. In 1994 some McNuggets tested by local health officials were declared 'unfit for human consumption'.

The court was told how the key to food safety was cooking at the right temperatures. But here there seemed some confusion: Colin Clarke, McDonald's' expert witness on food poisoning, was not called but it was said that he recommended 73° Celsius as the minimum internal temperature of the final product. When he had inspected three stores he had found some being cooked to 70°C. But the corporation's confidential *Operations Manual* set a minimum of 64°C for a cooked burger. US Senior Vice-President Robert Beavers said he was 99.8 per cent sure that this was safe but believed it had been raised a degree or two following the death of two customers at a rival fast-food chain.

And what about the health risk associated with chemical residues found in foods? Steel and Morris asked. Growth-promoting hormones and antibiotics were used to varying degrees in the US and the UK in treating cattle, pigs and chickens and traces of pesticides were found in milk, lettuce and other foods. While McDonald's was acting legally, and all residues were within government limits, the defence's experts stressed that residues in the food chain was courting trouble. Dr North told how 40 per cent of milk tested positive for organophosphate (OP) residues. These are related to military nerve gases; they attack human nervous systems. Separately, OPs have been linked with BSE. Steel and Morris also referred to a US National Research Council report on pesticide residues that at the time found beef ranked second on the list of foods with the greatest estimated 'oncogenic' (carcinogenic) risk. In his closing arguments, Rampton would dismiss Dr North's evidence on pesticides as 'inadmissible hearsay' because he had the 'wrong expertise'.

Finally, the defendants brought up the 'dangers' inherent in McDonald's UK using nine particular chemical additives in some or other part of their foods, as a preservative, colorant, stabilizer, thickening agent or flavour enhancer. Most of the nine were either officially banned or had had their use severely restricted in at least one other Western country. Dr Erik Millstone, an independent expert on food additives, said that there were safety doubts over all of them, but the UK regulatory bodies judged them on how they affected animals. It was assumed, he said, that if an additive did not produce adverse effects on animals then it would be harmless to humans. But some of the nine, he pointed out, had produced ill effects on animals and were still permitted in Britain. They should be banned, he said, but at the very least McDonald's should list all its ingredients on its packaging. The benefit of the doubt with food safety should always go to the consumer, not the compound or industry.

Rampton was unimpressed. His own witness, Professor Walker, was a 'world-ranking toxicologist' whose evidence fully supported the status quo. There was no contest, he said, between the two 'experts'. Besides, the defence evidence was quite irrelevant because the leaflet didn't refer to additives. Like 'foreign bodies', he said, 'this [was] just an(other) attempt by the defendants to cause gratuitous damage to his clients from a privileged platform'.

Chapter Nine

Seeing, Believing

'You can tell the ideals of a nation by its advertisements.'
— Norman Douglas, 1917

First, the facts. The Golden Arches of McDonald's have overtaken the Christian cross as the second most widely recognized symbol in the world. Only the five rings of the Olympic Games – which McDonald's officially sponsors – are better known. The corporation also claims that 96 per cent of American children recognize the arches. In the past twenty years, McDonald's has spent in the region of $20,000 million promoting itself – not far off the total aid given by industrialized countries to sub-Saharan Africa in the same period. In 1995, it spent $1,800 million on global advertising and marketing and it is one of the world's biggest advertisers. It is one of Britain's most visible businesses, too, spending about £54 million a year on promoting its image.

The marketing, advertising and promotion of the corporation – the next section of the McLibel trial – is precise and calculated. Eat in a McDonald's and, to believe the message, you may be linked to the Future (schools promotions), Care (hospitals), 'Fitness and Health' (sport) or 'Fun'. The techniques used are songs and jingles, a clown, gifts and collectable items, all designed to appeal to children. The confidential *Operations Manual* for McDonald's' operators says that 'offering toys is one of the best things to make them [children] loyal supporters'. 'Birthday parties are an important way to generate added sales and profits.' And in a section on making use of the Ronald McDonald character, the manual states: 'Ronald loves McDonald's and McDonald's food, and so do children because they love Ronald. Remember children exert a phenomenal influence when it comes to restaurant selection. This means you should do everything you can to appeal to children's love for Ronald McDonald.'

But so what? What's actually wrong with advertising? Nothing whatever, argued McDonald's, whose line never wavered from the fact that its advertising was standard to the industry, quite legal and regulated. Television, radio and other media all have bodies which monitor advertisements. The Factsheet, it said, had accused it of using gimmicks to cover up low-quality food, of directing its adverts at children to make them feel not normal if they didn't go to McDonald's, and of making them pressurize their parents to take them there. The basis of the corporation's case was that the very fact that its advertisements were shown demonstrated that McDonald's conformed to all the rules set by regulatory bodies. They denied that they exploited children in any way and all accusations that they tried to exploit so-called 'pester power'. Their advertising, as with all advertising, was part of everyday life.

The defendants, predictably enough, viewed things differently. They saw the problem as the way advertising in general was forced on the public, to get people to buy things they wouldn't otherwise buy. The particular objection here was, said Steel, to 'McDonald's' deliberate exploitation of children through the use of advertising and gimmicks to get them to pester their parents into taking them to McDonald's to eat junk food'.

Robert Beavers was the most senior corporation man to give evidence in the trial. The US-based Senior Vice-President and member of the Board of Directors of the McDonald's Corporation since 1984 opened the debate on advertising by saying that McDonald's had pioneered production methods and 'created an industry' which had 'helped to expand the eating-out sector'. Half of all meals in the USA are now eaten outside of the home, he said – an increase from one in every three around fifteen to twenty years ago.

He said this was a worldwide trend, that 'lifestyles are changing', and McDonald's had played a part in that. In countries where there had previously been no hamburger tradition, he said, advertising was part of the parcel in establishing company's influence on diet. Back in the 1960s, McDonald's had been 'the trendsetters in the food industry, in particular the fast-food service industry, in utilizing national television . . . It was at that time that we introduced Ronald McDonald.'

Kids, he said, had been and were vital to the corporation and he accepted that 'no other marketing factor had been more important in distinguishing McDonald's as a leader in fast food than its early decision to appeal to children through advertising'. He agreed that in the early days the company probably spent more of its advertising budget on children's ads.

Alistair Fairgrieve, McDonald's UK's Marketing Services Manager, gave some idea of the corporation's ambition. 'It is our objective to dominate the communications area . . . because we are competing for a share of the customer's mind.' He outlined research that showed what customers were thinking and the effects of advertising. They were asked about seventeen 'functional' and 'emotional' attributes which were ranked in terms of importance to McDonald's. 'At the top there are the ones by which we stand or fall. At the bottom were four categories: "Food is Filling", "Good Value For Money", "Use Top Quality Ingredients" and finally "Nutritious Food".'

John Hawkes, McDonald's UK's Chief Marketing Officer, defended the company's marketing practices and techniques and how it spent its then UK budget of £35 million per year (6 per cent of total income). The purpose of advertising, he said, was communication and persuasion to foster brand awareness and loyalty to increase sales: 'You have to keep your name in front of people's minds,' he said. Without advertising, he said, 'you might see the company decline completely'. He considered that advertising was 'a key element of free speech in this country'.

Hawkes said that McDonald's concentrated on TV as 'the most powerful advertising medium'. Charts revealed that the company advertised to children, in particular two- to eight-year-olds, most weeks of the year. A compilation of its TV ads was shown. The main techniques were the promotion of 'Happy Meals' with toys, and the use of Ronald McDonald and happy 'McDonaldland' characters based on food items. Ronald, he said, was not intended to sell food but to promote the McDonald's experience. All this was to entertain kids and to attract them, to 'make them feel McDonald's is a fun, colourful place to be, that they would like to go to'. Challenged by the defence, he said he could see no ethical problem with the use of Ronald and other characters.

McDonald's also brought in Ken Miles of the Incorporated Society of British Advertisers, a trade body. He described advertising as 'a legitimate part of commercial activity . . . valued by consumers'. In his view advertising performs 'a valuable role of information and persuasion for both parents and children, especially where food is concerned'. He added that laws existed 'to ensure that advertisements do not mislead', and are 'legal, decent, honest and truthful'.

Both sides were by now arguing from totally different points of view. Sometimes, as this interchange suggests, the conceptual gap was just too big, even for the judge to bridge. Here are Hawkes and Steel discussing the 'McDonald's experience'.

Steel: 'If your stores were filled with children and their parents who had come along for the experience but were not buying any food, would you be happy about that?'

Hawkes: 'No.'

Steel: 'Right.'

Judge: 'What is the point of that question?'

Steel: 'It is obvious that the whole point of the experience is to get them to buy the food.'

Bell: 'Yes. As far as I am concerned, you are pushing at a door which is absolutely wide open. I cannot see any point in McDonald's putting an ad on the television at all unless, either directly or indirectly, it was to increase their sales.'

Steel: 'It seems like that to me, as well, but it does not always seem like that to the witness.'

Bell: 'I do not think there is any difference between you and Mr Hawkes.'

The canyon was deep and wide. McDonald's quite simply equated its advertisements with effectiveness, therefore with success, and therefore they were a matter for pride. Just as surely, Steel and Morris equated that same effectiveness with cynicism and therefore as a matter for shame.

The point of the ads was to create brand loyalty even in children as young as two. Hawkes said that the company's ads created 'an image in the child's mind' to get them 'to encourage their parents to bring them into McDonald's'. He said that the company hoped that teaching them McDonald's songs would 'keep the memory of McDonald's at the forefront of their minds so they can again ask their parents if they can come to McDonald's'. No, the company didn't target eight-to fifteen-year-olds so much, Hawkes said. 'At that age, they do not pester their parents to go to McDonald's. It does not work in the same way.' 'They are not as brand loyal' as the two- to eight-year-olds.

Children, it emerged, were the company's way in to new countries. When McDonald's was launched somewhere the company would at first generally advertise almost exclusively to children. Said Hawkes: 'One tactic is to reach families through children.' The company also used promotions as a cheap form of publicity – Hawkes recognized McDonald's was 'riding on the back of Disney's popularity' by using Lion King and other movie-related toys in its stores. Furthermore, during the World Cup the company had run an advertising campaign showing a boy practising football. Hawkes said the company was trying to associate McDonald's with the World Cup and sport and agreed this was to associate McDonald's with fitness and vigour and to make people think 'our food is healthy'. McDonald's had been criticized for not sponsoring the Paralympic Games for disabled athletes, with allegations – which it denies – that this would not send out the correct message.

Sometimes, though, the company had gone too far. The UK Advertising Standards Authority had asked McDonald's to withdraw two of its newspaper ads: one in 1990 for claiming that 'chemicals only played a small part in their food', and the second in 1991 for making claims about the recyclability of their packaging.

McDonald's was taking no chances. David Green, the corporation's Senior Vice-President of Marketing, gave evidence for four days. Green said the company was the world's largest food service organization, spending close to $1 billion a year on advertising in the US alone. The idea was that adults and children would see several McDonald's advertisements a week. He agreed that young children of 'Ronald age' of two to eight years were 'impressionable', but he defended the targeting of 'Ronald age' kids and said Ronald was a 'friend'. (The company employed 100–200 Ronalds for local perform- ances and events.) 'But do friends usually promote multi- national corporations and sell their products?' Morris asked. 'I'm not sure how I can react to that,' replied Green.

Adverts directed at older kids ('tweens' aged nine to sixteen years) aimed to 'make sure they feel that McDonald's understands them'. In one clip, the company's 'Hamburger Patch' portrayed happy burgers growing on plants. Was this real? Green said that showing the burgers' origins (in slaugh- terhouses) 'would not be very appetizing'.

Green reiterated that McDonald's followed the rules. All the corporation advertising, he said, was very 'pro-social' and tried to promote family values at the same time as reinforcing the benefits of education, good nutrition and being part of the community. The corporation's code was there precisely to prevent the exploitation of children. Exhortative language was banned.

'Obviously children are an important target for our adver- tising as we want them to visit our restaurants. We attempt to convey the message to them that McDonald's is a comfortable and enjoyable place for them to come to eat with their families by promoting the fact that a meal at McDonald's is a fun social occasion to be shared by the family. We have long supported nutrition education for children through the devel- opment of school materials and national fitness and nutrition programmes. One of the best examples of this is a nutritional programme called "Healthy Growing-Up" which we have recently developed together with a number of outside experts for use in the classroom by teachers of kindergarten through third grade. It has been designed to teach children sensible and healthy eating habits by promoting balance, variety and moderation in their diet. We have also used the Ronald

McDonald character to promote nutritional education in an advertisement which we ran called "Ronald and the Nutrients" and featured a rock band dressed as symbols for vitamins and minerals to encourage children to eat food from the basic nutrient groups every day.'

He denied that McDonald's was 'manipulating people's emotions' or 'brainwashing' children with Ronald McDonald or having a 'hidden agenda' in the use of Ronald. But he recognized that McDonald's 'could change people's eating habits' and that children were 'virgin ground as far as marketing is concerned'.

Steel and Morris then tried to show what effect McDonald's' advertising had on children. They called Juliet Gellatley, former Director of Youth Education and Campaigns of the Vegetarian Society and now head of an educational charity. She had given talks to about 30,000 children of all ages in some 500 classroom debates and after the talks, she said, children often discussed changing their diets. On many occasions, of those interested in 'going vegetarian', some felt they couldn't because they would be the 'odd one out' or 'be laughed at' if they couldn't go to McDonald's. They often said this was 'because of the hype' and when questioned further they talked about McDonald's' advertisements which they had seen. She said she had been surprised that McDonald's was the only burger chain specifically mentioned in any of the talks, and that it came up so often.

The younger kids, she said, 'kept mentioning ... Ronald McDonald' who they obviously looked up to as 'just a pure and positive and fun character and something quite real to them'. Ronald was, she said, 'almost a mini-god'. What worried her was that younger children seemed to think it did not matter how much of McDonald's' products they ate, 'and that was ... healthy and good, because Ronald McDonald told them that that was so'.

She said that McDonald's' sponsorship – vouchers for schools, dentists and doctors to give children as 'rewards' – was just an advertising gimmick to get them to be loyal to McDonald's. She believed sponsorship was a particular problem in that it seemed to sanction McDonald's and helped children to feel not 'normal' if they did not want to go there. All this, she thought, helped make them see McDonald's . . . 'as a part of their life'. The majority did not question this, they just took it as fact, she said. Her conclusion? Children were being 'conned'.

But what about McDonald's' claim that it didn't exploit children because 'children are never encouraged to ask their parents to bring them to McDonald's'? 'The main purpose of advertising,' she replied, 'aimed at two- to eight-year-olds is precisely to encourage children to ask their parents to take them to McDonald's, otherwise what would be the point in advertising directly to such young children?' How could young children, she asked, differentiate between what was real and what was not, what was good for them and what was bad, and between being sold to and not being sold to? 'I think McDonald's play on that as much as they possibly can . . . this is what I mean by exploiting children.'

Many of the adults she had talked to had also mentioned the influence their children had in getting them to take them to what they termed 'a junk-food place like McDonald's', which advertising had succeeded in portraying as a 'treat'. 'A lot of parents think their children eat too much junk food,' she said.

Younger children, she said, were not aware that McDonald's' products came from once living creatures. She thought that singing, dancing 'Nuggets' which were happy to be eaten did not give children a clue what they really were. And just in case anyone in the courtroom still did not know what nuggets were – it has to be said that no one on either side looked like super-heavy McDonald's eaters – she said they were intensively farmed broiler chickens. 'Ronald McDonald is like a Father Christmas figure to them . . . he certainly wouldn't harm factory-farm chickens or slit the throats of cows, nor cause children any ill health'. Other food suppliers, she pointed out, did the same. She emphasized that it was the pressure from advertising and sponsorship which led to children wanting to visit McDonald's so often. No other burger chain 'seems to figure in their psyche', she thought.

Rampton declined to challenge her evidence. Instead, he showed a Vegetarian Society twenty-minute video used in some of Gellatley's talks – an educational film about the effects of the meat industry on human health, the environment, world hunger and on animals. Two words alluded to McDonald's' products but Rampton reasoned the video was 'principally aimed at McDonald's' and that Gellatley had a grudge against them. She denied this.

'In my view,' she said, 'McDonald's are involved in producing meat in such a huge quantity that they are involved . . . in killing millions and millions of animals, and all the environmental devastation which goes with that. And also . . . it is a junk food. I am putting the other side of the story, which is very rarely put to people because we do not have the money that McDonald's has.'

Steel and Morris were trying to show how the food industry 'exploited' children. They called on Sue Dibb, employed by the National Food Alliance (NFA) to research the effects of food advertising to children. To protect children's health, the NFA had called for a ban on advertising of sugary and fatty foods at times when large numbers of children were likely to be watching television. (Other countries, like Norway and Sweden, have severe restrictions on advertising to children, and in some instances outright bans.)

Dibb thought that the cumulative effect of much food advertising resulted in harm to children, 'in the sense that it encourages inappropriate nutritional practices which will have implications for children's health and their health in later life'. Public health should be given priority over the wishes of advertisers, she said, in the debate over the future of food advertising.

She related how children, described by one marketing company as an 'advertiser's dream', were effectively encouraged to wield 'pester power' over their parents. She quoted a recent survey suggesting that nearly half of the parents of children aged over five often gave in to buying foods they would not otherwise buy as a result of pester power. Almost two-thirds of those questioned felt there should be tougher restrictions on advertising of food and soft drinks to children.

Dibb had been to an advertising industry seminar called 'Pester Power – How To Reach Kids In 1994', where the most effective ways of reaching children had been discussed. It was clear from the title alone that the industry in general targeted children and aimed to get them to pester their parents into buying things. McDonald's, she said, used many techniques to 'draw children into the McDonald's world'. The use of characters (like Ronald McDonald) was a trend in children's food and drink marketing and could be said to 'play on children's affection and loyalty' to those characters and 'exploit their emotions'. Sections of the McDonald's *Operations Manual*, said Dibb, 'appeared to be a direct exhortation to managers to use children's emotions and particularly their love for Ronald McDonald to bring them into the store'. She did not think it was ethical.

Dibb criticized McDonald's' 'misleading' attempts to associate its products with health, fitness and sport. She was concerned about the 'underlying promotional message' in McDonald's' links with teachers, dentists and other professions, and in its increasing sponsorship activity. It was, she said, 'advertising in a covert way' that appeared altruistic.

Dibb was the author of a National Food Alliance report which looked at children's diets and the influences on their diets, including advertising. One survey had monitored a week of UK children's television ads. Food and soft drinks accounted for 53 per cent of the adverts, and in about ten hours of viewing there were 92 advertisements for food and drink. More than three-quarters of all the food and drink ads were for products high in sugars or fats or both. There were no ads at all for foods like fruit and vegetables. McDonald's' food was the fifth most advertised food during that period. The second survey, in May 1992, found that food and soft drinks made up 47 per cent of the adverts seen and that foods high in sugars and/or fats were about 80 per cent of the food advertised. There were no advertisements for unsweetened cereals or fruit and vegetables. In this period McDonald's was joint second in terms of the most heavily advertised food product.

She believed that the advertising regulatory bodies should look at the cumulative effect of advertising, not just at individual adverts. Children were getting a message that was very different to the nutritional messages that were being encouraged by government reports and policies as to what constituted a healthy balanced diet. She said that the effects of advertising this limited range of food products was to make fatty and sugary food more attractive and more desirable to children than foods which were not advertised.

She then came to documents which showed that McDonald's' adverts to children were shown forty-one weeks out of fifty-two in 1988. That was one of the most regular advertising campaigns she had known. Its effect was to 'fairly constantly' remind children of McDonald's and to present McDonald's as omnipresent. She referred to a study which showed that children were three times as likely as adults to recall adverts, and that a single exposure may have a natural life-span of some two weeks before it was lost from memory. Advertising forty weeks of the year, she said, would ensure that the company was not forgotten. The study went on to say that if the advertisement was reinforced by a second one, the child might have an 'effective recall' after four weeks.

Steel and Morris then introduced one of their 'star witnesses' – Stephen Gardner, former Assistant Attorney General of Texas. He told how in April 1986 a number of US states, including Texas, held meetings with the major fast-food companies to force them to comply with food-labelling regulations. They were told to provide ingredient and nutritional information to customers about each product sold. He said that McDonald's had been the most 'recalcitrant' and 'had to be dragged kicking and screaming into the fold'. Eventually, general agreement was reached and it was planned to make announcements to the press that the information was available from all the major chains.

McDonald's told the Attorneys General that it needed more time before it was ready. But the company then publically claimed it was voluntarily pioneering a unique project to provide this information. The public row which followed led to extensive press coverage attacking McDonald's. An internal company memo of the time was read in court. It revealed that McDonald's had produced ingredient brochures 'to help blunt the growing interest of state and federal lawmakers for ingredient-labelling legislation'.

Then in 1987, said the Assistant Attorney General, McDonald's began a major, but 'deceptive', advertising campaign. The company claimed it was an 'informational' campaign about the content of its food. But the company's own internal magazine stated that the aim was 'a long-term commitment beginning with a year-long advertising schedule' . . . 'to neutralize the junk-food misconceptions about McDonald's' good food'. The buzz words in almost all the ads were 'nutrition', 'balance' and 'McDonald's' good food'.

After the ads went out, the Attorneys General of Texas, California and New York wrote to McDonald's saying that they concluded that 'this advertising campaign is deceptive. We therefore request that McDonald's immediately cease and desist further use of this advertising campaign. The reason is simple: McDonald's food is, as a whole, not nutritious. The intent and result of the current campaign is to deceive customers into believing the opposite. Fast-food customers often choose to go to McDonald's because it is inexpensive and convenient. They should not be fooled into eating there because you have told them it is also nutritious . . . The new campaign appears intended to pull the wool over the public's eyes.'

A company memo, written in the run-up to this advertising campaign, appeared to back the Attorneys General's views. It stated: 'McDonald's should attempt to deflect the basic negative thrust of our critics . . . How do we do this? By talking "moderation and balance". We can't really address or defend nutrition. We don't sell nutrition and people don't come to McDonald's for nutrition.'

Attorney John Horwitz, Assistant Vice-President of the McDonald's Corporation, was flown in from Chicago to counter Gardner's allegations. Horwitz disputed Gardner's interpretation of the matters, which he had dealt with at the time. It was not a case of McDonald's being criticized, he said. McDonald's had not been pressurized into publishing ingredient information. He denied, too, that the 1987 advertising campaign was misleading – it was a coincidence that many of the adverts were altered or not rerun following the dispute and threats of legal action. He also implied that the three US Attorneys General were somehow part of some kind of vegetarian conspiracy against the fast-food company. Gardner laughed when this was put to him, explaining how he occasionally took his own kids to McDonald's.

Here, to give a flavour of the court, is a typical exchange. The talk is of children and balloons, of hats and flags. The judge, as so often when it came to Steel and Morris's case, is faintly mystified. What, he asks, is actually wrong with McDonald's giving away gimmicks? He can't see anything wrong with it as such. And Steel, one eye on the judge, one eye on a perfect world, warms to her subject.

'Whilst we would agree that giving and sharing is generally a good thing, and that there is nothing wrong with it, that isn't the case where it is done with an ulterior motive. It's clear McDonald's do have ulterior motives, they are not giving away these things out of love for the children, they are doing it out of love for the money they will be making out of the children or their parents through selling them junk food.

'I think the use of Ronald McDonald at fetes, school safety shows and charity events is insidious. Ronald McDonald makes his appearances wearing the company colours, he has the company logo on his clothes, he is the symbol, the personification of McDonald's. Clearly he is there as an advertisement for the company, but children will not realize that, they will think, as intended by McDonald's, that he is a fun character, that he is their friend, he gives them flags, sweets, toys, party hats, etc.

'The reality is he is *not* their friend, he is there to get them into McDonald's in order to sell them products. I think that in this day and age when parents warn their children of the dangers of speaking to strangers and accepting gifts from them, it is something of a contradiction that somehow it is acceptable for a complete stranger to speak to children and give them gifts just because he's doing it on behalf of a multinational company. The reality is that Ronald McDonald is one stranger parents certainly should warn their children about. We *know* he has ulterior motives, to seduce children into eating junk food in order to increase the profits of the company he works for.'

McDonald's was unruffled and Rampton summed up this section quite coolly. There was absolutely nothing illegal in McDonald's' advertising. So how could it be at fault? It was not the company's intention to get involved in the 'ethical' angle of the case, although it did stray into these realms occasionally. He posed this question: 'Is advertising to children intrinsically objectionable, in all circumstances?' He answered himself: 'Yes, if one took the view that children – especially small children – were unable to distinguish fact from fiction, reality from fantasy. . . . Are children so gullible,' he asked, 'that they will expect to find hamburgers growing in the back garden!?' The very suggestion, he said, was 'palpable (and ignorant) nonsense'.

Chapter Ten

In the Forest, in the Dark

'No brilliance is required to the law, just common sense and relatively clean fingernails.'

– John Mortimer QC

The anonymous handwritten letter that turned up in a bundle of documents sent over from McDonald's' solicitors just before the trial started was dynamite. Until that point in 1994 Steel and Morris had been finding it difficult to get first-hand or 'primary' evidence that would persuade Mr Justice Bell that the corporation should have to answer questions about the destruction of tropical forests for cattle ranching in Brazil. It meant tracking down landowners, suppliers and processing plants, getting lists of ranches and even finding out precisely what the vegetation was like. Their research resources were pitiful, they had little time and many of the people who had witnessed what had been alleged in the Factsheet were on the other side of the world.

Besides, not everyone wanted to talk.

Proof of the Brazilian connection seemed altogether too weak to even be considered part of their defence. They only had scraps of evidence to work from, the occasional letter from an environmental group which accused the corporation of involvement and had been rebuffed, or from individuals seeking assurance from the company that they were not buying beef from areas which were being deforested. Reluctantly, Steel and Morris had decided to concentrate their defence on deforestation in Costa Rica and Guatemala, where they already had some evidence of McDonald's' activities.

McDonald's had from the start, moreover, been allowed to withhold information about its operations in Brazil, claiming, when asked, that it was not relevant for this case.

Rampton had effectively ruled the destruction of the greatest swaths of forest on earth out of bounds. But right out of the blue a mistake by some unknown secretary or solicitor had opened the way for Steel and Morris to take the case into the heart of Brazil and into the dead centre of one of the most emotive environmental phenomena of the times. The letter had been written in 1984 in preparation for a libel action against the BBC. It stated simply that McKeys, McDonald's' sole supplier of beef patties in the UK, had in 1983 imported 80 tons of beef from Brazil for its UK stores. Ah ha. It was just the entry point that Steel and Morris needed. McDonald's' policy, they knew, was to say that each country sourced its own meat and that it never used any meat from cattle raised in former rainforests. Here was something that investigation might prove otherwise. On the basis of the letter that had fallen into their hands, they applied to the judge to amend their defence to include Brazil. Rampton tried to block them saying that they should never have been given the letter in the first place, but the judge ruled against him and from then on, and throughout the trial, Steel and Morris repeatedly and continuously requested 'orders for discovery' of documents on the basis that it was likely that there had been other similar sources and movements of beef for McDonald's' use.

McDonald's then had to disclose more information about the shipments. It emerged later that there had actually been five consignments of what was called 'balance sheet' beef from

Brazil to Britain in 1983 and 1984. This was cheap meat that the European Union allowed into Europe in very small quantities four times a year. It also emerged that the shipments were from Lord Vestey's ranches around Barretos, central Brazil. They were controversial for several reasons. After being subpoenaed by Steel to attend court Lord Vestey would later admit that he did not know where most of the cattle slaughtered at his plant had been raised because they were trucked in from elsewhere to be fattened up.

One letter that was disclosed referred to a cocktail party in Canada in 1983 when George Cohon, the head of McDonald's Canada, was introduced to Prince Philip, the President of the Worldwide Fund for Nature. In a rare moment of environmental zeal it seems that Prince Philip turned on the hapless executive saying (as recounted in the letter from the head of McKeys to a Vestey subsidiary): 'So you are the people tearing down the Brazilian rainforest and breeding cattle.' It is possible to imagine the President of McDonald's Canada turning as pale as an uncooked burger bun. Cohon is said to have replied: 'I think you are mistaken, sir.' Whereupon Prince Philip is said to have said, 'Rubbish,' and stormed away.

But the incident did not end there. Fred Turner, by then Chairman of McDonald's, heard about the corporation's social embarrassment and issued a worldwide edict from Hamburger House: no McDonald's plant outside Brazil was to use Brazilian beef. Nevertheless the imports of cheap beef from the Brazilian estates of Britain's noble butcher went through and the details were kept secret from Prince Philip, the Worldwide Fund for Nature, Friends of the Earth and the BBC. Prince Philip, following voluminous correspondence, later climbed down, saying that he could not recall having said what he was reported to have said.

As with so many other areas of McLibel, McDonald's and

Steel and Morris argued pretty much at cross-purposes to each other throughout the pre-trial hearings and in the two years during which evidence was taken. If it is possible to summarize in a few words one of the most sprawling, slippery areas of the trial, Rampton interpreted this section of the infamous Factsheet as narrowly and precisely as he could, while Steel and Morris interpreted the meaning broadly.

Briefly, Rampton argued that the words meant that McDonald's was actively destroying large areas of rainforest to make way for its cattle. The corporation regretted deeply that the forest was being felled but denied utterly that it had anything to do with it. Its bottom line was that its role was never active in its destruction. The plain meaning of the words left no case to meet, it felt.

This was easy enough to argue at times. The Factsheet identified McDonald's as one of many US corporations using lethal poisons to destroy rainforests. This meant, said Rampton, that McDonald's' people were (Rampton: 'literally and unarguably') cutting down the trees or spraying defoliants themselves. Impossible, he said. The corporation did not own and had never owned land – 'apart from restaurants and offices, the odd cricket pitch or football field'. So even if the corporation had wanted to, it was 'in no position to destroy a single rainforest tree directly'. Similarly with the Factsheet's allegations that McDonald's was helping cause 'starvation' in the Third World by evicting or dispossessing people. Were the defendants seriously arguing that the corporation was to blame for people not eating? How could they evict anyone when they did not own the land?

Steel and Morris said that the leaflet was obviously to be taken more broadly, to mean that corporations including McDonald's were collectively responsible and that it didn't matter who actually chopped down each tree. Tropical forests in Central and South America – colloquially known as rainforests, they said, are clearly being destroyed to a large degree because of cattle ranching; McDonald's, the world's largest user of beef, a corporation that spends billions of dollars annually promoting global beef consumption, was part of a system that leads to deforestation and encourages the land-use pressures that result in forest clearance: how can it claim no responsibility?

If their arguments were to infuriate McDonald's ('This is not a reasonable debate because the defendants have set out to use every issue as an opportunity to try and damage McDonald's,' fumed Rampton), so Steel and Morris were exasperated by McDonald's, which they claimed was continually moving the goalposts on what the issue in dispute was.

Ray Cesca, the man who drew up McDonald's' policy on using ex-rainforest land, came to the witness-box in February 1996. Court 35 was being well tutored in the environmental and social effects of beef production in tropical areas. Steel and Morris had called on some of the world's academics and researchers for expert reports. George Monbiot, one of Britain's leading environmentalists and an Oxford Fellow who had long researched Brazilian land use, was to tell how cattle ranching was ecologically disastrous; Fiona Watson of Survival International would say how it devastated indigenous communities; Dr James Ratter, an authority on biodiversity, would show the damage to vegetation; and Charles Secrett, the head of Friends of the Earth, was eloquent about rainforests generally.

'The Amazon' is something of a misnomer. There are, it should be noted here, many Amazons with several very different ecosystems. It is anything but homogeneous. Walk the floor of the tropical rainforest and you will find that flora and fauna change every few hundred yards. So, too, across the millions of square miles that make up Amazonia there are myriads of environments; there are the dense tangled biologically rich forests with labyrinthine, complex arboreal systems, highland forests, inaccessible cloud forest, rich floodplains, savannahs, places with no trees at all, flat grassy plains and bush. Some parts are rich in trees, others minerals, some are ecologically complex, some have weak soils that can barely support farming, others are fertile and as tough as old boots. All are important, and almost all are under threat. When Steel and Morris used the word Amazonia they were referring to an area that in Brazil alone (it stretches into several other South American countries) swallows a land mass equal in size to most of the United States, several million square miles of everything from biotic wilderness to arid lands – what the Factsheet, for all its possible literal ambiguities, referred to as a 'lush green belt of incredibly beautiful tropical forest'.

Into this immense variety of landscape that was already sparsely inhabited by hundreds of tribes, went the cattle ranchers, the gold miners, rubber tappers, settlers and adventurers. Some of the most powerful background evidence of the human side of the tropical region of Brazil was given by Fiona Watson, who told how the Gurani people once occupied 40 per cent of Mato Grosso do Sul, but had suffered such violence and displacement they now were confined to just 1 per cent, and by Professor Susanna Hecht, of the University of California, who had spent twenty years researching Amazonia and tropical land use.

Hecht stated that cattle ranching – an 'activity that exchanges enormous biological diversity for short-term gain' – has been the main form of land encroachment and dispossession in Amazonia for indigenous peoples, and most of the post-war encroachments have been in the southern flanks of the basin. Hundreds of contemporary ethnographers had provided detailed descriptions of cultural catastrophe, loss and marginalization. The front line of the social tension is cattle ranching – 'Amazonia is a zone of intense conflict, the scene of more than 75,000 threatening incidents and 3,000 violent deaths in the past five years' – and the conflicts are fuelled by livestock-land speculation. In her opinion the optimistic market forecasts and the real growth of the demand for beef for processed and fast foods, which McDonald's as the world's largest consumer and promoter of beef products stimulates, are an essential part of the impetus to large-scale deforestation and its biotic and social consequences.

But in legal terms Steel and Morris needed precise evidence of where the corporation had been getting beef from in Brazil, Costa Rica and elsewhere for the last twenty-five years. Could they show that the frequent McDonald's claims that it never used any 'meat from cattle raised in former rainforests' was wrong? Rampton had conceded at the start that the company had used ex-rainforest land in Costa Rica, some of it cleared about ten years before it opened its first stores in the country. More hard evidence about supply sources was still needed.

However, a previous witness had talked of seeing a map at Braslo's, McDonald's' Brazilian patty supplier for its 250 local stores. The defendants applied for it successfully. It showed seventeen beef supply plants, of which ten were inside Amazonia. And what was the significance of those? asked Steel. They were marked because they should *not* be used for McDonald's, was the unusual answer.

McDonald's was on the defensive now. Just before Ray Cesca took the stand, it disclosed a witness statement and another map from Senhor Roberto Morganti, Braslo's top man. This showed another 100 collection points in central Brazil. But while the statement mentioned supplies in the past from Cuiaba (inside Amazonia) the map showed no collection points in that region whatever. Even more strangely, just two points were marked for the neighbouring Goias state, and both were in the very south.

When Cesca took the witness-box he was asked where he

visited suppliers in Goias. He said he 'travelled around' in all directions. Had he said he only went down to the south, Steel and Morris would have been stumped. Now they proposed to Mr Justice Bell that his answer suggested there must be more sites. Morganti was contacted again. Yes, the Cuiaba abattoir had been supplied from places which Steel and Morris's experts identified as cleared tropical or rainforest land. And eventually a further list came. It showed another 120 collection points in Goias state (supplying Goias Carne Ltd. for McDonald's' use) that were not on the first list.

It was hard work, but now Steel and Morris had some real luck. By chance their last witness to be called after this new list arrived was Susan Branford, the highly respected Brazilian specialist and foreign correspondent for the *Financial Times* and the BBC. Steel and Morris didn't have time to talk to her but managed to get her the new lists. She instantly recognized that some of the areas mentioned – where McDonald's said it was still sourcing its beef – were places where she had travelled extensively over the past twenty years. She had seen forest being cleared and burnt for cattle ranches there from the mid-1970s until the mid-1980s with indigenous peoples being forced out.

Rampton argued this was new and inadmissible evidence but was overruled. It led to McDonald's seeking another statement from Senhor Morganti, who claimed that all the supplies that McDonald's would use would be from long-established farms.

Branford was backed up by a last-minute written intervention from Professor Hecht. 'I am certain that a substantial proportion of the cattle supplied to Cuiaba meat plants (1979–1982) and to Goias Carne for the last twenty years up to now would have been cattle from rainforest areas.' She added that the same would apply to the Vestey meat imported to the UK in the mid-1980s. McDonald's, it seemed, was caught.

McDonald's had other lines of defence. What, for instance, was meant by the words 'recently deforested'? Where the company had taken it to mean at various times 'a significant number of years', 'within twenty-five years', even 'within ten years', it was updated in the witness-box to mean 'since the corporation decided to open a restaurant in a specific country' and, in theory, just a year or six months before it opened.

Then in a series of arguments it considered the definition of the word 'rainforest'. It had, the company said, 'a precise meaning' for the 'ordinary person'. Tying it down, however, proved tortuous. Where Charles Secrett, for the defence, argued that the public understood the term in the broad sense of tropical forests, Cesca maintained it was ecologically very narrow, even inaccessible 'cloud forest'. Rampton would say that 'no technical definition' was necessary. It was said to be 'a forest characterized by or dependent on rain'. Then McDonald's considered two dictionary definitions, then one suggestion floated by the judge, 'a particular ecosystem where it produces its own clouds and rains', but finally decided to use *Chambers' Dictionary* – 'broad-leaved evergreen tropical forest with very heavy rainfall'. The obvious question was set up: Were the alleged trees that Hecht and Branford and others allegedly saw being allegedly felled actually 'rainforest' by this definition? Rampton believed not. Some of the witnesses, he argued, talked of 'dense humid forest', others of 'cerrado' or 'savannah', others of 'drier tropical forest' and 'semi-deciduous forest'.

Nor was there much chance, Rampton asserted, of McDonald's or its agents being remotely responsible for displacing or dispossessing indigenous or other peoples. Despite Monbiot, Watson, Branford and Hecht stating the scale and nature of the evictions due to cattle ranching in the areas under question, Rampton argued that the evidence was mostly 'hearsay', or 'inadmissible', or 'unspecific', or 'unsupported' or, he implied, barely worth considering. He was withering, professional: 'Ms Branford had in 1974 or 1975 come upon some pathetic Indians cooped up in a shack on a ranch near San Miguel' . . . and had 'seen someone killed on a crossroads somewhere near a ranch called Suia Misu'. How, wondered the defence, did he want his dispossessed Indians to be? He concluded, 'There is no more than a shade of a possibility that any of Braslo's meat for McDonald's . . . was derived from farms that had recently been occupied by (unlawfully dispossessed) Indians.'

The court then surveyed what was left of the Costa Rican forests. Rampton had admitted in his opening speech that some of the meat for the country's twelve stores came from areas deforested in the 1950s and 1960s. Steel and Morris pressed on and uncovered new evidence, this time courtesy of Ray Cesca's briefcase. What was in it? Morris asked when the US director took it to the witness-box. Cesca took out an official report (prepared for McDonald's) about Costa Rica. It had to be disclosed, and was found to identify cattle ranching as the principal cause of deforestation in the country. Other documents (not in the briefcase) showed that 20 per cent of the beef used in the company's Costa Rican stores was raised in the San Isidro region – which Cesca accepted as originally 'wet and rain forest'. The rest, said the company's local chief, came from areas of 'dry forest' cleared in the 1950s and 1960s. Steel and Morris showed maps suggesting deforestation in relevant regions, including San Isidro, continued until the 1980s.

Yes, but where did the meat go? The defendants hoped to prove much of it was exported to the US. They showed the court a 1983 film shown once on Channel 4 television called

Jungleburger. Here Senhor Quintana, then the sales director of McDonald's' local supplier, was interviewed, saying: 'We export meat to the US. Eighty per cent of the meat goes to . . . outlets such as restaurant chains such as McDonald's.' Cesca denied that this had ever happened. McDonald's had sued Channel 4 for libel and had got an apology. The film had not been shown again in Britain.

They needed more proof. It was well known, they said, that Costa Rican cattle farming had massively increased in the 1960s in response to demand from the US fast-food industry. Three defence experts attacked what they called the inadequacy of the US food-labelling system, in which imported beef is categorized as 'domestic' when it is inspected at the port of entry. Steel and Morris referred to a US Department of Agriculture directive that they claimed confirmed it. One of McDonald's' own big five suppliers in the US had also admitted that there seemed to be some 'discrepancy' over what constituted 'domestic beef'. (Cesca anyway denied McDonald's made use of any such imports.)

Enter Charles Secrett, the head of Friends of the Earth, who said it was a statistical inevitability that, whether knowingly or unknowingly, all the major US fast-food retailers had used imported beef raised on recently deforested land in countries like Costa Rica.

But it wasn't just cattle farming destroying the forests, the court was told. Cattle all over the world are fed soya, and – especially in Brazil – forests were being cleared and subsistence farmers dispossessed to make way for massive soya plantations. Cesca accepted that Germany was the main importer of Brazilian soya feed in the 1980s, and that much of it went to Bavaria, where most of the beef for McDonald's in Germany was raised. McDonald's is the largest corporate user of beef in Germany. The company had previously stated that no cattle used for their German burgers used Brazilian soya feed.

Secrett concluded that the McDonald's Corporation, as a global supplier of beef products to mass markets, must accept some responsibility for encouraging the deforestation of rainforests and the dispossession of people. Rampton was dismissive: Brazil was not a Third World country, he said. It was irrelevant to the case that hundreds of tons of Brazilian beef should be exported against company policy to Europe. McDonald's Brazil was only using a few hundred head of cows in the late 1970s and early 1980s. The chances of these few head coming from newly established ranches and being transported long distances to the places where its suppliers bought meat were very, very slim: 'There is not a realistic possibility, let alone a probability,' he said, and dismissed the rest of the defence as 'generalities' or 'insubstantial'.

In his closing arguments, he would question Hecht's academic qualifications despite her having twenty-two years of field research and six books published on the region, including one on the livestock sector in Latin America, another on the fate of the forest and a third on the social costs of livestock farming in the region. He tore into Branford's lack of expertise on trees, overlooking the fact that McDonald's had not put up one witness with a detailed academic or first-hand knowledge of Amazonian ecology. Who gave the only direct and admissible evidence? Who should the judge rely on for most matters? asked Rampton. Clearly, Senhor Morganti and Ray Cesca, the man who had defined the Amazonian ecological 'rainforest' border – beyond which the corporation should not take cattle – with a dead straight line across Brazil 2,000 miles long.

Nor, said Rampton, were there even remote 'shades of possibilities' that the corporation had been evicting people, causing starvation or clearing rainforest in Costa Rica and Guatemala. Again he argued that the corporation had no case to answer because it didn't own any land. Beyond that, he argued that any damage done had taken place years before, often before 1940, much of the land was not rainforest anyhow and that, as in Brazil, the corporation could not possibly bear any responsibility for the forest clearance.

The company policy was that meat should be sourced locally, so it could not have happened, and, said Rampton in his summing up, 'there isn't even a theoretical, never mind a sensible, probability that McDonald's in the USA has ever used imported meat'. Nor was Rampton impressed by defence witnesses who testified how the US beef labelling system allowed imported beef to be relabelled domestic beef and then sold on, including to fast-food chains. Equally, he considered 'irrelevant' evidence by David Rose, the London *Observer* newspaper's Home Affairs Editor, who testified that he had been told by a McDonald's PR person that the corporation used cows raised on land that had been rainforest up to the 1960s.

It was time to leave the jungle.

Chapter Eleven

Middle England

'No one's nature has been made the better by the case of
Jarndyce and Jarndyce.'
— Charles Dickens, *Bleak House*

WINTER 1995

Sometimes the exhaustion gets to everyone. Tempers fray.
The mindset of being a continual, professional adversary can
drag people down. There are luminous days, OK days, angry,
scratchy, tetchy days. And always day-to-day problems: how
do you keep track of the mounting piles of transcripts, the
legal points? Will it ever end? Is there life outside Court 35?
Beyond McLibel? The early estimates of the length of the trial
– first measured in days, then weeks – now seem from *Alice in
Wonderland*. McLibel has been 'confidently' expected to end
(a) by Christmas 1994, (b) March 1995, (c) summer 1995, (d)
Christmas 1995 and now as late as (e) summer 1996. Some,
more perceptively, say (f) even later.

And just as the possible finishing date stutters forward, so
Steel and Morris 'um' and hesitate in their cross-examinations
and falter with incomplete sentences. Sometimes they seem
painfully slow, lost in the enormousness of their cause. Then

the scale of their undertaking becomes apparent, and the slick, consummate skill of the professional advocate is seen.

Morris: 'I'm continuously aware of a hundred things that we should have done. We're just struggling each evening to keep up with the next day.'

Steel: 'The whole thing is stupid; having to spend days in court arguing whether for instance we can say that McDonald's' wages are low. The law is basically there to protect business as usual.'

Morris: 'It's not so much David and Goliath as Prometheus. I feel chained to this rock that's trying to crush me.'

Steel: 'I get fed up having to listen to their corporate propaganda and waffle. It's worse than a job, you can't get away.'

Morris still keeps an hour a day sacrosanct for Charlie's bedtime story. Father and son live with two friends in a three-bedroomed flat above a carpet shop on a busy main road where the cars are never quiet and wind whirls the litter down the gutters. The landlord hasn't been overzealous with repairs; the kitchen ceiling is coming down, and the wallpaper and the walls are not always together. There is no central heating but it's unmistakably a happy home – one very purry cat and one very active child. Charlie is being read his bedtime story. Morris ('Dave' as his son calls him) is reading *Aladdin and the Lamp* and by turns puts on a high 'princess' voice and a low 'genie' voice. It is hard to tell who is enjoying the performance more. However, Morris knows it's only when his son's gone to sleep that he can get down to his preparations for the next day.

The house is physical evidence of Morris's twin lives; as father and as political activist. In one room is a huge photocopier, rented at special rate for the duration of the trial. There are bookshelves, a large atlas and boxes and boxes of court files. Around the walls in all rooms are Charlie's drawings, alongside A4 fliers for demonstrations; a witch's hat sits next to pamphlets reading 'Decent Homes For All'. There's a guitar on the wall, and in the hall a credit-card sized sign reads:

> *Don't Quit – when things go wrong as they sometimes will,*
> *When the road you're travelling seems all uphill . . . do not quit.*
> *(Author Unknown)*

Ray Kroc would have liked that.

McLibel has taken its toll. Morris has barely had a break in four years. 'It's just McDonald's, McDonald's, McDonald's,' he says. He describes it as 'exhausting and a nightmare; tedious and unfair, relentless, continuous, and very complicated'. It involves massive amounts of paperwork, and organization and legal research. Preparing questions for witnesses has been time-consuming. But he says, 'We're just driving ourselves on. The issues are so broad and the unknowns so huge that barristers have told us, "We just don't understand how you can do this – it's beyond all precedent," and it is.'

He doesn't think of it as sacrifice. 'If you want to achieve something you have to put work into it. If I have to work myself into the ground I'm going to do it in order to expose the truth.' The trial has, he says, helped him to see 'just how strong ordinary people can be if they're determined to achieve something and they stick by it whatever the consequences'. He concedes that the consequences, even the sacrifices, have been particularly hard for Charlie. 'We've lived in the shadow of the case for four years, and he's been very understanding, luckily for me. It's been very unfair on him and I'm angry with McDonald's about that – they've forced themselves into our life.'

Only occasionally do Morris's two worlds meet. Once Charlie broke his leg and was unable to move around, needing twenty-four-hour care. Steel applied on behalf of Morris for a five-week adjournment, backed up by a consultant's letter. Mr Justice Bell gave them just three days off after McDonald's offered to pay for a childminder. Steel and Morris interpreted this as a cynical ploy to keep up the pressure of the trial. Another time, Morris had to bring Charlie into court. His school's central heating had broken down and he couldn't find a childminder. The judge's clerk ended up looking after Charlie all day. 'He got taken into the room behind the judge's chair,' says Morris, 'he felt very grand.'

Shortly after Charlie was born, his mother had been ill and unable to look after either herself or the child. For the first – most difficult – two years, Morris was looking after them both. Eventually he and Charlie's mother split up and Morris has been his sole parent for most of the last four years. 'I think my relationship with Charlie has suffered because of the case. I used to be very in tune with him and I took a lot of time to explain things to him about life and about our society but he's gradually drifted away. At the end of the trial I will have to spend time with him just recovering our relationship. I want to spend real time with him because he's growing up in a very hostile environment – all the images that are forced on kids from advertising, from shops, schools, the media, it's all bombarding him ... telling him the way the world should be. I have a responsibility to encourage him to question things and to think for himself and not just be obsessed with the next *Power Rangers* toy. He's been pushed to one side, and he hasn't had the attention that he deserves.'

Steel lives about a mile away in one of the poorer areas of North London. This is a world of renting-by-the-room and Housing Benefit from cash-strapped local councils, and litter everywhere. The yard outside her house is bare. You go in, down a cold, shared corridor full of bicycles to her tiny one-bedroom flat. One room is kitchen, plus office, plus eating plus talking space.

There are files everywhere, the claustrophobia of court clutter. Apart from the files, there are boxes, piles of paper about two feet deep, transcripts, witness statements and press cuttings. The paraphernalia of a solicitor's office seems to have squeezed out so many of the usual warmly personal things which make a home home.

One of the most difficult things for her since the case began has been trying to forget McDonald's: 'I can't get them out of my head. For the past four years, I've had no time to see my friends or family. For the first few months of the trial, I wasn't doing anything else. I felt I was going round the twist continuously thinking about McDonald's.' Partly because of this, and partly because she felt there were lots of other issues that were just as important, she took on another early morning task.

'There was a strike of fast-food distribution workers about two miles from where I live. It was totally unconnected to McDonald's. They were having pickets starting at 5.30 in the morning. So I have been going down and joining them before I go to court.' Rather than being an impossible addition to her day, it has been a relief. It gives her some time each day when she is not thinking about McDonald's. 'I ended up dreaming about them as well, which was really horrible.'

About a year after the trial started, she got a West End bar job, on Friday and Saturday nights. It gives her a very modest income, but the bonus, she says, is that she is too busy serving drinks to think about the trial. 'It does get a bit much from time to time,' she says. Those who know her say it is a great understatement.

In one attempt to keep herself, as she says 'sane and effective', she took her bicycle to Scotland in a break from the trial. 'Every time I thought about McDonald's, I said to myself, "Stop, don't think about them,"' she laughs. 'But I climbed Ben Lomond and I was only up there a few minutes and this guy strolls up wearing a Flintstones McDonald's T-shirt. It said *McDonald's – 90 billion people served.* I happened to have a couple of leaflets in my bag so I gave him one. I thought it was quite funny in a way. But I dunno, climb a bloody mountain and there's still a reminder of them.'

There are other times which she can't laugh about. She has broken down in court several times with stress and exhaustion. Once she applied repeatedly to the judge for an adjournment. 'Despite the fact he could see with his own eyes I wasn't in a fit state to carry on, and despite the fact that I had a letter from a doctor, he wouldn't give an adjournment, and I lost all remaining respect for him then, because it's no way to treat another human being.' He refused to give an adjournment unless her doctor came to court and gave evidence and could be cross-examined by McDonald's. 'There was no way,' said Steel. 'I didn't want McDonald's to know my doctor's name and address. I was prepared for the judge to know, to verify that she was bona fide, but not McDonald's. Our lives have been intruded on far too much.'

The case is devilish for the urbane Richard Rampton, too, even if there are compensations. He will have earned himself the better part of £1 million by the end, but he must negotiate professional elephant traps. Taking on 'litigants in person', people who represent themselves, is notoriously tricky, a bit like Newcastle United of British football's Premier League taking on the amateurs of Kettering Town from the lowly Vauxhall Conference League. Mark Stephens, senior partner in law firm Stephens Innocent, says that a barrister in these cases must totally adjust their style to ensure they are not seen to be taking advantage of weaker foes. They should, he says, be doubly careful, triply polite. Moreover, the rhythm of a case can be lost; there must always be interruptions as the judge helps the amateurs through the legal points. It's easy to become overconfident and impatient. Richard Rampton does not seem naturally patient.

Nor can Rampton much further his career. For all his professionalism, his Dickensian interjections, his theatrical, staged gruffness and loud – but not too loud, mind – asides, Rampton is becalmed. This nightmare case against two legal beginners runs against his nature. Where he relishes the confrontational, the adversarial, and the banter of equal, well-trained legal minds, here he is pitted against people of passion; admirable enough: but Steel and Morris are people with a cause and not remotely to his taste politically, socially or intellectually. 'Is Rampton bored?' is a question frequently asked by observers of Court 35. Does the judge wear red?

Besides, at this rough mid-stage of the trial Rampton has everything to lose. He has the real legal advantage in that he has dealt with many of the points before in his career, but he cannot be seen by the public to genuinely win. He may score point after legal point, like a boxer jabbing away to the head, but even though the judge notices and may appreciate them, he is denied the public stage he loves. No one will stop him in the street and say well done this time.

And even if he and the well-oiled McDonald's' corporate legal machine were to win 90 per cent or more of the verdict, few people are ever going to consider that it has been a level playing field, argues one of Britain's top QCs, Michael Mansfield. The public will say, he suggests, 'Ah yes, but there was such an imbalance between McDonald's' resources and Steel and Morris's that the inference will always be that Rampton won unfairly.'

Rampton has long made his name and will not be bothered, whatever he may feel personally about the use of the court, the way Steel and Morris have conducted their case or his own predicament. He will harrumph in public, be full of bonhomie in private, take a break and return to gobble up more libel cases as he always did; but questions will be raised if the defendants lose, such as what would have happened if Steel and Morris had had the money to track down all the relevant witnesses especially overseas, if they had had full-time professional back-up, if – imagine – Rampton had been arguing for the defence.

It is a no-win situation, too, for Mr Justice Bell. Like Rampton, he is professionally becalmed, but it's unfortunate that the legal wind has gone before he has really sailed forward as a judge. He should have done hundreds of trials by now; instead he has one great behemoth on his shoulder before he has made a judicial name for himself. It is popularly believed that the senior judiciary feels somewhat guilty about McLibel. Bell, it is said, drew the short straw of this case because he was a newcomer, and that the powers know that they have dumped this nightmare on him. It's little compensation that they congratulate him for holding it together.

It is hard personally, too. There are ominous signs that everyone in Court 35 is getting decidedly fed up with everyone else. Steel and Morris feel that he has not been even-handed enough. This may have more to do with the judicial system that he represents than personal, but he is human, loyal to the system he presides over, and it rankles. If he thought the defendants plucky at first, as the case grinds on it becomes harder to appreciate their very real legal disadvantage and to uphold the unwritten convention that judges should proactively assist litigants in person. 'He could have helped more,' argues Keir Starmer, Steel and Morris's shadow lawyer. 'Sometimes he puts them down too quickly. They see him as biased.' To most observers he is patience itself.

And Steel and Morris do not have much faith in the courts now, and sometimes you can see why. On one occasion they were appealing on a ruling. They had eight points to make but the night before the hearing in the Appeal Court they decided to abandon seven and concentrate on one. They went to the court, said their piece, and the court adjourned for a few minutes. It then returned to give a particularly detailed judgement (against them). They thought it strange, but left it at that. As they were going out of the court, an official returned them their original papers. Tucked in with them were some other documents that they had not seen before: they were judgements done on all the eight points they had originally listed with only a few details to be filled in. All had been decided in advance, without anyone hearing their case. It was another slap in the face for the defendants. 'It read like a script,' says Starmer. Steel and Morris took the matter up with the Lord Chancellor, and it is still being batted backwards and forwards.

As if it's not enough to have two professionally and politically aggrieved defendants continually shouting foul, Mr Justice Bell also has one formidable libel lawyer to contend with. Rampton, to start with at least, knew far more about libel than Bell, who had to rely on him heavily. It is not unusual for a judge to rely on leading counsel, but it can seem unfair to those who do not know the law. Moreover, Rampton has been a powerful presence from the very start, always ready to push his skills and provoke adversaries. He and Bell are not natural allies, but they respect each other, and have drawn closer over the years. The body language is telling: when Rampton talks, Bell leans back, an evident, relaxed equal. With Steel and Morris he leans forward, on one level saying, 'Yes, I am here to help'; on another, illustrating his superiority. Without a jury he has a double responsibility – to be the arbitrator of both fact and law.

The absence of a jury is a vexed question. At one point Mr Justice Bell was to say: 'In fact, I do not think any jury would have survived a case as long as this.' It's an interesting point. What would have happened if there had been a jury but the jurors had not been able to survive the length of the trial?

Bell expresses how the difficulty of being untrained litigants in person is far greater in a libel suit than in any other type of case. 'For better or worse,' he says, 'the law of defamation has grown up in its own special way over . . . the last hundred and fifty years, and whereas in ordinary negligence claims if you don't know what the law is you can say what you think is sensible and there is a ninety per cent chance of you being right, I am not sure the percentage isn't the reverse of that in the law of defamation. But there we are.'

Certainly he sees that the case raises questions about the libel laws that others may want to address later. 'There may be an argument, or a view,' he says, 'that some people hold, that very large corporations should not have the right to sue for defamation under English law, but that is not a matter I am going to enter into. If ever there was a matter for Parliament to decide as the elected representatives of the people, rather than an individual judge, it would be something like that.' Above all, though, he can be sure that whatever judgements he gives, both sides will claim to have won. It is all very, very messy.

Why is McLibel taking so long? It's certainly not because anyone wants it to. The short answer must be that it has become a monster of McDonald's' making, says Keir Starmer. The case is extraordinary for several reasons. Usually in libel there is just one issue between the parties. McDonald's, he says, chose 'the scatter gun' legal approach, without giving itself fall-back positions or thinking the case through. They chose to object to virtually every sentence in the Factsheet, regardless of how basic the point being made. Did anyone in the corporation ask what would happen if Steel and Morris decided to fight? It seems not. When McDonald's slammed in so many witness statements before the trial started, did anyone wonder what would happen if (as it did) the defendants matched them with their own witnesses? Didn't the corporation realize that the untrained and unresourced Steel and Morris would take far longer to make their legal points, to cross-examine witnesses, to sum up? It seems not. The pair say the trial was taking so long because their strategy has been to gain admissions and information from McDonald's' executives and witnesses. 'It takes us days sometimes to break down their slick PR speak.'

Meanwhile the monster is still growing and records have been tumbling. McLibel became the longest UK libel case at 102 days, the longest UK civil case at 199 days, it has celebrated its first and is about to celebrate its second anniversary; soon it will become the longest English case of any kind at 292 days. It has been continuously interrupted with legal and procedural submissions and 'interlocutory' matters both by Rampton and by Steel and Morris. There have been numerous applications for 'discovery' of further documents, arguments over the admissibility of evidence, more arguments over the meanings of parts of the Factsheet, debate over scheduling and the need for preparation days and all manner of complaints and requests to the judge. Steel and Morris have said that Mr Justice Bell seems to be allowing McDonald's to ignore their counter-claim – Rampton will later emphasize their 'right' of 'privileged self-defence' for the right to issue de-famatory material because they were 'under attack' by the defendants.

Starmer sees the defendants irregularly, sometimes several times a week, sometimes not at all for a few months, and often speaks to them on the telephone. Occasionally Steel and Morris drop in to his chambers after the day's hearings, where they may have intense discussions on the course of legal action to take. Often they all disagree, and he says he has watched them develop into potentially 'very good' lawyers. Both have an extraordinary grasp of detail and Steel, especially, is able to spot a legal point now as quickly as anyone in the business. He doesn't advise them to try to be Ramptons. They would never succeed. Far better to be themselves, arguing from principle, shouting out that the law is wrong or that this case is impossible or that the British judiciary should become more human.

The only group which finds itself in a win-win situation is the McLibel Support Campaign (MSC), which is fast becoming a movement in itself. MSC was set up in 1990, shortly after the writs were served, partly to raise money, partly to publicize the case and partly to continue the campaign against the corporation. Six years later it's developed into an essential morale-booster for the defendants, the very image of a pesky 'in-yer-face' 1990s grass-roots phenomenon. About fifteen people are closely involved, another hundred or so in London help from time to time and thousands of active supporters in the UK and around the world chip in with donations or by their local campaigning.

As the trial has gone the distance, so MSC has mush-roomed, with new groups starting in the USA, Canada, New Zealand, Spain, Ireland, Norway, Scotland and Australia and now in thirty countries in all. There's no membership, but supporters are sent mailings from time to time. They, in turn, do what London Greenpeace did years ago – distribute leaflets and make McDonald's' operation as uncomfortable as poss-ible. And in what must be one of the loudest backfires in corporate history, leaflets that McDonald's found so offensive have now been handed to at least 2 million people in the UK alone and no one can hazard a guess how many elsewhere. Hundreds of groups and individuals have signed 'Free Speech Pledges' saying they will continue campaigning whatever the verdict; there have been protests in twenty-five countries, marches, campaigns to send back McDonald's' litter, a union-inspired support network has started for McDonald's workers, there's a Kids Against McDonald's group; protesters have even 'adopted' 300 out of 750 of McDonald's' UK stores. You can almost hear the corporation scream as Lilliput exerts its revenge on Brobdingnag.

Apart from helping to coordinate legal volunteers and assistance for Steel and Morris, MSC has helped raise about £30,000 in six years – about as much as McDonald's spends in a week on the trial – which pays for Steel and Morris's witnesses to get to court, for photocopying and phone calls and, especially, court transcripts. The operation is run from a small North London flat by the unfailingly courteous Dan Mills, a former corporate lawyer. Mills worked in the New York branch of Lovell White Durrant, a top firm of British solicitors. He wrote *The Vegan Guide to New York*, but returned disillusioned with his job, heard about the case, was intrigued and joined the Support team full time in September 1994. Now, apart from handling the media, Mills advises, cajoles, coordinates and helps others. MSC works closely with the Nottingham-based Veggies group. It, too, has distributed hundreds of thousands of leaflets, and sends volunteers to London to help Steel and Morris in and out of the courtroom.

It's hard to quantify the damage – if any – done to the corporation by the campaign and the trial. McDonald's' profits have soared every year since the trial started. Since 1990 it has added more than 5,000 restaurants, improved its profits by more than 25 per cent, become one of the largest hundred corporations in the world, one of the forty most profitable companies in the USA, and it employs more people than ever before. It would be hard for anyone to show that the activities of a small group of anarchists had done any harm at all. But the steady dripfeed of negative publicity festers and works in mysterious ways.

At this rough halfway stage, McLibel is for Steel and Morris at least a battle also for hearts and minds. Like all campaigning groups, they thrive on the oxygen of the media and they have developed a love-hate relationship with the ('Establishment', 'middle-class', etc.) press and television. On the one hand they criticize most of the media for concentrating on the David–Goliath aspect of the story and for not looking at the 'issues'; nevertheless they relish the fact that some 800 (Establishment etc.) newspapers and dozens of television stations around the world have featured the case.

McDonald's keeps quiet. To some it seems a dignified response to the zeal of its critics, to others damage limitation or bunker mentality. Following the failed settlement attempt, a corporate decision was made to say nothing to the press to exacerbate the rash of bad publicity or allow it to spread. But the reason for such corporate silence is revealed in a leaked McDonald's memo about media interest in the trial that was featured in an Australian TV documentary: 'Contain it as a UK issue' . . . 'We could worsen the controversy by adding our opinion' . . . 'We want to keep it at arms' length – not to become guilty by association' . . . 'This will not be a positive story for McDonald's Australia' . . . 'The aim is to minimize any further negative publicity', it says.

And now there's McSpotlight. The ultimate 1990s campaigning tool is the brainchild of 'Jessy', an Oxfordshire computer fanatic. With the independent McInformation network – sixty volunteers from over a dozen countries – she assembled in 1995 a massive, growing, Internet Website with 2,500 files on McDonald's: a hundred megabytes of information including videos, interviews, discussion groups, transcripts from the trial, films, and so on, through 'issues', 'debates' and extracts from all the banned articles. To cap it all, 'What's wrong with McDonald's' leaflets are ready to print off the screen in a dozen languages. Morris and Steel are ecstatic at its untouchable status: 'It is of crucial significance for freedom of speech and the public's access to full information about the trial and McDonald's,' says Morris.

For the corporation, still insisting that the trial is not about freedom of speech but about 'the right to stop people telling lies', it is McHell. The most comprehensive collection of alternative material ever assembled on a multinational corporation is gaining global publicity in itself, and is totally beyond McDonald's' control. By the end of the trial McSpotlight will claim that there have been more than 7 million 'hits' on the site. Many are thought to be McDonald's workers, who even have their own 'debating room' on the site. The corporation launched its own Website a few months later, but it's still unsure what if anything it's able to do about McSpotlight.

On 15 April 1995 McDonald's celebrated its fortieth birthday and there were celebrations and demonstrations all over the world. Steel and Morris were flown to America by their US supporters to join an 'anti-birthday' event outside the first store opened by Ray Kroc and the McDonald's Corporation, in Des Plaines, Illinois. They have their picture taken in front of the Ray Kroc 'shrine', they stamp on a birthday cake with forty candles, they go to the corporation's HQ, they walk through some forests for a break and they try to avoid the 'M' word for one whole day.

Chapter Twelve

Eee-i-eee-i-oh

'Litigation, n. A machine which you go into as a pig and come out of as a sausage.'
– Ambrose Bierce, *The Devil's Dictionary*

26 March, London: The British are in the grip of the biggest scare in a century. Four days ago the Health Minister, Stephen Dorrell, told the House of Commons that the most likely explanation for ten deaths from Creutzfeld–Jakob disease (CJD) in people under forty-two was exposure to BSE-infected products. The reality, well known to government, is that hundreds of thousands of cows have been fed the diseased brains of sheep and are suffering from 'mad cow disease' (bovine spongiform encephalopathy). There are forecasts that very many thousands of people will die after eating infected beef even five years ago.

The government, having known about BSE and CJD for ten years, is accused of being too close to industry and not on the side of the consumer. It maintains that most British beef is perfectly safe but the industry is in meltdown as consumers panic and officials consider killing all 11 million cows in Britain. Europe has imposed a complete ban on all British beef. Sales have dropped by 40 per cent in a few days, farmers are facing financial ruin and politicians and scientists are in a spin. It is an environmental and political scandal which over the next year will cost more than £3 billion. McDonald's, along with most other burger chains, has announced that regrettably it will not serve British beef for the time being.

Howard Lyman, the Campaign Director of the US Humane Society, the largest animal welfare group in the US, with 2.5 million members is in the witness-box in Court 35. Lyman, fifty-seven, is a former cattle rancher, a fourth-generation farmer, who built up his family ranch to a huge corporate agriculture business with a $1 million a year chemical bill. It was one of the biggest farms in America, with 1,000 cows out on the range and 5,000 in a factory feedlot. But in the midst of all his financial success, tragedy struck. Lyman was paralysed from the waist down with a tumour on his spinal cord. He recovered after surgery, but the experience affected him deeply. He sold up and decided to spend the rest of his life warning the world of the 'danger' of modern intensive farming and promoting 'sustainable' organic agriculture.

Lyman tells the court that he has visited hundreds of slaughterhouses and meat-processing plants. As senior lobbyist for the US National Farmers' Union in Washington, he met and talked to thousands of farmers. If anyone knows the state of beef farming in the US, he implies, he does. He talks of his concerns for the environmental impact of modern cattle-production methods, how he has seen the soil being eroded by cattle hoofs and turned into dust by overuse of chemicals, how water supplies are being contaminated and the wealth of nature is being lost. 'Animal husbandry practised today is only concerned with economics,' he concludes. The comfort and welfare of the animal is only important if there is the chance that the animal will fail to achieve profitability.

'For many years I believed that the ends justified the means; today I regard the methods used in most animal production as barbaric and inhumane.' He gave examples: dehorning animals without anaesthetic, castrating them with no regard to the pain, putting them in confined spaces, transporting them great distances and putting them on unnatural diets. Metaphorically, the court pricks up its ears. Where Britain is going through a beef crisis, America, he alleges, is setting itself up for one, also feeding its cows to its cows, as a low-cost, high-protein diet. 'Fourteen per cent of all cows by volume are basically ground up and fed back to other cows,' he tells the court.

Outside the court, Lyman is forthcoming. He is convinced that a brain disease not dissimilar to BSE is infecting parts of the US herd, and a bizarre and fatal condition called Downer cow syndrome is killing 100,000 apparently healthy US cows each year; a high proportion of these cows are ground up and fed to other cows: but in the US, he says, there is at best, ignorance, at worst, a cover-up protecting the large companies with a vested interest. While none of the Downer's cows has exhibited symptoms like those in mad cow disease (BSE), researchers in Wisconsin, he claims, discovered that minks given feed containing the remains of Downer cow syndrome (DCS) feed did. The crucial evidence was that Holstein cows whose brains were injected with 'mad mink' brain died after eighteen months of an encephalopathy disease.

It seems clear to Lyman that there is some kind of brain disease infecting parts of the US herd. He doesn't totally trust the US government's figures that of 2,700 DCS cows analysed, zero had BSE. He says he was once asked to provide cows for McDonald's but refused. Rampton will tell Mr Justice Bell in one of his discreditings of defence witnesses that Lyman is 'no more than an enthusiastic amateur', and has, along with many of Steel and Morris's main witnesses, 'no academic or professional qualifications' and 'no direct knowledge of McDonald's' suppliers'. This despite Lyman's testifying that he believed he had visited 50 out of the 175 slaughterhouses that were providing meat for McDonald's at the time. McDonald's will, further, call Morris and Steel's reading of the evidence 'selective' and 'misleading', and will argue that, in general, everything in the McDonald's empire must be fine concerning animal welfare because the government and other professional bodies regularly test and inspect premises and no one is suggesting that the corporation or its suppliers are illegal; therefore, as everything is within the law, all must be well.

Over the animal welfare issues, as in the nutrition part of the trial, McDonald's had changed its statement of claim. Originally it claimed that the Factsheet contained words meaning: McDonald's 'are responsible for the inhumane torture and murder of cattle, chickens and pigs'. Now they claimed it meant: McDonald's 'are utterly indifferent to the welfare of the animals which are used to produce their food ('the animals'), with the results that (a) the animals, especially chickens and pigs, spend their whole lives without access to air and sunshine and without any freedom of movement; and (b) the animals (chickens, pigs and cattle) are slaughtered by methods which are grossly inhumane' and that this was untrue and 'defamatory' of McDonald's.

Steel and Morris did not accept that the Factsheet was saying this. 'There is nothing stated in the Factsheet about McDonald's' state of mind towards the animals,' said Steel. 'The "defamatory" meaning of that section of the text was that animals were suffering and McDonald's were responsible.' She added though 'as it happens we do believe McDonald's are utterly indifferent to the welfare of animals'. The main objection was that McDonald's was once again moving the goalposts, this time in order to gloss over an earlier admission by Rampton in his opening remarks that it was perfectly valid for people to hold and express a view that animals suffered at the hands of the meat industry.

Edward Oakley, Chief Purchasing Officer and Senior Vice-President of McDonald's UK, also responsible for the Quality Assurance Department at McDonald's, was called as a witness for the plaintiffs. As part of his remit he said he had a responsibility for animal welfare. He claimed that the company 'had a very real feeling that animals should be kept and slaughtered in the most humane way possible' and so had published an animal welfare statement two years previously. When questioned about this Mr Oakley admitted that the 'animal welfare policy is, in fact, just a policy to comply with the laws of the various countries in which McDonald's operate', and added 'we do not go beyond what the law stipulates'.

Steel argued that the scale of the McDonald's cull – what the Factsheet called 'the constant slaughter, day by day, of animals born and bred solely to be turned into McDonald's' products' – was staggering. McDonald's was the world's single biggest user of beef. In the US, the corporation used beef from 3 million cattle a year, outside the US slightly fewer. It was the world's first or second biggest user of chickens: something like 80–120 million chickens were being killed each year in America for the corporation. The menu for Britain alone reads like a grotesque feast: take 2,777,832 pounds of pork or 180,378 pigs; 59,751,272 pounds of beef, equivalent to 331,951 head of cattle or over 6,000 head a week.

David Walker of McKey Foods, McDonald's' sole UK supplier of beef and pork products, agreed with Steel that 'as a result of the meat industry, the suffering of animals is inevitable'. This one statement from a McDonald's witness was to act as a backcloth for everything that followed. McDonald's did not try to disagree, but argued that this was a libel case, not a public inquiry into the company, and the real question was first what the degree of suffering was, and second whether that suffering was such that the 'ordinary person' (not, they made a point of saying, 'the vegetarian animal-rights campaigner') would say it was 'beyond the pale'. The allegation, in short, said Rampton, was that McDonald's 'condoned a degree of suffering in the animals that are used for their purposes which any "right-thinking member of society" would agree was wholly unacceptable'. However, having teased the admission that the level of suffering was a matter of opinion, Steel then argued that whatever the so-called 'ordinary person' might accept (if they even knew the methods used), if other people, be they vegetarians or not, felt that animals were suffering they had a right to express that opinion.

Rampton's strategy, as with other sections of the case, was to heap scorn on his opponents' witnesses, beef up his own and argue that provided no laws are broken no wrong has been done. McDonald's did, however, make concessions, in this case that the company used eggs supplied by chickens kept in battery cages where the chickens had no freedom of movement, fresh air or sunshine.

But what were the animal conditions like? Oakley famously said that he thought that chickens kept in small battery cages were 'pretty comfortable' but Dr Neville Gregory, McDonald's' expert witness on the rearing and slaughter of animals, painted another picture. He said that the abattoirs supplying McDonald's beef supplier used mainly ex-dairy cows. He accepted that dairy cows were subjected to stress, pain, exhaustion and disease due to being forced to be almost constantly pregnant and milked. When they became unproductive after only a few years they were sent to be slaughtered for McDonald's' burgers. Electric goads were used to force the cows into pens where they were stunned with a captive-bolt pistol to the head. The accuracy of shooting was not always good, it transpired. Half of the skulls examined showed an inaccurate aim.

There began a long procession of witnesses, each telling a more or less predictable story depending on which side of the fence they sat. Timothy Chambers, Quality Assurance Manager from Midland Meat Packers Ltd. (the largest of dozens of abattoirs supplying beef for McDonald's' hamburgers), said that 600 to 800 animals were killed there daily. Cattle were transported there live 'from all over the country', sometimes hundreds of miles. His company, he said, 'care about the animals' welfare, for commercial reasons as much as anything else', because if they are 'subjected to stress' prior to slaughter the meat can become dark and 'aesthetically unpleasing', and therefore 'devalued quite considerably'. He admitted his company did use electric-shock goads to move cattle around, despite claims by McDonald's that this practice was banned by its suppliers.

Dr Alan Long, an independent animal welfare researcher and biochemist for over forty years (in McDonald's' view with no qualifications to 'educate the court'), gave evidence for the defence. He, too, had studied conditions for cattle and pigs on farms, at markets, in transportation and slaughterhouses. Long thought that animals had been turned into production 'machines', subject to stress and distress, disease, abuse and a short and totally unnatural life. Dairy cattle (as used for McDonald's' burgers) had, he said, a particularly 'exploited' existence based on continuous forced pregnancies and almost constant lactation until exhausted, and then transported under extreme stress to be 'burgered' at five or six years old. What state were they in? he was asked. 'They showed signs of great distress when their calves were taken from them at a very young age, frequently mooing and bellowing, sometimes for several days.' 'Cows kept without such stress have a lifespan of twenty-five to thirty-five years,' he said.

The dairy cow might have started as a wild animal but it was now something else entirely. The court heard how a whole series of what are termed 'production diseases' affected them – brought on, said Long, by 'excessive pressures of production'. This included mastitis (a painful udder condition), which affected approximately 35 per cent of dairy cows in Britain. Dr Long said output from a modern dairy cow is about 5,500 litres a year, about twice what it was at the end of the 1940s. Sometimes the strain on the udder caused it to drop and then, in order to avoid kicking the udder, the cows would walk in an unnatural way which caused lameness.

And so the case moved to pigs. In Dr Long's opinion, intensively reared pigs (which McDonald's uses) generally suffer a similar fate to cows. At the end of the 1980s, the time of the alleged libel, over 50 per cent of sows spent nearly all their lives in stalls and crates, with no freedom of movement, unable even to turn round. He criticized animal-slaughter practices, stating that noise and handling methods (including the use of goads) led to high levels of stress and even terror. He was also highly critical of inefficient stunning methods. 'Humane killing' is 'a lie', he said. He believed that 'consumption of such cruelly derived foods is unnecessary' and that whilst he would welcome any improvements in conditions for the animals, they had a right to a life of dignity and freedom – to relax and to root in the open air, to play, to socialize and to rear their young.

During his opening speech, Rampton had claimed that the London Greenpeace Factsheet was libellous because it stated that some of the animals reared for McDonald's' products – especially chickens and pigs – spent their lives in factory farms with no access to the open air. He asserted: 'Whilst it is true that a lot of chickens live in large sheds, it is not true of pigs. The pigs used for McDonald's' food, in this country at least, live in the open air in fields.'

This was now to be tested. Dr Neville Gregory, Mc-Donald's' chief witness, had visited the company's pig-meat supplier, G. D. Bowes Ltd., to prepare his expert report for the court. It seemed that he had only been shown the outdoor farming system. Under cross-examination by the defendants, Ashley Bowes, Director of G. D. Bowes Ltd., admitted that there were 'two separate buying channels for pigs' (indoor and outdoor) and that McDonald's bought indoor pork and would only get outdoor pork if there were some left over.

The company, said Bowes, weaned piglets at twenty-four days. They were then reared in what he called 'indoor kennels', with roughly twenty weaners in each kennel, until they reached 30 kilograms. Bowes said that he was aware of some suppliers using the flat-deck system for rearing weaners until a few years before: they would be kept 'fifteen or twenty' in an area 'roughly 12 by 14 feet', normally on a metal or plastic-mesh floor without any bedding.

At 30 kilograms (9 to 10 weeks) the piglets were transferred to indoor 'finishing units' where for the last part of their lives there was only 0.52 square metres of floor space per pig, plus an enclosed and roofed dunging area. They remained in the finishing units until they reached 90 kilograms liveweight (at around twenty-two or twenty-three weeks old) when they were sent for slaughter. According to Dr Gregory, all Bowes Ltd. pigs had their teeth clipped and one in four had their tails docked.

After the life, the court heard of the death of the pigs. They were stunned using 'head-only stunning' and killed at a rate of 220–240 an hour at the company's own slaughter-house. The government's Codes of Practice state that for head-only stunning the current should be a minimum of 1.3 amps, otherwise the pig 'is unlikely to be stunned effectively', but when Dr Gregory, McDonald's' expert, visited the plant he calculated that the current used to stun the pigs was 0.45 amps. Bowes claimed that Dr Gregory's figure was wrong because he hadn't taken into account the fact that Bowes sprayed the piglets with water before stunning, which he said 'improved the conductivity'. Dr Long, for the defence, stated that he had 'a great deal of concern' about this, because there was a danger that 'the current tracks round the conducting wet surface instead of going through the more resistant part of the head', so the pig 'would not be properly stunned and would be stuck while it still had a sense of feeling'. Bowes testified that some pigs were stunned with the tongs 'on each side of the neck'. The Codes of Practice state 'electrodes should not be applied behind the ears or on each side of the neck, otherwise the animal may be paralysed without being rendered unconscious and may suffer severe pain'.

Bowes also said that his company had used growth promoters (such as clenbuterol) until 'about five years ago' when they were banned by the EC. He admitted that until that time 'it was fairly standard practice in the industry'.

And so to chickens. McDonald's, it emerged, used some 27 million a year in Europe. Gregory said that those used to make Chicken McNuggets and McChicken sandwiches were put into sheds, with less than the size of an A4 sheet of paper per bird and no access to daylight. Forty-four per cent of them had leg abnormalities, and other health problems occurred. Chicks rejected by the company were dumped into dustbin-sized containers and gassed.

Life was short for those chickens that were accepted. At six to seven weeks birds were transported to the slaughter-house, where they were hung upside-down before being electrically stunned in water. Up to 14 per cent of the chickens raised by Sun Valley Poultry received pre-stun shocks, which cause distress and can be painful. One per cent of birds (around 1,350 per day) were decapitated without being stunned, which Gregory agreed could cause suffering. A further 1 per cent were not dead on entering the scalding tank. He agreed that the stunning and killing methods used did not always comply with the government's voluntary Codes of Practice, and might lead to distress and pain for the birds.

Dr Gregory said McDonald's' egg suppliers kept chickens in battery cages, five chickens to a cage with even less space per bird than the broiler chickens and with no freedom of movement and no access to fresh air or sunshine. Mr Oakley said McDonald's had thought about switching to free-range eggs, but not only were battery eggs '50 per cent cheaper' but, he claimed 'hens kept in batteries are better cared for'. He said he thought battery cages were 'pretty comfortable'.

Dr Mark Pattison, Group Technical Manager of Sun Valley Poultry Ltd., in Rampton's words, 'a scientist of some distinction', gave evidence for McDonald's about the conditions under which chickens were reared to produce the meat for chicken McNuggets and McChicken sandwiches. He said that SVP hatched 'in the order of 200,000 chicks each day', four days a week. Eggs that did not hatch out were put through the macerator, which he agreed might include chickens still alive in the eggs. The company killed an additional 200–300 unwanted chicks each day, by gassing them with carbon dioxide.

Chicks were then taken to the broiler units when they were a few hours old. On arrival, they were routinely given antibiotics in their feed for the first week of their lives in an attempt to reduce infectious disease. 'For broilers we normally have 20–25,000 [birds] in a modern shed' of '14,500 square feet'. Broiler houses were generally stocked with roughly twice as many males as females with a partition between them.

Females are taken out for slaughter at 42 days old, weighing approximately 2 kilograms. The males were slaughtered at 52 days, weighing approximately 3 kilograms. Throughout their lives there was never any 'opportunity to go outside', Dr Pattison admitted. He agreed that 'farmyard' chickens 'can live up to five to ten years'.

Despite being on the committee of the Farm Animal Welfare Council which produced the Report on the Welfare of Broiler Chickens (for the government) Dr Pattison accepted that SVP was not complying with its recommendation that the 34 kilograms per square metre stocking density 'should not be exceeded at any time during the growing period'. The stocking density at SVP was 'about 36.5 kilograms per square metre'. He accepted that the birds 'have less space each than an A4 sheet of paper', but said, 'I do not believe it is cruel.' Dr Pattison said 'economics are a very important factor, of course' in why the company had not reduced stocking density.

Clare Druce, a researcher for the Farm Animal Welfare Network ('no practical experience of broiler or battery chicken farming' – Rampton), claimed that the 'modern broiler chicken was a genetic freak, the product of generations of selection for fast growth. Birds are frequently diseased, lifeless and crippled', she said, and 'suffer from painful and crippling leg weaknesses' due to their unnatural weight, and also suffer from a number of common diseases. Some of these diseases 'may remain sub-clinical yet cause serious diseases in humans eating contaminated meat', especially in 'the young, pregnant, old and immuno-compromised'.

As a result of her own research, including raising former battery and broiler chickens, Druce had concluded that chickens' 'ancestral patterns are never, never outbred, never lost by changes in habitat – they are still there, precisely the same'. This only served to underline the cruelty of modern systems and the right of chickens to live a natural life.

Rampton submitted that McDonald's' standards were as high as any in Britain, and the defendants argued that modern farming systems were unmitigatingly awful. Somehow, Mr Justice Bell would decide.

Chapter Thirteen

Spy vs. Spy

'. . . You can learn all you ever need to know about the competition's operation by looking in his garbage cans. I am not above that . . .'

– Ray Kroc, *Grinding It Out*

May 1996: when London Greenpeace was infiltrated in 1989, Steel and others were suspicious, but it never occurred to anyone that the spies were working for a corporation, let alone McDonald's. They had assumed that the police were keeping tabs – as they always do – on the protest movement. So what? they thought. Even if some of the infiltrators acted at times like clowns and the episode resembled a bad movie, they believed that they were well within the law and had nothing to hide.

But the picture changed when it emerged in the pre-trial hearings that the spies were working for McDonald's. What right had a large corporation to spy on its public critics? Some of the spies, it transpired, had been to many more meetings than some of the anarchists themselves and – crucially – had taken an active role in the group. Where Morris, for instance, had been only eight times in one year, the spies between them had been to almost all London Greenpeace events. One, Anthony Pocklington, had been to twenty-six meetings in a seven-month period. More to the legal point, some of the spies by their own admission had helped distribute the anti-McDonald's leaflets, either stuffing them in letters or for example running a stall at a well-attended public event. McDonald's must have known. Did this mean that the corporation condoned the sending out of the leaflets that it was trying to stop?

But the first question that came up when Sidney Nicholson gave evidence in this section was about the role of the police in the corporation's pursuit of its critics. Nicholson, a UK vice-president who was Head of Security at the time, had worked in the Metropolitan Police for twenty years, and before that in the South African police in the apartheid years. He told the court how many people in McDonald's' security department were ex-police. They had 'many, many contacts in the police service ... I would not ask them who their contacts were'.

Where other senior McDonald's men had access to ministers and exchanged information and opinions with government departments, Nicholson would turn to his police contacts for information: 'If I wanted to know something about someone I would almost certainly make contact with the local crimes beat officer, the local CID officer, the local collator,' he said. It emerged that McDonald's had been sent the Factsheet by the secretive right-wing Economic League and had been advised on London Greenpeace by Special Branch, the arm of the UK's police forces charged with monitoring 'subversives' and international crime operations.

In a classic infiltration operation, McDonald's hired two private-eye agencies – King's Investigation Bureau and Bishops (part of Westhall Services) – and instructed them both that this was to be a very secret operation. Neither agency, however, was told that the other was also working on the case. It led to inevitable farce at London Greenpeace meetings with spies spying on spies and being observed in turn by suspicious anarchists. Sometimes there would have been as many – or more – spies at a meeting as anarchists.

At least seven spies were employed and between them they spied on the group between October 1989 and spring 1991. Their activities ranged from taking or 'borrowing' letters sent to the group about McDonald's, which were then photocopied for the company's files, to breaking into the London Greenpeace office. One agent, Allan Clare, admitted gaining entry to London Greenpeace's office by using a phone card to 'swipe' the lock. He said in court: 'The door lock on the office to London Greenpeace was basically not very strong and it was decided by me and my principals that entry to it would not be a problem.' Another reported that the office window had no security lock on it. In his report he had said that he thought the next-door office was occupied twenty-four hours a day. Asked why this information was relevant he denied that it was to advise anybody interested in getting into London Greenpeace's office to burgle them. Nicholson said that he had given the agents categorical instructions to do 'nothing illegal and nothing improper'. But, he added, 'people do make mistakes.'

Steel and others were suspicious, but one of the spies, Michelle Hooker, found her own way to stay above suspicion, embarking on an affair with Charlie Brooke, one of London Greenpeace's active members. It lasted several months before she abruptly ended it. What did the spies make of London Greenpeace? One of the 'enquiry agents', as McDonald's called them, who had taken part in many events organized by London Greenpeace, described the group as 'sincere, friendly and open'. He testified that to do his job, he felt it would be beneficial to show willing and help out . . . in the office. He spent time answering letters and sending out anti-McDonald's leaflets.

Another, Frances Tiller, ended up as a witness for the defendants, testifying that she found the whole operation distasteful: 'I felt very uncomfortable doing that particular job,' she said. 'I did not like the deception, prying on people and interfering with their lives.' She added: 'I did not think there was anything wrong with what the group was doing . . . I believe people are entitled to their views.' Ironically, she had 'introduced' Michelle Hooker to the group.

The legal point that the spies' activities raised was important. McDonald's' original statement of claim – their original case against Steel and Morris – was that they were responsible for handing out the Factsheet on a handful of specific occasions in 1989/1990. If they failed to prove this – and it was proving hard – the whole McDonald's case might fall apart. Halfway through the trial even the judge had expressed concern over why the 'publication' issue – as this was known – hadn't been scheduled right at the start of the trial. A bizarre situation could occur where the defendants might have no case to answer, he suggested. In which case everything heard so far would be a waste of court, corporation and individuals' time.

McDonald's was allowed to amend its statement of claim to say now that Steel and Morris were responsible for the production and distribution of the Factsheet 'wheresoever and whensoever' it had taken place since 1987. The defendants appealed, but were refused. However, Mr Justice Bell ruled that Steel and Morris could amend their defence to claim that because McDonald's' spies had been actively involved in the group and had helped to circulate the Factsheet, McDonald's had consented to its distribution.

The defendants then applied to join three of McDonald's' spies as 'third parties to the action' (effectively becoming co-defendants), due to their admissions of distributing the Factsheet. This would make them liable to contribute to the payment of any damages awarded against the defendants (were they to lose) by the judge at the end of the case. The judge refused to join them as defendants at this stage, ruling that the appropriate time for such an application would be after his verdict.

'Why should we be liable to McDonald's for something that was done with their own consent? It's ridiculous,' said Steel. Morris: 'It's a weird situation where McDonald's were hiring people to do the very thing which they wanted the group to stop doing. A couple of the spies went to heaps of meetings, took part in mail-outs and leafleting. If anyone was to be sued it should have been them, not me.' Nicholson thought that four of them stayed in the group after writs were served on the defendants in order to monitor the response.

One of the worst moments of the whole trial for Morris came when one of the spies was giving evidence. Roy Pocklington had agreed that people had been followed home to get their addresses. Steel and Morris recalled that he had once handed a parcel of baby clothes over for Charlie, Morris's son. They questioned Pocklington about this and he replied, 'As far as I recall, it was an attempt to discover Mr Morris's address.' Morris was sickened. 'I just went cold. I thought that was the most disgusting, cynical thing. I was disgusted that my son could have been wearing clothes sent by a McDonald's agent. I'd heard a lot during this case, but that, in terms of the personal effect it had on me, really capped it.'

Chapter Fourteen

Loads of Old Rubbish

Rampton (in his opening speech): 'I state the issue this way: "Is the plaintiff's use of resources significantly detrimental to the environment?"'

Morris: 'We can't believe that McDonald's seriously disputes that unnecessary production and disposal of fast-food packaging inevitably leads to environmental problems like pollution and litter.'

Edward Oakley, a senior vice-president of McDonald's UK, may appear in a British legal footnote as one of the few people who raised a laugh in Court 35 between 1994 and 1997. His sayings and wise words in days of terrible humour hunger are now collectors' items.

Q: 'It's pretty rough being a cow?'

Oakley: 'I am not a cow.'

or:

Q: 'Mr Oakley, do you think chickens suffer at the end of their lives?'

Oakley: 'I do not have the ability to talk to chickens.'

Or:

Q: 'So, Mr Oakley, McDonald's' animal welfare policy is in fact to comply with the laws of the country you operate in?'

Oakley: 'Yes.'

Or even:

Q: 'Does reducing the fat content in McDonald's' food concern you?'

Oakley: 'I do not think it's a concern.'

Q (surprise): 'You do not?'

Oakley: 'Why do we need to reduce the fat content?'

But one of his best lines was reserved for the section of the trial that examined the corporation's attitude and response to environmental concerns like recycling, waste, litter and packaging. Oakley, the company's Chief Purchasing Officer for Northern Europe, as well as the man responsible for animal welfare in the UK, was asked about McDonald's' corporate environmental policy. Ever the man to give a direct answer, he said he didn't know when this was introduced but he knew it existed because he'd seen it on a wall at HQ.

The cross-examination went on:

Steel: 'So, Mr Oakley, there is no problem with dumping lots of McDonald's' waste in the ground?'

Oakley: 'And everybody else's waste, yes. I can see the dumping of waste to be a benefit. Otherwise you will end up with lots of vast empty gravel pits all over the country.'

Steel: 'So it is an environmental benefit to dump waste in landfill sites?'

Oakley: 'It could be ... Yes ... it is certainly not a problem.'

Oakley was relatively light relief in a section of the trial that had both sides practically weeping with frustration at the misunderstandings and different starting points. At times, the debate seemed insane. Of course people litter streets with McDonald's' packaging, Steel and Morris would say. It's obvious, isn't it? Why on earth has McDonald's tried to deny it? But how can a corporation be held responsible for its customer's actions? McDonald's would say. It's equally obvious.

Formally, though, McDonald's had objected in the strong-est terms to the Factsheet's saying that the corporation did not care for the environment. It objected strongly to words like 'McWasteful' and 'McGarbage', to an allegation that it 'didn't tell the whole truth' about its use of recycled paper, to an allegation that 'it takes 800 square miles of forest to keep McDonald's supplied with packaging each year . . . much of which ends up as litter'. Indeed, many of the objections to the company opening in a neighbourhood have nothing to do with alleged cultural imperialism, the Americanization of society, 'McJobs', the quality of burgers or the suffering of animals, but simply whether the streets were clean. Litter is something that occupies the minds of many people who live near McDonald's' restaurants, just as it seemed to confuse people who worked for the corporation.

On day 5 of the trial, McDonald's UK's President, Paul Preston, had declared that if 1 million customers each bought a soft drink at McDonald's, he would bet no more than 100–150 cups would end up as litter. Steel could hardly believe what she was hearing: 'It was incredible. At the time he said this the company had 550 stores and served a million customers each day. If what he was saying was true then each day on average there would be only one cup ending up as litter for every four stores.' She put photographs to Preston which showed twenty-seven pieces of McDonald's' litter on one stretch of pavement alone.

But how far was a restaurant responsible for its customers' actions? asked McDonald's. Rampton thought the defendants' argument had an *Alice in Wonderland* quality about it: 'It can be summarized in a syllogism that the Queen of Hearts/Red Queen might have been proud of:

'McDonald's uses packaging

'Litter is composed of packaging.

'Therefore McDonald's are to blame for the litter.

'(Off with their heads!)'

Colin McIntyre, of the local residents' group in Chelsea, London, and a former executive member of the National Union of Journalists, gave evidence for the defence. He saw the problem differently, effectively saying:

'McDonald's wasn't on the King's Road in the 1980s.

'There was very little litter then, the store came and the litter is now terrible.

'(Away with their licence!)'

But before he took the stand, Messrs Siddique and Stump, the former managers of the Chelsea restaurant in question, told the court just what a problem litter was for McDonald's and how valiantly they tried to control it with litter patrols. It was hard going, it seemed. Local residents, the court heard, complained bitterly and Mr Siddique went so far as to lay on a candle-lit dinner to try to build rapport with them. But the complaints continued: even local MP and government minister Nicholas Scott wrote to complain.

The McDonald's managers told how about 1,500 sales a day at the store were takeaway custom. Takeaways were at least half the store's business and represented something like 10,500 potential items of litter a day.

Stump recognized that 'there was a lot of McDonald's' litter' and admitted that there were times when so much litter was being generated that the store could not cope. Both managers claimed that 'trash walks' (litter patrols) to pick up all litter around a set route of nearby streets were done about every thirty minutes.

Rubbish, said McIntyre, who told how, at the start of the 1990s when McDonald's planned to open in Chelsea, the local residents had opposed it, in part because they predicted it would create litter problems. Since the store had opened, he said, rubbish in his street had got 'incredibly worse'. 'I would say approximately 70 per cent of litter is McDonald's'.' He produced photos.

It looked bad.

The company had started with good intentions, with litter patrols two or three times a day, but this did not last, he said. Despite continuous complaints, there had been no litter patrol down his street for two and a half years (which the manager had claimed to be on the 'trash walk' route map at the store). Apart from the council, the only people he had seen picking up litter were his neighbours. 'I have seen one McDonald's litter cleaner, it was enough of a joke we all made a note of it in our diaries.'

McIntyre told how local residents' associations were also angry about the store causing increased traffic, noise and cooking smells and how they eventually set up an action group to consider legal action. 'I object to litter in front of my house and in my basement,' he said. 'I do not really see why I should be condemned to litter for the rest of my life.'

Professor Graham Ashworth, head of the 'Tidy Britain Group' (TBG), a government approved organization – which used to be called the 'Keep Britain Tidy' group but changed its name when it became clear that Britain was no longer tidy – is dedicated to keeping the litter down. TBG got £250,000 a year from McDonald's but the professor agreed that it was in the 'top 1 or 2 per cent' of all companies whose products end up as litter, and that the rise of fast-food business was a factor in Britain's untidiness.

So, Professor, what should be done? Ashworth told the court that as much packaging waste as possible should be removed, and that it was 'obvious common sense' that the order of priorities in dealing with packaging and waste was (1) prevent, (2) reuse, (3) recycle, (4) incinerate (preferably with energy recovery) and lastly, (5) landfill.

Professor Ashworth said he believed that McDonald's was involved with TBG out of genuine concern with litter; 'they have been willing to sponsor programmes that we have devised and which we have wished to have sponsored because we needed additional financial resources from those available to us through the public sector. They have been willing to assist us in broad educational activities, frequently through the medium of their restaurants, and they have been willing to encourage their staff to support campaigns that we have been running where their staff have been located in areas where those campaigns were operated.'

The scale of the packaging problem became clear when Robert Langert, McDonald's Corporation's Director of Environmental Affairs, testified that the average company store produced about 140 pounds of waste packaging a day. During closing speeches, Morris said that as there were some 20,000 stores worldwide, this represented some 2.8 million pounds every day, worldwide, or over 1 billion pounds worldwide every year. It was unclear whether this astronomical figure (approximately 450,000 tons) included the bulk packaging used during transportation and delivery. But, Langert had said, it definitely excluded takeaway packaging, and in the USA takeaways were 50 per cent of its custom. Clearly the total amount of packaging waste produced was even higher.

By now, the court was entering Gee-whizz Land. Steel dug up a document produced by McDonald's UK in 1985. This claimed that if all the hamburgers sold by McDonald's since 1955 were lined end to end they would stretch to the moon and back five times. In that case, she said, she wouldn't like to hazard a guess as to how many times the packaging would stretch to the moon and back now, bearing in mind that the packaging was bigger than the burgers and that the company had expanded massively since 1985. She also pointed out that whereas hamburgers were eaten, packaging actually stayed around a lot longer, maybe for ever.

Oakley insisted that McDonald's was an environmentally responsible company. The corporation (to its credit) had moved faster than anyone in the fast-food business to phase out the ozone-layer destroying CFCs in its packaging. Its own ozone expert, Professor Duxbury, had said that in 1988, at the time of the alleged libel, the company's CFC usage (for packaging) was 'significant'.

Moreover, the court was told, McDonald's was using a growing percentage of recycled paper. It denied that vast areas of forest were required to maintain its packaging operations, and denied that polystyrene has a negative environmental impact. But the corporation was in a bit of a quandary here. The UK company's own McFact Card No. 4 stated that it'd switched to polystyrene in the mid-1970s 'because of serious concerns from environmentalists'. Yet the US company's '1991 Waste Reduction Action Plan' said it was phasing in paper-based packaging 'for environmental reasons'. Oakley suggested it was 'six of one and half a dozen of the other'. Indeed it was, and it emerged that the corporation was 'searching for alternatives' which were safe for the environment.

But had the corporation's environment policy had any direct effect on the purchasing department? Oakley: 'It certainly did on the communications department' – i.e., the PR department. Morris leapt in: coming from their Senior Vice-President in charge of McDonald's' purchasing in Northern Europe, was this not an admission that their policies were for propaganda purposes only?

Oakley denied that.

The McDonald's policy was to reduce packaging and solid waste, to reuse materials where practical and to recycle. Since 1990, the corporation had made 'considerable reductions in the amount of plastic packaging used by making bulk deliveries and using thinner plastic. A further 334,000 kilograms was being saved through the development of light waste and unbleached food-wrap paper and by standardizing carryout bags'.

Anne Link, the Science Co-ordinator of the Women's Environmental Network, told the court about the negative environmental effects of McDonald's' packaging. She was concerned about dangerous chemicals and excessive amounts of energy used in production processes, and also about the damage caused by the disposal of discarded materials. She criticized the sheer volume of company packaging – much of which she thought was unnecessary – and the fact that McDonald's used disposable items instead of reusables.

She said the aim in all Western countries was to create a 'no-waste society'. She said she would conclude from McDonald's' official documents that the company was 'waiting until forced to change by increasing environmental awareness', and 'could be using its international structure to spread good environmental ideas rather than bad ones as at present'. Not at all, said Ed Oakley. McDonald's used large quantities of packaging and colourful cartons with company logos 'to put the brand across directly to the customer'. The logos were 'for image, brand image'.

Enter, for the defence, Theo Hopkins, an independent researcher on the degradation and destruction of temperate and boreal forests. Hopkins had analysed McDonald's' annual use of hundreds of thousands of tons of paper packaging in Europe and the USA. Generally, Hopkins said, large-scale commercial forest exploitation led to the reduction of natural 'old-growth' or ancient forests, which were still being logged all over Europe, North America and elsewhere. This had gone on despite protests and official 'protection' measures. Mono-culture plantations had, moreover, replaced natural forests, but could not match such forests for their biodiversity, or social, ecological, cultural or spiritual value – they could not, he said, be described as 'sustainable' even under official international guidelines.

McDonald's said its products used paper sourced from such forests. This, said Hopkins, was 'self-evidently damaging to the environment'. Only since the late 1980s had the forest industry publicly had to recognize these problems, faced with publicity and pressure from the public. In 1989/1990, at the time of the alleged libel, there was virtually no concern by government and forest industry for ecological sustainability, he said. Whilst some problems were now being recognized, this had only just started to have some effect on the 'forest floor'.

He outlined some of the environmental problems in countries which provided the source materials for Mc-Donald's' packaging in North America and Europe. There was much logging and clear-cutting of natural forest in the US and Canada; forests were being cut down faster than they could regenerate in the Czech Republic; very little ancient forest remained in Finland and Sweden; over 40 per cent of what little ancient woodland which existed in the UK had been felled since 1945. Plantation forests as replacement were no solution, he explained.

Hopkins quoted expert concerns over the scale of world pulp production (which had 'increased by five times over the last forty years', being 'the major use of timber' from managed forests) and anxieties over the effects of pulp production 'due to the highly polluting milling processes'. In order to protect forests, he said, the first priority is to reduce paper consumption, especially in rich countries which consume vast quantities.

Forestry experts on both sides now crawled over the oak pews of Court 35. Terence Mallinson, formerly with one of Britain's largest tropical timber importers and now an industry spokesman, told the court that 'ecological sustainability was seldom, if ever, on the agenda of government or industry before 1988/9'. His claim that the timber industry was 'getting better' was evidence, said Morris, that the situation was bad when the writs were served. Mallinson argued that more trees were being planted than felled nowadays, albeit in plantations.

But the big question was what area of forest was needed to keep McDonald's in paper packaging each year. The words complained of in the Factsheet were: 'It takes 800 square miles of forest just to keep McDonald's supplied with paper for one year.' This meant, the defendants argued, sustainable forest area, not forest which is cut down – the area of maintained agriforest it took to keep McDonald's supplied with the relevant annual volume of paper it needed, indefinitely.

The court was in for some big statistics and lessons in 'sustainability' and 'forest cover'. First, though, both sides – remarkably – agreed that in order for a forest to be sustainable, it had to have a 'cycle' period. This is the time it takes for the forest to become mature, to be continuously cut for timber, yet for the overall area to remain the same.

So far so good. Mallinson had said that McDonald's got most of its timber from 'thinnings' and 'toppings' of trees, not from cutting trees down to the ground. Morris claimed Mallinson had admitted that the area needed to get this 'sustainable' timber was 80 to 100 times the cubic feet of trees actually cut down each year. The judge didn't accept this, and

Rampton refuted it outright. The judge seemed to side with Rampton.

Rampton did his calculations. First he took the total cubic feet of US timber (831 billion); he divided that by the total acreage under timber (483,000) and got the timber yield. This gave him the pulp yield, and so the pulp yield per acre. Then he factored in McDonald's' use of virgin pulp (88,761 tons from their main US supplier in 1992). Therefore, he concluded, triumphantly, 6,058.8 acres were needed to yield that weight . . . therefore the real figure for the amount of land McDonald's needed to provide its US paper packaging was . . . 9.46 square miles of virgin wood.

Oh no it's not, said Morris, who took an altogether different route to reach a wildly different answer. It was difficult, he prefaced his calculations, because McDonald's didn't take into account things like their overestimate of 'recycled material, the non-inclusion of packaging handled by the corporation's other suppliers, the amount of wood lost in production, and Mallinson's evidence that 10 per cent of "forest area" was actually paths or rivers or picnic spots . . .' and so on.

The true figure, he computed ('after much analysis of documents and expert testimony'), of commercial managed forest area under plantation needed to keep supplying McDonald's – worldwide, not just USA – in paper packaging every year was: (wait for it) '20 square miles × 1.5 (taking account of all other suppliers) × 1.7 (to include the whole non-recycled content) × 1.1 (left on the forest floor) × 2.5 (to include the non-pulpwood uses of wood extracted) × 1.1 (forest area percentage not used commercially) × 2 (material lost in production) × 80 to 100 (forest cycle sustainable area needed) . . . which equalled about [the A-level mathematician paused] between . . . 24,684 and 30,855 square miles'. This was an area almost the size of Cuba or French Guiana, or

Austria – almost, indeed, a third of the size of the UK. It didn't mean, explained Morris, the whole area was being managed solely for McDonald's' use, but that the company required stable access to products sourced from such huge plantation forest areas.

It was seriously different from the 9.46 square miles that Rampton had estimated.

By now, the judge was getting the hang of it. Yes, he said to Morris, but it was not put to a witness that if the life cycle was forty years, you would need forty times the area, if it was eighty years, you would need eighty times the area or if it was a hundred years, you would need a hundred times the area. 'I mean this is Morris on forestry, not a witness on forestry.'

Then there was downright confusion when Rampton said that the sentence 'It takes 800 hundred square miles of forest, etc. . . .' would be OK if it appeared in a specialist forestry publication, but not in a public leaflet as 'ordinary people' would not be able to understand the technicalities. It was pointed out that this suggested that McDonald's was suing not because the figures were absolutely wrong but because Joe Public couldn't understand. As ever, the two sides had foundered over perceived meanings. If the leaflet was referring to the area of economically sustainable forest then, said the judge, the leaflet was 'understandable'. If it meant that this was the area 'actually, physically chopped down each year', then he did not feel it had been proven. Just which meaning the leaflet had, he would decide on.

If the concept of sustainable forest was confusing for the court, polystyrene was almost its undoing, and anyone who ventured in during the evidence around this time was liable to faint with statistical overload. The UK President, Paul Preston, now said that styrofoam packaging was 'less environmentally damaging' than using plates, knives and forks.

This view was not shared by a defence witness from the

USA, Brian Lipsett, who explained how the 'McToxics' campaign in the US had galvanized thousands of protests and official bans and had forced McDonald's to withdraw its polystyrene-foam food packaging. He identified the problems associated with styrofoam (toxic wastes, damage to the ozone layer and smog pollution, the leaching of styrene from the packaging into the foods packaged in the foam) and the serious disposal problems (the sheer volume of the material and the lack of a suitable method of disposal).

McDonald's has continued to use styrofoam in many countries, including the UK. Professor Walker, McDonald's' toxicology expert, agreed that styrene can migrate from polystyrene packaging into food (especially fatty foods), and can metabolize in the human body into styrene oxide. The defence toxicology expert Dr Erik Millstone testified that the International Agency for the Research on Cancer had classified styrene oxide as probably carcinogenic to humans.

McDonald's had admitted that recycling polystyrene was now feasible, yet it was not doing anything about it in the UK (or elsewhere), despite claiming to have pilot recycling schemes, argued Morris. It was an environmentally irresponsible attitude, he argued.

Judges, barristers and environmental scientists do not talk the same language. The following was an exchange which showed the gulf in comprehension between the two sides when it came to ecological literacy. Rampton was questioning Brian Lipsett, an environmental specialist from the US who was speaking for Steel and Morris. One side saw the issue of packaging as being a problem of volume, the other side as a problem of content . . . To the casual observer, it is exquisitely cross-purposive; a metaphor for so much else in Court 35:

Rampton: 'For a given volume, the greater the density of material, the greater the weight of material within that given volume, correct?'

Lipsett: 'Sorry, would you ask that question again?'

Rampton: 'The more you squash things, the more things you can get into the hole?'

Lipsett: 'Is that the same question?'

Rampton: 'Yes.'

Lipsett: 'The more you squash things, the more you can get them into the hole, yes, that is right.'

Rampton: 'McDonald's' polystyrene foam waste does not lie around the United States of America in uncontrolled mountains, does it?'

Lipsett: 'Well, it depends at what point you are talking about in the disposal process. If you are talking about styrene foam lying around in mountains in a landfill, no, the landfill is a compilation of a large body of waste from a number of sources. If you are talking about McDonald's' foam in its dumpsters, then you are talking about uncompacted foam. If you are talking about McDonald's' foam in recycling facilities, you are talking about very large piles of foam.'

Rampton: 'Those are transitory stages. The landfill is supposed to be the terminus, is it not?'

Lipsett: 'Yes.'

Rampton: 'So, whatever the volume in cubic feet of the polystyrene foam in its transitory state, what one must look at to judge fairly McDonald's' contribution to the municipal waste stream is how it ends up?'

Lipsett: 'Yes.'

Rampton: 'That is either by incineration, where its volume is reduced to practically nothing, or else in a landfill site?'

Lipsett: 'Its volume is not reduced to practically nothing. Its volume is transferred into the air.'

Rampton: 'In terms of billions of cubic feet, incineration reduces those billions of cubic feet, whatever other substances may be liberated, in terms of volume of polystyrene foam.

Incineration reduces the polystyrene foam to practically nothing in terms of volume?'

Lipsett: 'No, according to the laws of physics, the incineration of polystyrene foam cannot destroy the matter in the foam such that the volume of the package is made to no longer exist. It is merely transformed into another phase.'

Mr Justice Bell: 'Yes, but hold on a minute, quite a proportion of the volume is just air, I mean, what we call air?'

Lipsett: 'I would say that what is released in the gases is a combination of all that is not left as residual ash, OK? It is actually transferred into the air. It is transferred, based on whatever degree it breaks down in the burning process; obviously that is a matter of contention here. The substances that are released are a matter of contention. However, they are released into the air.'

Bell: 'Quite a lot of the volume which is released on incineration, without getting too technical, is what you and I are breathing at this very moment?'

Lipsett: 'I hope not.'

Bell: 'I had understood from the evidence we had earlier that quite a proportion of what is in the little bubbles in foam – correct me if I am wrong, Mr Rampton – it is not just a blowing agent, it is what I will continue just to call air.'

Rampton: 'That is right, is it not?'

Lipsett: 'I am sorry?'

Rampton: 'In the composition of polystyrene foam, a high proportion is just air, as his lordship calls it?'

Lipsett: 'Well, air is a very general term.'

Mr Justice Bell: 'I know, that is why I said what we are breathing now is pumped into the foam together with the blowing agent and is held there in the foam?'

Lipsett: 'OK, I have seen that . . .'

Bell: 'Is that right or not?'

Lipsett: 'I see them as different matters.'

Bell: 'So when you burn that?'

Lipsett: 'When you burn polystyrene foam, the issue is not whether or not what is in the package is mostly, as you say, air, and only whatever percentage of that product is another substance; the issue is what happens to the material, the polystyrene material, when you burn it and when you release it into the air.'

Bell: 'I am sticking on volume?'

Lipsett: 'OK.'

Bell: 'Let me accept for the moment, without examining with any particular care, that the actual polystyrene is by incineration changed into something else and, therefore, becomes some other form of gaseous matter?'

Lipsett: 'Right, yes.'

Bell: 'There is still in that volume a significant proportion of what I will continue to call air which does not fall into the same category?'

By now the witness no longer has a clue what is going on. He has a counsel who does not understand too well the laws of physics, and a judge who has become obsessed by air. He just wants to make the point that you don't just get rid of polystyrene foam. The noxious substances revert to the ash or go into the air, damn it. Will not anyone understand him?

Lipsett: 'I am a little lost.'

[*Exeunt.*]

Chapter Fifteen

Heigh-ho, heigh-ho, it's off to . . .

Steel: Do you ever wonder why groups campaign against McDonald's?
Preston (President, McDonald's UK Ltd.): No.
Steel: You do not wonder?
Preston: No. Why would I wonder about that?

If McDonald's only had 'kitty customers', life for its 1.5 million mostly young employees would be blissful. Kitties, writes an anonymous McDonald's worker on the Dan McGripe Internet site – set up specially for disgruntled employees – are the most polite of McDonald's customers. Kitties say please and thank you, kitties think that McDonald's provides a service and so should be stroked. Kitties appreciate low prices, know that the McDonald's crew work under enormous pressure, and that mistakes happen . . .

But, Dan's correspondent continues, life for the McDonald's employee is a 'living hell' because kitty customers are practically an endangered species. It seems the typical McDonald's customer falls into one of two other groups. First there's the 'jackass', 'completely oblivious to what goes on in the background, what the crew must go through to produce the vast amounts of food being ordered'. The jackass sees the entire establishment as a bottomless food depository and is oblivious not only to the abilities of the crew people but also to the laws of physics: 'The jackass will order some outrageous quantity of food with no more thought than if he/she were putting a coin into a machine . . . it is these ignorant types who make employment at McDonald's a wearing experience.'

But even jackasses are lovable compared to the object of this virtual writer's real scorn, the third type of McDonald's customer. 'There is no magnitude of pure ignorance that can produce the amount of grief, anger or madness that results for the truly evil, inhumane persons of society . . . the one and only bastards of bastards, the asshole customers . . . no, not just assholes, the fragmentations and incarnations of the soul of his Assholeness, Satan himself . . .'

McDonald's has its full share of Satan's customers, according to Dan's correspondent. 'They are unbelievably impatient and unforgiving: "I want five cheeseburgers AND GIVE THEM TO ME WITHOUT ONIONS!" they will say . . . they will stand there barking at the management . . . they rant and rave . . . they ask for a refund . . . The grill team knows they're out there, and receive their grill requests with a "God D*mmm*t! What a f******* bit of sh*t." No number of kitty customers could ever balance the shadow of pure evil and misery these minions of Lucifer cast over McDonald's. They are what makes McDonald's Hell on Earth. They are what drives the employees to a slow painful insanity . . .'

The anonymous McDonald's worker interestingly regards the customer as the most disagreeable aspect of the McDonald's employment experience. But for Morris and Steel and many witnesses called to Court 35 over two years to give more than eighty-five days' evidence on the corporation's working practices, the problem is the absolute opposite; the system of work itself, they believe, led to widespread dissatisfaction. The trial should not be of the customer so much as of the corporation.

But McDonald's was trying Steel and Morris. The Fact-sheet had itemized three areas that McDonald's found offensive: it had said the corporation 'opposed unionization', 'paid bad wages and provided bad working conditions' and was 'only interested in cheap labour'. It denied all, vehemently.

Steel and Morris, trade unionists, tried to paint Mc-Donald's as a pioneer of employment practices based on 'low pay and few rights' coupled with arduous work. About 40,000 employees work for the McDonald's chain in the UK, and 1.5 million worldwide. The sort of jobs characterized by hard work, low pay, no guaranteed hours and no unions or rights have been popularly described as 'McJobs'. 'We'd thought,' says Morris, 'right the way back in 1990, there should really be no difficulty in showing that the company which gave the world the word "McJobs" was fair game to be criticized for exploiting their staff.'

The defendants were following a well-beaten path. Think-tanks, analysts and others around the world had identified the casualization of global workforces. Out were going the improved wages and conditions (Steel and Morris would say won by a hundred years of strikes and 'struggles' by organized labour), in was coming low-paid, non-union, temporary or part-time work with few guaranteed rights and poor conditions. Such is the upside-down post-Communist world that revolutionary anarchists can these days be in agreement with the UN, most political opposition parties in the West and even right-wing newspapers.

The trouble was that McDonald's was making Steel and Morris prove what so many commentators were saying without mentioning the corporation specifically. It argued precisely that the leaflet was defamatory because it meant that it paid *bad* wages and provided *bad* working conditions, took advantage of the absence of any specific union for its workers and prevented unions getting in by getting rid of pro-union workers. Moreover, it argued, the leaflet claimed that it had taken advantage of there being no legal minimum wage in Britain to pay what it liked, helping thereby to depress wages in the catering trade. Finally, it said, the leaflet claimed that McDonald's was only interested in recruiting cheap labour, and to this end exploited disadvantaged groups. Prove it, it said, knowing that in the letter of the law, a team of experienced advocates, let alone two legal amateurs, would find it next to impossible.

Faced with a semantic hell where words like 'high' and 'low', 'bad' and 'cheap' could be interpreted either as fact or as expressions of opinion and were themselves open questions for the judge alone to decide on, Steel and Morris (as usual) clambered straight for the high moral ground. But unlike in the rainforest and advertising sections, where they had to try to prove particular points of the Factsheet with general arguments, here the defendants had to try to prove the McDonald's system itself was at fault. It was to take eight months' detailed analysis of documents and statistics relating to numerous McDonald's stores. Dozens of current and former employees were lined up.

In one sense the defendants were fortunate. More than in any other section of the trial there was ample evidence of things frequently going wrong in the fast-food industry. As one after another disaffected McDonald's worker, trade unionist or expert paraded through Court 35, so they found McDonald's boxing carefully from the legal ropes and arguing that there could be nothing fundamentally wrong with the way it operated because it was inside the law.

Yes, it would concede in the final speeches, there might be

isolated examples of this and that going wrong; yes, it was a problem getting good staff in some areas; yes, the odd mistake – even illegality – had undoubtedly been made in such high-pressure, intense environments, but it would be inhuman to expect otherwise; and to show fault in a few things was in no way to prove fault in the system – which, after all, had served something like 100 billion meals with few complaints in two generations. McDonald's would argue: 'We work within the law, therefore we cannot by definition pay low wages. We are not anti-union because the law is not anti-union and we are not illegal. And the working conditions for our staff ['crew'] are good because the law and the regulatory bodies demand standards that we meet and we respect our workers because they must be respected.'

The showdown in Court 35 started at the top. For Morris, the old Post Office union branch secretary, it was heaven itself to have the chance to grill – perhaps even to flip – a 'boss'. First to the witness-box in July 1994 came Paul Preston, McDonald's UK's President. He was direct enough. Of unions he said: 'It's not that I don't like communicating with unions, it's just that I would consider it as failure if we did.' No, he said, he did not think the current starting wage of £3.10 an hour to be 'low pay'. Nor did he think his own salary (he refused to reveal what it was) to be 'high'.

But he could easily brush off most of the political sparring:

Steel: 'Why can't crew members be paid higher wages out of the $1 billion global profits McDonald's made last year?'

Preston: 'People are paid a wage for the job they do.'

Morris: 'Why doesn't the company use its $1 billion advertising budget to pay higher wages?'

Preston: 'Without advertising the company would have no business.'

Preston had stated that it was 'policy' to ensure staff were never paid below the minimum wage in any circumstances. *How could McDonald's be anti-union when everyone had the legal right to join one?* Of course it was policy to communicate with staff constantly.

In the witness-box he became ever more careful. No, he didn't think that a pay rise of 5p an hour in two years (less than 1 per cent a year) was 'low'; no, he wouldn't tell the judge if any of his workers actually belonged to a union; yes, he *might* have said to the *Financial Times* that McDonald's' financial results would be affected if unions were to spread in the company; and rather than 'keeping wages as low as possible' he *preferred* to say that McDonald's 'followed the market'. It was corporate-speak, defensive play, but legally measured and hard to break down.

Enter Sidney Nicholson, the UK Vice-President with several jobs. As Head of Security he had employed the spies to follow Steel and Morris around and as former Head of Personnel he was now the spokesman on pay and conditions. He denied that McDonald's' crew were low-paid but said that everyone complained about money everywhere, didn't they? He, Sidney Nicholson, could say he was not getting enough. So how much was he getting? Nicholson wasn't saying.

Nevertheless, in 1993 McDonald's' senior management mostly had salaries over £75,000 a year (about £36 an hour) while at the other end of the scale, the starting rate for crew members outside London at the same time was £3 an hour for over eighteens and £2.65 for sixteen- and seventeen-year-olds.

McDonald's, it emerged, set its starting rates either the same as or just a few pence over the minimum rates of pay set at the time by the Wages Council (a statutory body enforcing minimum wages and conditions). At the time in question, the company couldn't pay crew aged twenty-one or over lower wages without falling foul of the law, said Nicholson. Indeed, when the government abolished the legal protection of a minimum wage for under-twenty-ones (in 1986) he said he was 'quite content . . . because it simplified things'.

In Britain about 80 per cent of crew are part-time, averaging about twenty hours per week. Approximately two-thirds of McDonald's crew are under twenty-one, and nearly one-third are under eighteen. Nicholson denied the corporation chose to employ a high percentage of young workers so that they could exploit them for lower wages and make greater profits. Nevertheless crew have no guaranteed hours or pay, get no money for meal breaks and managers can – and do – compulsorily cut or extend workers' hours as needs dictate.

Q: 'Has not McDonald's UK admitted that it was convicted of seventy-three offences in relation to the employment of young people in the early 1980s?'

Nicholson: 'Since that time I have no knowledge of any infringements of the regulations.'

Steel and Morris remained unconvinced and continued to press for the official employment records. 'When we eventually persuaded the judge to get McDonald's to produce the documents – clock cards, schedules and so on – they revealed breaches of company policies, contractual obligations and the law. If we'd had that at the start of the trial it might have saved a lot of time.'

Nicholson was supported by the most senior McDonald's man to give evidence in the trial. US Senior Vice-President Robert Beavers joined McDonald's in 1963 and has sat on the board of directors since 1984. He told the court how McDonald's US workers generally started at the legal minimum wage of $3.35 per hour and the company would not be allowed to pay less. 'I do not consider it ($3 – $4 p.h.) to be low pay. It is a fair wage for the work that is expected,' he said.

The relationship between the company and its young staff was crucial. In America in 1995 it was training 400,000 people a year to be part of its system, and more than 10 per cent of the entire US workforce are believed to have got their first job at McDonald's. The mutual dependency is great and growing. The corporation, said Beavers, 'depends for their profits on the labour of young people'. Beavers took on Morris for the moral high ground.

Morris: 'Do you think the McDonald's Corporation has had a positive input on [sic] society?'
  Beavers: 'Yes, I do.'
  Morris: 'Can you give some examples of the influence it has had, then?'
  Beavers: 'We have introduced production methods around the world that have been adopted and replicated that have helped to reduce costs as well as improving basic services, the quality of goods. I think we have been a good corporate citizen. Wherever we have located our restaurants, we have tended to become a part of the community, to be much more than just a business in the community. We have tried to be a good corporate neighbour in reaching out and working with various organizations and Church groups within that community. We have provided thousands and thousands of jobs across the world, across seventy-nine countries in which we operate, jobs that did not exist. We have provided oppor-tunity—'
  Morris: 'The jobs did exist, did they not?'
  Beavers: 'Pardon?'
  Morris: 'There were jobs in catering before McDonald's came along?'
  Beavers: 'Yes, but we create—'
  Morris: 'You replaced the kind of catering that was going on with a different kind of style?'

Beavers: 'Well, actually, I think we have created an industry. We have provided additional jobs over and above the jobs that were part of the catering industry. We have really helped to embellish a way of life, the way of life in America, and some countries where we have located. In addition to the jobs that we have provided, we have provided a great deal of advancement opportunity for people who are willing to work hard and exhibit good, you know, good work habits . . .'

What McDonald's interpreted as worthy of pride or evidence of its success was interpreted by the defendants as the opposite. When told that on their first day all new crew are shown an official McDonald's 'orientation' video to inject 'a family feeling', Steel and Morris latched on to it as the corporation 'brainwashing' staff – something flatly denied by the McDonald's executives. Beavers explained how workers' attitudes were important, how crew were marked on their attitude towards store 'success' and their desire to 'progress'. Yes, he said, people failing to identify with the corporate goals could be fired. The cultural gulf between corporation and critic yawned widely. Steel and Morris thought this was taking advantage of a 'vulnerable, inexperienced' sector of society and that what McDonald's was really doing was teaching young workers how to be 'a cog in a machine, to be obedient, not to question the idiocy of the job . . . and to basically be a slave for the company'. Beavers did not.

It took Sidney Nicholson to explain the corporate discipline needed to work in the stores. Workers had to get permission to have a drink. Management could change crew hours of work at will; the *Crew Handbook* listed dozens of examples where management could direct, restrict or ban employee activity and behaviour (under threat of disciplinary action and summary dismissal). Did workers have rights beyond those for which there was statutory protection? Nicholson could not think of one. Beavers had earlier said that US crew workers had no guaranteed employment rights. 'They do not have guaranteed employment or guaranteed conditions of employment.' To the corporation this meant an increase of 'flexibility', which benefited everyone.

Nicholson admitted that store managers were under pressure from higher up to keep labour costs down. Company documents revealed that a former UK manager in Newcastle had been told amongst other things to get his labour costs down 'within targeted labour guidelines' (of between 14–16 per cent of sales) or face dismissal. Internal company documents showing profit and loss projections for 1992 revealed that the company had planned to reduce the overall crew labour costs nationally as a percentage of turnover (at about 15 per cent of sales) whilst increasing the management percentage.

But as fast as McDonald's hires staff, it seems it loses them, argued Steel and Morris. UK and US crew turnover in December 1989 was about 190 per cent, and had been higher in the USA. The corporation had managed to reduce the percentage somewhat since, but, said Morris, UK figures were still three or four times the catering industry average. McDonald's claimed this was due to the high number of students employed, but much of the catering industry has a similar youth profile and company documents suggested that only 23 per cent of the turnover was due to staff saying they were leaving to go back to education. Beavers admitted that 'consistent and important' reasons given by staff on leaving (as noted in the company's *Operations Manual*) were: 'poor treatment – lack of recognition, poor people practices, dissatisfaction with pay, low and/or infrequent raises', 'no job enjoyment or satisfaction' and 'poor working conditions – faulty and missing equipment'.

Rampton would argue that low pay and bad conditions did not lead to the problem of high turnover of staff. 'People do not leave in droves simply because someone thinks their pay and conditions are poor,' he said in his closing speech. 'For these reasons, the assertion can only be that the pay is low and the conditions are bad in absolute, or objective terms; that is, as a matter of fact. Taken together in context they fuel the image of deliberate (improper) exploitation, and are therefore part of the defamation.'

In short, he said, if everything was really so bad at McDonald's the following would be true:

a. the workforce would be hopelessly depressed, etc.

b. staff turnover would be higher, recruiting would be extremely difficult, etc.

c. the restaurants would be understaffed and dirty

d. service would be dreadful, etc.

e. food would be awful

f. there would be thousands of prosecutions, worldwide, for breaches of food safety, Health and Safety and employment laws and thousands of ex-employees would be clambering over themselves to come to the witness-box, when in fact there was a total of fourteen from the UK

g. the customers would walk out never to return

h. the company would go out of business.

None of which was true, he said. The Steel and Morris picture of working life at McDonald's was a gross misrepresentation. It was, he said, self-evidently not like this.

Whether or not the arguments were legally telling, Steel and Morris were scoring bonus points for revelations with the imaginary jury. They produced time sheets revealing five breaches of the law relating to the employment of young people in one week alone at Orpington, Kent, in 1987. Other documents showed that in 1993, on average two or three under-eighteens in London were showing up on company records as working more than ninety-six hours in a fortnight which until 1990 was illegal, and was still, according to Mr Nicholson, against company policy.

According to Nicholson, McDonald's never had to pay overtime, despite the statutory (now defunct) Wages Council setting minimum overtime rates for anything over a thirty-nine-hour week. But what happened, it was posed, if people did work more than thirty-nine hours a week? Nicholson said that company policy set a maximum of thirty-nine hours a week for all crew. Steel and Morris then showed payroll reports that showed that at least 5 per cent of hourly paid staff (that is, they said, a quarter of all full-timers), in London and the South of England worked over thirty-nine hours each week. McDonald's took it squarely; Nicholson said it was a rare occurrence. But the defendants pressed their claim: did not payroll records for one store alone show that nine out of fifty-three workers worked over seventy-eight hours in a fortnight (thirty-nine hours per week)? When asked if it would concern him if 17 per cent of McDonald's workers were working more than thirty-nine hours a week, in breach of policy, Nicholson commented: 'It would not concern me.' He also stated 'it is only policy'.

Industrial relations expert Phil Pearson was called by the defence and told the court how in 1992, when McDonald's was paying crew members around £3 per hour, a decency threshold was being defined by the Council of Europe as £5.52. It seemed to him, as a former member of the now abolished catering industry Wages Council (which was a statutory body enforcing minimum wages and conditions for low-paid workers), that McDonald's' failure to pay any overtime in the late 1980s was 'apparently, from the figures [official McDonald's documents], systematic abuse, systematic underpayment . . . non-application of the law'. Failure to pay the appropriate remuneration was, he said, punishable by fine or prison.

It was damaging. McDonald's had broken the law at times and consistently underpaid some of its staff for various periods of time. In many cases the amounts were low, but Mr Justice Bell worked out that one particular employee had been underpaid for overtime £175. The judge had included ten years' compound interest. Steel and Morris believe there may be thousands of people in the same position: 'They could all demand payment for what they are owed,' says Steel.

For McDonald's, though, a certain number of mistakes had to be put into the context of the massive size of its operations. Seen as a proportion of the whole, such faults were relatively insignificant. Furthermore, as Preston argued, these 'irregularities' were the result of accident, not of policy. For example, here is the UK President being cross-examined about eighteen-year-olds unlawfully working late at night:

Q: 'Is it true there have been times in the past where McDonald's' restaurants have employed young people illegally in conditions that were illegal?'

Preston: 'Well, what do you mean by "conditions that were illegal"?'

Q: 'For example, working illegal hours?'

Preston: 'We have admitted, I believe, for the case, historic circumstances where things went wrong, things happened. I do not contest them. We are not perfect. Certainly in the scale of things, McDonald's' management personnel do not set out in the morning to say: "How can I break the law? How can I make people's lives miserable?" Quite the opposite is true. Unfortunately, we are dealing with human beings here who make mistakes.'

Rampton was to sum up the overtime controversy: 'This

is not something to be brushed aside; and it would be something of a black mark against McDonald's, but for the fact that their method of payment had, in effect, been [officially] sanctioned.' Picking his way through pay rates and notional shifts, he calculated that the number of workers receiving less than their minimum statutory entitlement after 1986 was, in reality, 'close to negligible'.

Steel and Morris were not through, in grand substance or in minute detail. They had concentrated much of their defence on three English stores (Heathrow, Colchester and Bath) to try to show what sort of employer McDonald's was. The specific allegations of their two dozen witnesses (mostly ex-employees) were long and detailed, and ranged from what might seem the most trivial of malpractices (like staff being told to use 'out-of-date' onions or skimp on the lettuce) to the far more serious allegations of grill temperatures being wrongly set, the undercooking of burgers and the systematic docking of wages; of under-eighteens working illegal hours; and of understaffing and an authoritarian and pressurizing management style. In between came claims that staff were ordered to water down syrups and mustard, not throw food away, reduce portions and double-brew coffee. The trial hit the front pages when ex-workers testified that on one occasion they had to prepare burgers whilst standing in sewage from an overflowing drain.

The Colchester store was the company's 'Store of the Year' in 1987. The court heard from former managers how special clean-ups were ordered when senior management were due to visit, how breaks were sometimes shortened and hours compulsorily cut or extended. Siamak Alimi, former crew member at Colchester, told of the high pressure of work at McDonald's, long hours (including twenty-hour shifts) with few breaks and low pay; of crew members under eighteen working illegal hours; and of threats of the sack for joining a union or protesting against in-store conditions.

Rampton would later paint the lack of breaks as a benefit: 'Since breaks are not paid, many people will not want to take their full entitlement ... many people will also find, say, forty-five minutes sitting in the crew room boring, and will want to get back down to the job as soon as possible ... If an eighteen-year-old decides that he doesn't want a forty-five minute break because he's bored or because he wants to work for all the money-generating hours in his shift, or both, that is his business – and it won't do him any harm, either.' Steel and Morris countered that it was a basic right. It was hot, pressurized work, and breaks were needed for safety reasons.

Kevin Harrison worked in 1986 and 1987 at McDonald's branches in Colchester and Ipswich as an assistant manager. Pressure to reduce costs all round led to the secret cutting of food servings and using out-of-date food, he said. He criticized managers' use of 'hustle' to get work speeded up. 'McDonald's,' he stated, 'is a very pressurized environment, and nowhere else are you expected to work at that level for such long periods of time.' He left, he said, due to 'the job, the hours and mounting dissatisfaction with the company philosophy in general'. McDonald's called half a dozen of their own witnesses to deny, admit or at least explain the problems at this 'Store of the Year'.

Kevin Perrett, a McDonald's 'breakfast manager' at its Bath restaurant, was quoting and countering defence witness Michael Logan, who'd worked at the store for four years up until 1994: 'Michael says that McDonald's treats its employees as a cost not a resource, giving little regard to their rights and well-being. This has not been my experience. If it had, I would have left McDonald's years ago. I feel that I have had the opportunity to progress and I am treated with respect by both managers and crew. I do not feel exploited. I feel that the communication in the restaurant is good and I have always felt able to talk to any manager if a problem arises. As far as I'm concerned, there has always been a safety culture at the restaurant.'

Other current employees, almost all managerial grades, who gave evidence for the plaintiffs agreed that they did not feel exploited and denied that they were treated with little regard for their rights or well-being. Others described the company as a culture of opportunity. They felt there were high levels of safety and there was good communication. In short, the working conditions at McDonald's were 'good'.

Christopher Purslow, an experienced hygiene and safety consultant, and a past chairman of the Institution of Environmental Health Commercial and Industrial Centre, gave evidence for the corporation. 'McDonald's' procedures,' he said, 'when taken in combination, reflect a very real commitment to principles of health and safety, a commitment that in my professional opinion places them as one of the leaders in the industry. I would particularly point to the standards of training and procedures laid down as being models of their kind. That being said, it would be surprising indeed if across 450 stores and 30,000 staff there were not problems from time to time. These are, however, closely monitored and appropriate and effective action is taken, including if necessary the allocation of considerable capital sums ... The law requires the employer "to do everything 'reasonably practicable' to secure the health and safety at work of their employees". I believe that McDonald's fully reflect that commitment, a belief that is endorsed by the lack of formal EHOs [Environmental Health Orders] over the years, in a sector of the industry which is always vigorously scrutinized by the enforcement authorities.'

*

On 12 October 1992, Mark Hopkins, a McDonald's worker in Manchester, was electrocuted on touching a fat-filtering machine in the 'wash-up' area of the store. A McDonald's memo from the north-west region dated 17/2/92 was quoted which revealed that 'there have been several recent instances in our restaurants where members of staff have received severe shocks from faulty items of electrical equipment'. Following an investigation of the death, the Manchester Environmental Health Department issued a Prohibition Order forcing McDonald's to install 'Residual Current Devices' on all electrical equipment in wash-up areas. In its view an offence had been caused because there was 'a risk of serious personal injury' without them. They were fitted nationally following Mr Hopkins' death.

Jill Barnes (McDonald's UK's Hygiene and Safety Officer) was challenged over a previously confidential internal report into Mark Hopkins' death. Not shown to the inquest jury following the accident, the report had catalogued a number of company failures and problems, and concluded: 'Safety is not seen as being important at store level.' Additionally, a confidential 1992 Health and Safety Executive report about the company made twenty-three recommendations for improvements. One was: 'The application of McDonald's' hustle policy [i.e., getting staff to work at speed] in many restaurants was, in effect, putting the service of the customer before the safety of employees.' Steel and Morris referred to McDonald's' Crew Training programme which stated: 'When do you use hustle? (All the time.)' Beavers said that the 'hustle' policy of fast working came from the US and applied to over 1 million crew workers. But he was unaware that the 'hustle' policy had been lambasted by the UK Health and Safety Executive.

The sheer weight of claim and argument was, here more than anywhere else, phenomenal. Steel and Morris produced witness after witness to testify that things went wrong on every level of day-to-day operation. Rampton and his team riposted with more than 240 pages of legal arguments defending the company policy and unpicking their opponents' allegations one by one. The price of Mr Justice Bell's determination to let everyone have their fair say was now deep cross-examination and evidence gathering about blocked drains, lavatory cleaning and whether people were harassed to work ever faster. It was, depending on your starting point, painful or painstaking, and is hard to imagine the great QC Richard Rampton reduced to defending allegations that grease traps were occasionally bunged up or that one pickle rather than two might have been used at times if a restaurant was running short. But McLibel was as much a trial of individual stamina as anything else.

The most contentious issue of all was unions. McDonald's' battles with organized labour have been long and sometimes fierce. Neither party has much respect for the other. Because Steel and Morris had to show up the company system, they went back to the start of the McDonald's story, trying to show that the corporation was rooted in anti-unionism. They questioned at length the Senior Vice-President Beavers.

Did not the corporation employ in the 1970s a man, John Cooke, who had a responsibility to keep the unions out? And was not Mr Cooke quoted in the book *Behind The Arches* (written with McDonald's' backing and assistance) as saying: 'Unions are inimical to what we stand for and how we operate. They peddle the line to their members that the boss will be for evermore against their interests'? Did not the book state that of the 400 serious organization attempts in the early 1970s, none was successful? And, asked Morris and Steel, had not McDonald's set up a 'flying squad' of experienced managers who were dispatched to restaurants as soon as word was received of attempts to unionize?

Beavers agreed.

And did not company managers in those days use 'lie detectors' (half-hour polygraph tests) on current or potential employees? Did not the practice only cease 'when it was obvious that the law was going to be passed making it illegal'? Did not, indeed, Cooke send a memo to top executives stating 'I think [the union] was effective in terms of reaching the public with the information that we do use polygraph tests in a Gestapo-type manner' and suggesting stopping their use?

Beavers admitted that in some cases refusal to take such a test would have led to dismissal. He said he did not know about a 1974 San Francisco Labor Board hearing at which McDonald's workers apparently testified that lie detectors had been used to ask about union sympathies, following which the company was threatened with legal action.

Enter Stan Stein (McDonald's US's Senior Vice-President, Head of Personnel & Labour Relations). Why the hostility to unions, Stan? Stein, who was grilled for nearly two weeks, said that he had worked for McDonald's since 1974 and in that time none of the company's restaurants in the USA had been unionized. In his view, McDonald's workers just happened not to want union rights. But whenever unions almost anywhere in the world made serious attempts to organize McDonald's workers, Mr Stein would likely jet into town. He had visited very many countries over the years.

Mr Justice Bell took over the questioning of the UK President on this issue.

Bell: '. . . are any members or any employees of McDonald's in this country [the UK] members of a union at all?'

Preston: 'They may very well be. I do not know. It is their right to join one if they so choose.'

Bell: 'I asked you whether any employee of the English company was a member of a union?'

Preston: 'I said they may very well be.'
Bell: 'They may very well be?'
Preston: 'It is their right to join if they so choose.'

The court later heard about serious disputes with unions in fifteen countries and how McDonald's had frequently been to the labour courts in its attempts to challenge unions. Nicholson told the court dead straight, too, that the company was not anti-union at all and all staff had a right to join one, at least in Britain. He insisted that McDonald's was 'very, very much in support of performance-related pay. Those who work well are paid well,' he said. 'For that reason we would rather not deal with trade unions.'

So, he was asked, what would any McDonald's workers interested in union membership actually be able to do? They would not, he said, be allowed to collect subscriptions, put up notices, pass out any leaflets, organize a meeting for staff to discuss conditions at the store on the premises . . . or inform the union about conditions inside the stores (which would be deemed 'gross misconduct' and a 'summary sackable offence'). In fact, Nicholson agreed, they would not be allowed to carry out any overt union activity on McDonald's' premises at all. But at one point he stated: 'If a majority of the staff of a restaurant had an election and voted to be represented by a trade union, then they would be represented by a trade union.' Later he said that 'if every single member of crew in a particular restaurant joined a union [McDonald's] would still not negotiate with the union', but he did recognize that if there was a massive national drive and a very large proportion of McDonald's employees joined a union and took industrial action, McDonald's 'might be left with no short alternative but to negotiate'.

Morris and Steel knuckled down to some gritty labour relations with Nicholson. On three occasions, in Hackney in 1985, East Ham in 1986 and Liverpool in 1988, the ex-policeman visited stores where he'd been told that employees were interested in union representation. He went with other management or security officials to talk to the crew 'to explain our point of view to them'. No, he said, people would not have felt intimidated by his presence or that of management or security. (Indeed, he said that he took an area security manager to Hackney only to help him find a place to park his car.) But did the company refuse to negotiate with trade unions because they would be more effective at arguing for better wages and conditions than individual workers? Nicholson thought not.

He claimed that company 'rap sessions' (meetings for workers to give their views to a manager or supervisor) meant there was no need for unions, and he denied any crew felt 'exploited' or 'pushed around', or felt they got 'low pay', because 'no one has said to me they do'.

He remembered banning a union official from leafleting or talking to staff inside a London store, even during their breaks, but said he had no objection to him leafleting or recruiting outside – 'We are quite used to people outside our stores giving out leaflets.' Wry grins all round. He stated, 'I want to know everything that happens at a store.'

The procession of international trade unionists, industrial relation experts and former McDonald's workers paraded through Court 35 to tell of pay, turnover and conditions. The court heard that although there were 'low wages, poor conditions and high turnover' throughout the catering industry, unions had sometimes won recognition and improvements. McDonald's was accused of denying people basic human rights.

Terry Pattinson (former Industrial Editor of the *Daily Mirror*) told the court about an interview on 16 December 1986 with Sid Nicholson (at the time McDonald's' Head of Personnel), who stated: 'We will never negotiate wages and conditions with a union and we discourage our staff from joining.' Mr Pattinson testified further that Paul Preston (McDonald's UK's President) had stated much the same to him in conversations in May 1990.

Sarah Inglis, a Canadian worker, testified how in 1993 at the age of sixteen she signed up a majority of the workers in her McDonald's store (Ontario) to a union. In response, managers organized a bizarre and nationally controversial 'anti-union' campaign, which included creating a climate of fear against pro-union staff, getting some of the workers in that store (the majority of whom were under eighteen) to lie outside in the snow forming the word 'NO' (to unions), putting on special anti-union video and slide shows and temporarily allowing improved conditions in the run-up to a secret ballot in the store for union recognition. McDonald's denied much of this.

Hassen Lamti, a current McDonald's crew member in Lyon (France) told how five McDonald's managers were arrested for trying to rig union elections in July 1994; how he was harassed for union activity; how McDonald's offered him a bribe if he renounced the union; how the union branch, now established, has so far won over twenty court judgements against the company to stop harassment and illegal business practices.

Calm, calm, urged Rampton in his summing up. The corporation's position is essentially neutral towards unions: 'Its position in Britain is that it would rather do without them because they would prefer to run their own business, but the policy elsewhere is that attitudes vary from country to country. The corporation had agreements with unions in seventeen countries.

He played down the troubles both sides had had over the years: 'In some cases the birth of the agreement was a bit of a struggle because, as ever, each side wanted more than the other would give, and each fought its corner. But just as often because McDonald's perceived that the agreement proposed by the union was inappropriate to its business or disadvantageous to its employees.'

Rampton's summing up suggested that contrary to defence witness statements and evidence, McDonald's did value its staff: 'It is the full-time staff at McDonald's who are the core of the business.' These staff must be reasonably content. 'They are not exactly queueing up to join unions. So if the unions cannot claim any significant numbers then one may reasonably conclude, there can't be very much wrong with the pay and conditions.'

It had been the longest section of the trial – detailed, intense and debilitating to anyone who was not intimately involved, and exhausting to those in it.

Chapter Sixteen

But it's not just McDonald's

'They [corporations] were invisible, and . . . had no soule;
and therefore no subpoena lieth against them, because they
have no conscience nor soule . . .'

C. B. Manwood, 1614

What will £3,000 buy? On the arid plain in the north of
Burkina Faso it will buy a deep well for the village of
Tamassogoo with a bit left over for a better seed store. It will
save Madame Genevieve and 150 other women having to
walk seven miles a day to collect brackish water. It would,
say Oxfam, immunize 300 children against most of the
world's killer diseases, provide emergency shelter for more
than 4,000 refugees, too. But in 'McWorld', a system of free-
market economics and globalized trading, where businesspeo-
ple live and breathe vast profits and dream like Ray Kroc of
going global and dominating their competitors, money talks
differently.

Specifically, £3,000 will buy one person the chance to go
to a few hours of lectures spread over two days at The World
Management Summit conference being held in the ballroom
of a central London hotel. Here people are gathering to learn
how to become a transnational corporation.

The conference is fully subscribed and includes talks by

the high priests of globalism and laissez-faire capitalism. They are no longer the radical thinkers of the 1960s and 1970s Chicago School of Economics. The Milton Friedman model of monetarism is now outdated but the principles of a borderless world, of open access to markets, of governmental retreat from social affairs that he and others were theorizing about while Ray Kroc was building his empire are now Establishment. Here at the conference are Nobel laureates in economics, business leaders, professors and wannabe legends.

The gurus of market globalism are billed to talk on how to 'take charge of the world's future'. Everyone wants a slice of the global pie and such is the hype that many people are here because they fear being left out. In the new economic order where the 'free world' of McDonald's and Ray Kroc, of Thatcher and Milton Friedman, has 'defeated' collectivism and Socialism, where the secretariat of GATT and the World Trade Organization, the IMF, the World Bank, the European Union and every other global body is predicting that the global economy will grow by trillions of dollars a year, everyone wants a fix on the future. 'Welcome to McWorld,' says an English banker to his colleague.

It is an odd collection. Widget-makers rub shoulders with advertisers, banks with auto firms, and all, nuclear industries, water companies and accountants, analysts, media and property groups, expect tips from Paul Preston, President of McDonald's UK, on 'how to successfully manage the globalization of corporations'. Harvard Business School's Jeffrey Sachs ('probably the most important economist in the world' – *Time*) is due to speak and Peter Drucker, at eighty-three the guru of old business gurus, is promised in a live screen link-up with the US.

The speakers, some of whom earn several million dollars a year, are being paid about £5,000 to talk for forty minutes. Uninvited, but coming anyway by train and bike from Cambridge, is Patty from the Baby Milk Action pressure group and Helen Steel from the McLibel trial, which is not sitting today. Patty's beef is the Nestlé Corporation (even bigger than McDonald's, turning over $42 billion a year). Where some might talk of 'penetrating new markets' she would read 'selling health-threatening diets to African, Chinese and Indian mothers'.

Both groups talk of the Real World. For those who have paid £3,000 it is the reality of 'downsizing', hard-nosed economics and tough competition, of there being no alternative and having to follow the market. For those outside it is everything that is swept aside when the first principles of open democracy are ignored. The Real World, says Patty and her group, would be a lot safer without the unaccountable, socially irresponsible, profit-greedy global megacorporations which are stuffing their faces inside. It'd be a lot easier without protesters, says an irascible and late businessman making his way through the small crowd.

Inside the ballroom, 120 suits are buttoned up, there is a fog of corporate jargon and Bernard Fournier, MD of Rank Xerox, is talking at £2 a second. The title of his talk is 'Ensuring Your Business Plan For Sustainable Profitable Growth Into The 21st Century Exploits And Leverages Your Core Competences To The Maximum'. To the outsider it's incomprehensible corporate jargon. No one admits to knowing what it means, because it isn't meant to mean anything, says one of the conference organizers. Who thought it up? She did, she says. The words, she says, were 'chosen randomly to appeal to the suits. It just gets them going. They love it, don't they?'

Outside the hotel, Patty and Helen and others wave more banners which are written in brisk, no-nonsense English: 'Health before profits'; 'Stop baby milk death'; 'People before profit'. They wait on the pavement to greet Mike Garrett, head of Nestlé, billed as a speaker. Hoping to see Mr Preston of McDonald's is Dan from the McLibel Support Campaign. For Preston's conference fee, Dan could fly in seventeen witnesses from the US. They talk to passers-by. They laugh a lot.

It's getting technical. Fournier flashes questions on a screen. The phrases are in English but this is globospeak, accessible only to advanced corporate zealots. 'Is there life after the quality journey?' he asks the audience. Eyeballs shift. 'What is the Rank Xerox 2000 Vision Team D?' No one murmurs. Suddenly the few impartial observers in the hall hear words they think that they recognize: 'Face the truth, live the experience, involve change agents, be flexible,' Fournier advises proto-globals. All too soon, it is over. The screen above him flashes 'thank you' three times.

Then it's on to Akio Miyabayashi, the MD of Minolta Europe, who has had a vision of the Real World. He sees every future market dominated by four or five global corporations, each 'infinitely caring' for billions of customers. 'Global corporations must love people,' he says. What does he mean by love? He means make even more money. He tells a story of a Japanese restaurateur who, recognizing that a customer's false teeth were loose, quickly changed the menu to softer food: he beams, 'That's love.' 'Successful companies imagine.' He repeats it twice. 'Creativity is the key to globalization. Think local, act global,' says Miyabayashi. But doesn't globalization mean worldwide sameness? 'Yes. Loss of old identity. New identities created.'

Gary Hammell of Harvard University says US and British managers have produced executives obsessed with 'downsizing, delayering, decluttering and divesting', all of which mean sacking people. A company, he says 'must get to the future not only first, but for less'. Sachs talks of global integration and a Kodak man tells how his team set new standards using 'realtime process, feedback systems and robotics'. Preston of McDonald's is one of the few who will consider anything but good coming from globalization. He thinks one downside may be that local incidents can soon develop into international crises. The man from Shell should know. He is still reeling from the Brent Spar affair, when a massive consumer boycott of the corporation in Europe forced the world's second largest company to think again about where to dump its rubbish. And now Shell is being hauled over the coals for its involvement in Nigeria.

But this being lunch, the suits file into the mahogany-panelled Gents for relief and to adjust the poppies that they uniformly wear to remember the millions who died when war was twice globalized earlier this century. When asked, no one from the Business Summit is aware of the Ogoni, or the death sentences just passed on Ken Saro-Wiwa and eight others who stood up to Shell or the fact that hundreds of thousands of people demonstrated peacefully to tell the corporation to leave Nigeria. Some are not even aware of Patty and her friends outside. 'They're like the homeless, aren't they?' says a senior economic analyst who was given a leaflet about corporate responsibility that morning and dumped it in the bin. 'Protesters are something that's just there now. We haven't got time to take on every issue.' At another lunch table a group of executives are guessing what Ogoni are: 'They are an Amazon tribe?' asks a Dutchman. 'No, a river,' says a Swiss. 'A vegetable,' decides an Englishman.

The global corporate culture is so threatening, says one man. 'People fear to speak up in this environment,' says a woman from Arthur Andersen, a $12 billion a year corporation which advises international firms how to compete better in the global market. Andersen has developed a 'total knowledge base', with everything the company 'knows' downloaded on to CD-ROMs. There are millions of pages, says her colleague, enthusiastically. So how does Andersen's advise corporations to handle writers, demonstrations or deaths on the orders of military dictatorship? It doesn't. 'We do feel helpless,' says one executive who admits to Greenpeace leanings. 'Yes, we are all a bit narrow,' adds another. 'But then what can we do?'

Indeed. Corporations do not have to think like individuals or feel guilty or bad about their actions, and the increasingly global economy allows them to operate with their own ethics and a social responsibility that may have nothing to do with the people who use their products. There are those that profess great social awareness and are addressing their new responsibilities, but by definition a corporation must tailor its actions to the pursuit of money-making. There can be no corporate conscience or doubt, no emotions. Success and failure must finally be defined fiscally. Maverick operations like the Body Shop can trade on a professed morality, some may try to embrace 'fairness' or 'equality' or 'humanity', but to social reformers and anarchists like Steel and Morris the whole structure of laissez-faire capitalism is so wrong that root and branch surgery is needed.

In fact it is well argued that it is now the corporations who are practising anarchy in the old meaning of the word anarchism as 'the absence of government'. In their drive for survival and profits their tendency has been to seek to limit restrictions to markets and to regulations and hindrances to growth thrown up by governments. And in its purest form, as seen in the Chicago boys or in Thatcherism, anything erected by governments or the civil society that stands in their way – tariffs, borders, regulations, criticism, dissent – may be interpreted as a potential denial of their freedom to operate.

When Kroc set up and the Chicago School of Economics still hadn't won a Nobel prize, the world was less complex and bound together. Communications were slower, and more hazardous, so the physical distance between peoples seemed greater. A greater cultural diversity was tolerated. The world was more agrarian, conservative, and ecologically and culturally stable because of this diversity. Two fundamental political belief systems may have thrown their cloaks over great geographical swaths of the world, but a myriad of lesser cultures were thriving much as they had done for centuries. Forty years later the global economy is concentrating power in ever fewer hands. Of 5,000 ethnic groups, all but a few say they feel their uniqueness threatened. Globalism promises the world 'consumer choice', technological advancement, travel, access, information and entertainment, but it also threatens the very base of how we have lived.

First some statistics. Fewer than ten transnational corporations control virtually every aspect of the worldwide food chain. Four companies control 90 per cent of the global export market for corn, wheat, coffee, tea, pineapples, cotton, tobacco, jute and forest products. The same companies that control the trade in these commodities also handle the storage, the transport and the food-processing facilities. Four companies between them control almost 90 per cent of all beef slaughtered in the US; two companies provide more than 65 per cent of all US breakfast cereals.

Take the privately owned Cargill Corporation. The eighteenth largest corporation in the world – turnover $45 billion a year, which is greater than Colombia – employs 57,000 people, trades more than half the world's grain and is a major dealer in seeds, coffee and sugar. Or Philip Morris. In 1994–5 more than 10 per cent of all the money spent by Americans on food went to the Philip Morris corporation, which is also one of the largest tobacco manufacturers.

This is the scale of market globalization that Steel and Morris object to, as much for the inequality and lack of real choice and the social disorder that they say must accompany a system that is based on capital not social responsibility. The largest 500 companies are now responsible for 42 per cent of global wealth, controlling over $10 trillion, or two-thirds of global trade. Of the world's largest hundred economies, fifty are now corporations. The world's largest hundred companies had $3.4 trillion of global assets in 1992; the turnover of the ten biggest corporations is more than the total of the world's hundred smallest countries. Shell, the world's number two, owns or leases some 400 million acres of land, which makes it larger than 146 countries.

Only twenty-seven countries in the world now have a GNP greater than the sales of Shell and Exxon combined. One company, General Motors, had sales revenues ($133 billion) roughly equal to the combined GNP of Tanzania, Ethiopia, Nepal, Bangladesh, Zaïre, Uganda, Niger, Kenya. And Pakistan. That's more than 500 million people. The fifty largest banks and financial institutions control 60 per cent of the $20 trillion a year global capital. And twelve of the world's most important industries – ranging from cars through aerospace, electronics, steel, oil and computers to media – are each more than 40 per cent dominated by five or fewer corporations. McDonald's is a relative baby: its $30 billion a year turnover is about the same size as Tanzania, Burkina Faso, Mali and Sudan combined.

Bizarrely, they are becoming far more successful at centralized planning than Moscow, Beijing or Havana ever were and are beginning to make Communism seem transparent. The sales of just five Japanese corporations in 1991 were roughly the same as the entire GDP of the former Soviet Union. Cuba and North Korea, still clinging to centrally managed systems, would rank seventy-second and less than nowhere on the list of the world's largest corporations. Only China would make it into the list of top one hundred economies. Moreover these bodies, which can control more money than so many national economies, are barely subject to outside scrutiny, unaccountable, unquestioned and barely watched.

The vision of centralized control that many now have is far greater than anything that Socialism or Communism ever aspired to. So immense are they, and such is their skill in levering vast markets, so grand their resources, so great their influence in government corridors and so sophisticated their power to lobby, cajole and influence government departments and world bodies that they are now effectively units of governance. But they have avoided, so far, the messy business of having to be moral or socially accountable to the public – except perhaps once a year at an annual meeting when a few institutional shareholders turn up to lob questions about the financial returns they can expect.

Financial power without social responsibility – the pure, free-market doctrine of the 1990s style transnational corporation – is great for profits, but even governments are beginning to see how the transnationals are becoming potentially ungovernable, reports Andrew Rowell in *The Green Backlash*. Rowell quotes a report by the US Office of Technology Assessment which in 1993 found that they were 'growing in power and authority' so fast that lumbering old nation states, still grappling with ideas like social responsibility and accountability, 'were unable to keep up with them'. As David Korten has spelled out in *When Corporations Rule the World*, 'the global trading system is now being worked out on the level of corporations and not governments. A massive transfer of power is taking place from governments to corporations without so much as a by your leave to the people.' It is axiomatic that as corporations increase their power, says Korten, so the power of others – in this case people with a single vote every four or five years – decreases.

What this means to democracy is debatable. In the past

only a few people saw corporations as political institutions, and few demanded their social accountability. Today there is a serious move within a few companies to examine the social impact of their operations, but the overwhelming agenda of the majority is business as usual. Nevertheless, the perceived social crisis in so many Western countries is making people aware of the global free-trading, free-wheeling agenda. 'When corporations are bigger than nation states you have to ask who governs them, and for whom. And when these corporate states eschew democracy in favour of central command you have to wonder how long they will last,' writes Charles Handy, author of *The Empty Raincoat*, in the *Economist*. He notes that no government could get away with disenfranchising 40,000 people in a stroke, like General Motors, Ford or AT&T might do when 'downsizing', 'rationalizing' or switching operations from one country to another.

Handy is not too bothered by globalization, seeing advantages in the way that corporations can redistribute their assets around the world, bringing new technology to new markets. Because they are answerable only to themselves, he says, they are able to act faster and further and bolder than governments. Which presupposes, of course, that maximizing profit alone is beneficial to society because it maximizes a corporation's worth which increases its contribution to society's welfare.

But if the nation state remains for the while the dominant economic unit, its interests are increasingly being tied to those of the corporations. Politics inevitably follows financial power and governments are being forced to mirror wider global or corporate demands. So states will now openly bribe companies to set up within their borders, offering them sweeteners, tax breaks and more. Sovereignty itself may not be greatly in danger because the corporations are not interested in visible political or social influence, but there is a realistic scenario of two political economies developing. One (that of corporations and global bodies) is unaccountable and growing in influence; the other (that of national governments) is increasingly slave to it, must respond to it within tight parameters and is declining in influence. Where the former hides behind a massive bureaucracy or legal 'commercial interest' and works in relative secrecy, so the other is facing increasing pressure from below to be accountable and transparent. In the meantime there is the extraordinary vision of nation states, gripped by the laissez-faire market dogma pushed by a few corporations, handing over their traditional responsibilities and functions like social services, health, pensions, even prisons and crime, to corporations which are often only nominally based within their borders and effectively stateless. It is one of the most dramatic shifts in power relationships since colonialism began or, indeed, since Communism ended.

Transnationals could not, of course, have reached the position they are in without having got into bed with the politicians. What the gurus of globalism at the Park Lane Hotel were not prepared to spell out was that to operate across the globe a corporation must be able to capture government subsidies, manage demand, open new markets, centralize power, enclose new environments and evade regulations.

Nicholas Hildyard, the Editor of the *Ecologist*, makes the good point that all the sleaze scandals that have racked most Western political parties in the past decade have been rooted in the pollution of the political system by corporations. The merging of interests between business and government – the notorious 'revolving door' – is seen in the way MPs everywhere openly represent business, hold directorships, pass effortlessly from front bench to boardroom. In the newly 'liberalized' former Communist states, MPs own much of the stock of the industries they have privatized. In old Europe, donations to party funds, cash for questions, corrupted foreign aid, the machinations of lobby groups have all undermined the already low reputation of politicians and suggested to people that they cannot trust the decision-makers. By and large the politicians get blamed for sleaze rather than the corporations who try to seduce them. Somehow we expect our politicians to be rotten nowadays, and we excuse anyone who may tempt them.

Domestic political scandals are more likely to surface if only because that small part of the press and the media which has the resources and the guts to concern itself and risk everything to investigate corruption in high places has far less access to City boardrooms and the new centres of power like the World Trade Organization and the European Union than it has to national parliaments which have long been more or less scrutinized.

It is here, though, even further removed from the person in the street, that the trade and political policy decisions are being made, in secret, without accountability, and mostly by and for the interests of the corporations. Hildyard cites the European Round Table, a powerful lobbying group of industrialists and free-market globalization ideologues in the European Union set up in the early 1980s when the prospects of economic integration in Europe seemed to be faltering. Senior EC bureaucrats and executives of the largest European-based corporations then combined to lobby the politicians. Two industrialists drafted the original proposal for a single European market. The Round Table has been responsible for pushing massive infrastructural projects that financially benefit mostly the small club of people who build the roads, the power stations and the dams and who propose the development of certain favoured regions and industries. The power of the ERT is undoubted: when the ERT brings out a report whole passages are frequently reproduced in European common policy papers. The European Union is now driven by the interests of the corporations who aspire to be pan-European, says Hildyard.

It is similar in the US, where the Business Round Table is one of America's most exclusive, least diverse and most powerful organizations. Its 200 members include forty-two out of fifty *Fortune* 500 US industrial corporations. Seven of the eight largest commercial banks, nine of the eleven largest utilities, five of the seven biggest retailers are there, and so on across each major industry. BRT describes itself as 'an association of chief executive officers who examine public issues that affect the economy and seek to reflect sound economic and social principles'. But as David Korten, author of *When Corporations Rule the Earth*, perceptively points out, membership of the club that knows all about sound social principles is limited to white males over fifty whose salaries are at least 170 times the US average.

The corporations that employ them stood to gain substantially from globalization, in particular from the signing of the North American Free Trade Association deal (NAFTA) with Canada and Mexico. BRT officials lobbied furiously for the agreement that would open the Mexican market to services, allow them to export companies, relocate in cheaper labour markets and dump heavily subsidized products on the market. All but four of BRT's 200 members sat on NAFTA advisory committees.

Since NAFTA was signed in 1994, the free market has done just what the corporations said it would do; the GDP of Mexico has risen, but the social price, which was not fully considered by the political or business elite of either country, is clearer. In 1992 Mexico imported 20 per cent of its food. In 1996 it imported 43 per cent. Since NAFTA, 2.2 million Mexicans have lost their jobs and around 40 million, as opposed to 30 million, are now in 'extreme poverty'. Meanwhile the US–Mexico border is still a circus place of American industry and agribusinesses taking advantage of lower environmental standards that are barely policed. 'Everything has been left to the market, on the demand of agribusiness corporations. Eating on imports is not eating at all for the poor in Mexico,' says Victor Suares Carrera, of the National Association of Peasant Producers.

But it is on the international level that the transnational corporations execute their corporate activism most success-fully. The Bretton Woods organizations, especially the World Bank and the International Monetary Fund – both packed from the start with corporation men – have worked ceaselessly to deepen the dependency of low-income countries on the global system that Milton Friedman and the Chicago boys advocated, and then open their economies to corporate colo-nization. For all its blandishments about 'progress', 'develop-ment' and 'institution building', the World Bank is in business to loan countries money to increase the purchase of goods from the Northern industrial countries. It has lent billions of dollars to countries knowing that they will never be able to pay them back.

Having created a need for its only product – money – by allowing countries to get into fearful debt, it then lent even more so that indebted countries could pay back their loans. In ten years (1970–1980), low-income countries increased their debt from $21 billion to $110 billion; middle-income countries' debt rose from $40 billion to $317 billion. It couldn't go on, so the World Bank and IMF stepped in to impose what they called 'structural adjustment'.

In its earliest, most dogma-driven days, structural adjust-ment demanded that countries shift economic incentives away from the small towards the large, and from policies that fostered self-sufficiency to export in almost every sphere. Even the IMF can see some of the damage that has been done, but country after country for more than a decade has been made to displace its small farmers and marginalize even further the weakest in society. Countries were made to rewrite trade policies, fiscal policies, environmental regulations and budgetary policy. The result has been that countries have had to cut back on social and health programmes, and there has been less education and more unrest. To meet its own needs, the Bank advanced the integration of domestic economies into the global one. 'It was a double act. Damn fine banking,' said one corporation executive at the fiftieth birthday party of the bank in 1996, where $20 million was blown on the festivities.

On their own terms of reference the Bank and the IMF got it right, just as the Chicago boys did and Ray Kroc and his successors at McDonald's did. The global economic elite correctly predicted that higher economic growth rates, expansion of exports and debt repayment would follow their policies. GDPs have risen, in some cases dramatically. But the measures of success are narrow and increasingly absurd. In bank terms a polluting factory can add more to a country's wealth than a clean one, in that the pollution clean-up counts as a benefit. In economic terms, war might be considered financially efficient in that a country is probably importing arms, spending heavily on drugs and turning forests into coffins.

Even the Bank recognizes today that the social conditions have everywhere deteriorated for those at the bottom and the gap between rich and poor has everywhere increased. Undeterred, it has trotted out the mantra from the economists that things would be a bit tough on the poorest until economies picked up. How long might that be? one journalist was prompted to ask at the UN Development Programme's fiftieth birthday party. At least a lifetime, came the off-the-record answer.

But having wrung its hands in mock sorrow at the

widening gaps between rich and poor, the breakdown of institutions, the worldwide deterioration of the environment (the failure, indeed, of just about everything it has tried to do), the bank has proceeded to increase loans for those countries which had successfully carried out structural adjustment. Indebtedness in low-income countries rose to $47.3 billion in 1992, requiring $18.3 billion a year repayment. The transnational corporations couldn't believe their luck. Grateful that a more or less unaccountable global bureaucracy could do their work out of sight and above the heads of elected rulers, the corporations have marched in wherever they smelled resources.

Meanwhile a global trade body with legislative and judicial powers above those of the nation state and with a remit only to meet the needs of the world's largest corporations was being developed parallel to the creation of debt and the dismantling of countries' economic policies. Enter the GATT, one of the most extraordinary post-war triumphs of the few over the many. The General Agreement on Tariffs and Trade is a global trade body whose members have been sitting in permanent session since the 1950s, mostly tinkering with trade liberalization policies in long-running 'rounds' of inter-governmental talks. Under pressure from transnationals it went for broke in the Uruguay Round.

Dangling the carrot of immense economic growth in front of the donkey of the political elite, the national barriers to trade between countries began to come tumbling down in 1994 when the Uruguay Round was finally signed. The corporate bonanza is still going on; the playing field for capital is being smoothed out at the expense of the social. The new trade agreements and regulations cover 22,000 pages and it's only now that the full results are being seen. Just as the civil society – the people without any vested interest – predicted, more than a hundred developing countries are paying more for their food imports; the price of tropical export crops will be lowered and hard-won environmental safeguards are being challenged. The global economy has undoubtedly increased in volume, but the benefits are not being shared.

Corporate interest in GATT was huge. Of the 111 members on the US advisory committees ninety-two represented individual corporations and sixteen represented trade industry associations. The chemical industry fielded ten members. For the most part, governments followed their advisory committees.

GATT was signed without ever being fully discussed in most northern parliaments yet it was claimed by corporations and governments that it would be good for democracy everywhere; indeed there are elected MPs who to this day had no idea what it really did. Many are paid handsome stipends to look after the interests of corporations who have done very nicely from it. 'GATT has served to create and enforce a corporate Bill of Rights, protecting the rights of the world's largest corporations against people, communities and democratically-elected governments,' says Korten. 'In a stroke, the rights of corporations around the world were increased over the rights of citizens.' By late 1996, a dozen hard-won environmental and social protection laws were being challenged in the world courts by corporations.

The GATT died as it gave birth to the World Trade Organization. This massively powerful organization works by a series of committees comprising government appointees who are mostly corporations. A recent straw poll of British politicians from three parties produced no one who knew where it was based, what its powers were, who sat on its panels, what its remit was or to whom it was responsible. Answers included 'It's a company selling bananas', 'It brokers arms deals', and 'It's an industry lobby group'.

The last response may have been the closest. Consider Codex Alimentarius, the WTO's health and safety standards group which it inherited from GATT. Codex sets the standards that the world's food should be grown to, what should be put on labels and how much additives food companies should be allowed to put into food. It is run jointly by the UN's Food and Agriculture Organization and the World Health Organization. Claiming neutrality, it is little more than a corporate club sitting in secret session. Of 2,587 individual participants in Codex meetings between 1989 and 1991 only twenty-six came from public interest groups. There were 445 industry representatives on national delegations, but only eight from public interest groups. More than 140 of the world's largest multinational corporations are participants. Codex standards are some of the lowest in the world and are being promoted by chemical companies as the standard to which everyone should work.

But the corporations aren't finished yet. Backed by the global organizations that they influence so strongly, they are now assaulting the rights of governments to decide who and how people should operate within its borders. The Multilateral Investment Agreement (MIA) is, effectively, a direct assault on the sovereign state and is being heavily promoted by the European Union and its most powerful corporations on the basis that it would lead – as always – to greater foreign investment in developing countries. In the logic of the pure free marketeers and the corporations it makes complete sense. Most countries, after all, are doing their best to attract foreign investments.

But what the MIA seeks to do is to give transnational corporations a legal right of entry into any country on the same basis as a local company. There would be no difference made between, say, McDonald's Corporation and a fish and chip shop. Both would have the right to trade. No country should be able to protect a local company against a global corporation; the natural resources of any country could be mined by anyone; land and property anywhere could be bought by anyone.

At the moment, no country in the world allows totally free access to its resources by foreigners. The rules vary from country to country. They may insist that a certain percentage of a company is owned by nationals. Many developing countries have policies developed after the colonial period, favouring local companies. Often countries have tax breaks for locals, or local firms might be given preference in government businesses or contracts. Conditional policies like this have so far been justified on the grounds of sovereignty – that a country's population has control over a significant part of its own economy.

All this would go out of the window if the European corporations, inevitably backed by their peers in Japan and the US, have their way. 'It is breathtaking,' says Martin Khor, of Third World Network, one of the South's leading non-governmental citizen groups. 'It would be a true return to a colonial era, where the master country's government, through force, enabled their companies to enter and to take over everything. No longer would governments have the freedom to choose their particular mixture of policies on foreign investments. There would be strong implications on culture as the proposed treaty would not allow exclusion on religious or moral grounds nor for the media, communications and information sectors.'

Whether or not it is passed, as with GATT and the WTO, there will probably be no full debate in national parliaments unless enormous resources are mobilized. Increasingly, indeed, the citizen is not only being left out of the decision-making process but is not even being told what the implications of decisions by remote bureaucrats might mean. Only the vigilance of a coalition of 200 groups including environmentalists, farmers, women's groups, development agencies and human rights activists managed to stop the European Parliament nodding through a chemical industry proposal to allow the protection and promotion of genetic engineering to be written into the centre of European industrial policy-making in 1995.

If the corporations had gained their clause – which they fully expected to, such is their arrogance – it would have given a huge official boost to one of the most controversial and untried industries, which has barely been debated in public. How many corporations would have benefited? Perhaps four. Undeterred, the corporations are lobbying heavily again, stepping up their pressure, will not let go.

The civil society may record small, temporary triumphs but the tide is still in favour of those who would homogenize, standardize and globalize. It is definitely against anyone trying to steer industry or government away from the path of maximum immediate profit towards social gain. Once corporations and governments between them have decided something is good for them 'and the national economies' it is effectively done. Besides, the trend in government today is wherever possible to transfer power to larger, more centralized, less accountable, more powerful institutions who are accessible to even fewer people. This may include supranational political trade bodies. Or most likely corporations themselves.

The global food industry, in which McDonald's is an important player, has been through the most extraordinary transformation in the past hundred years. On the one hand it has grown massively – from $65.4 billion a year in 1972 to $323 billion by 1995 with forecasts that it will double again by

2015 – and on the other hand it has shed jobs as if people were a plague. The scale of what has happened to the one industry on earth that no one can do without is immense.

More statistics: between 1935 and 1989 it is estimated that more than 40 million small farmers went out of business in the US and Europe. More than 30,000 are still being lost each year in America and it is reliably forecast that more than 75 per cent of US agriculture (one of the world's largest industries) may be in the hands of fewer than 50,000 farmers and controlled by a handful of firms within a few years. For a comparison, Britain in 1996 had 100,000 farmers.

When farmers leave the land, local suppliers and whole rural communities go with them. In Britain, where more than 70 per cent of the food market is now controlled by five corporations, less than 3 per cent of people work on the land and 500,000 small farmers have left since 1945. It is now quite possible to travel the length of the country without ever seeing anyone working in the fields because farm work has become automated, or any animal on the land because most are now reared indoors. As in the US, more than 800,000 small shopkeepers have gone to the wall directly or indirectly because of the industrialized food industry. The blood-letting continues as supermarkets and hyperstores find new ways to grow at the same time as reducing the number of real full-time, protected jobs.

The forecasts are similar everywhere. The Philippines must, under new global trade rules, import a minimum of 59,000 tonnes of rice a year. This, it is known, will force 25,000 Filipino farmers to leave the land each year (there are 350,000 in all). In return for allowing in American, Japanese or European rice or staple crops, the country will have new access to OECD markets. But it is only the rich farmers who will be able to export the flowers or salad materials or 'exotic' vegetables that the faddish West wants. Ditto another two dozen countries.

These economic migrants will head to the cities with their own social problems or will find work abroad, perhaps in the Middle East. Even countries whose rural economies seemed unassailable, like France, have been unable to do anything and must watch their cultural diversity diminish as the food industry globalizes, intensifies and brings all the associated breakdown of the rural society. Peasant farmers in India and elsewhere are beginning to mobilize against the power of agribusiness, but many accept that now it is a rearguard battle.

The same pattern is being repeated everywhere and at all levels of society. Hundreds of millions of people are being discarded by a global industry that can operate without them. The new industrial landscape that has emerged at national and international levels is made very much in the image of the corporations. The thrust of modernization has been towards automation and new technologies. Partly as a consequence of labour problems since the 1950s, they have sought to rid themselves of unions and rebellious workers.

Just as Ray Kroc developed a system that could minutely control and rationalize burger-making, so the system that the food corporations have instigated is ideally suited to mass-production of standardized products. In under fifty years farming in the rich countries has got into a never-ending spiral of ever higher output, with farmers forced to increase production to maintain their incomes. It is now deeply embedded in Western agriculture that farmers should produce as much as possible even though it may be ecologically or socially damaging. The rewards of farming now almost exclusively go to the largest farms. In Europe, 80 per cent of the $40 billion support to farmers in agricultural input and crop and livestock production went to 20 per cent of farms: 80 per cent of all farms received less than 10 per cent of agricultural subsidies in 1990. In the US in 1995, 58 per cent of the agricultural support went to the top 15 per cent of farmers. The Washington-based Worldwatch Institute reports that in 1995 Western governments spent in the region of $300 billion a year subsidizing ecologically unsound agriculture.

And of course it is the largest producers who need to be able to sell their products somewhere else, so they encourage the politicians to lower barriers, tariffs and protection systems everywhere on their behalf. The system works like a dream for a few. The biggest agribusinesses collect their subsidies from the state, drive people off the land, fill up supermarket shelves at the expense of the environment, overproduce and then seek new markets overseas to sell their produce. So they need to promote free trade. The most 'efficient' agribusiness corporations make money at both ends of the system – selling chemicals to the farmers and buying back 'cheap' food. Worldwide, government policies shunt at least $500 billion a year towards activities that harm the physical and social environment. Because mining, farming, logging, energy utilities and agriculture are dominated by ever fewer corporations, these handouts are mostly at the expense of the vulnerable or the weak.

And just as Ray Kroc found that the really big profits came only when he controlled real-estate and had bought the McDonald brothers' trade marks, signs and names, so corporations are now positioning themselves to patent the ultimate real-estate – life itself. We may be moving into what the *Ecologist* calls a 'new global order', where food supply and health are effectively dominated by a handful of corporations. The twin keys – which must be turned at the same time to unlock the box of promises – are gene manipulation and patenting, both of vegetable and of animal life.

The prize is said to be infinitely productive crops and animals without the need for half as many chemicals to make them grow or to pollute the environment. The claimed benefits for society are legion – crops engineered to resist weeds and weevils, even flourish without water; animals to produce drugs, or three times as much milk or meat without fat; trees that will grow plastic, tomatoes that never go soft, and so on. But the dawning of the Bio Age is also, potentially, the dawn of even greater totalitarian control of the many by the few.

The final insult of the Uruguay Round of GATT was to use the talks to extend the international patent protection of genetic materials, including seeds and natural medicines. It is now possible for corporations to patent trees, crops and whole lengths of DNA. The effect is that companies will be able to control the future genetic research over entire species and over any useful products.

Few people, let alone politicians in the North, have understood the implications or know what intellectual property rights are. In India, however, where farmers have saved the seed from one harvest to another for generations, it was immediately seen that anyone replanting the offspring of a patented seed would, under international law that supersedes national law, violate the law. More than 800,000 farmers protested. Professor Vandana Shiva, a leader of the Indian opposition to the patenting of life forms, sees it as 'a blatant effort by a few corporations to establish monopoly control over the heritage of the planet. GATT creates a global structure in which hazards increase in the Third World, the rights of corporations increase globally and their responsibilities decrease everywhere.'

Just as McDonald's can trade mark the word 'Royal' or 'You', so corporations have moved quickly to try to patent whole species of plants and sequences of DNA for commercial purposes. With legal protection, pharmaceutical groups have been scouring the world to identify and then patent genes in plants and in people, the chemical companies have been trying to patent the genes that lead to inherited illnesses and agribusiness has been working flat out to develop designer crops. In some cases monopolistic powers are being granted; one company now has the rights to all future genetically engineered cotton, another has soya bean. Many scientists, reports the *Ecologist*, do not agree with the patenting of genes, but are finding they must follow suit to prevent others patenting their own work.

Pharmaceutical, agribusiness, chemical and food-processing companies are even now merging to take advantage of gene technologies. It is, says the *Ecologist*, a worldwide complex of scientific expertise, technological capability and transnational capital accumulation constituting a (new) bioindustrial complex.

But as corporate power and globalism increases and reaches deeper into people's lives, so it is inevitably being opposed. You can see why: OECD figures suggest that world trade has increased by a multiple of twelve since 1950 and economic growth by five, yet there have been massive increases in poverty, unemployment, social disintegration and environmental destruction. Few people in the North believe that their quality of life is improving and in the South the wealth disparities and the numbers on the economic edge are growing.

As will be seen later, those standing up against globalism or its effects are not governments (who mostly approve, having given the corporations the authority) but non-governmental groups, which are being pushed into the role of social justice watchdogs, moral arbiters and spokespeople for those without a voice. The concerns of the civil society increasingly converge as the system that is being promoted worldwide becomes more successful.

But if globalism is growing, so, too, is the repression of those who stand against it. Corporations, with the most to gain and lose, are retaliating to the growing dissent. Their tactics range from murder and outright intimidation at worst, to harassment, expensive PR exercises, the funding of think-tanks and scientific research in others. In Europe and America in particular they are employing lobby groups, the media and especially the law to protect their interests and promote their message to the public. Andrew Rowell, author of *Green Backlash*, reports on the increasing number of corporate front groups, and the demonizing of environmentalists and new democracy groups or individuals as 'terrorists', 'Communists' or 'dissenters'. He illustrates how dirty tricks, physical and legal harassment and the use of violence are on the increase everywhere.

Where corporate activity is criminal, killers and thugs are paid to silence critics. Many people have been killed for opposing illegal logging or destructive mining in Brazil and the Far East. Environmentalists, journalists, priests, ecologists, charity workers and leaders of indigenous groups are frequently labelled subversives and worse for exposing or opposing illegal logging or mining. More subtle, legal and common is the silencing of critics with what are being called SLAPPs – Strategic Lawsuits Against Public Participation.

These were first identified by two US academics, who noted that an increasing number of environmentalists around the world were being named as defendants in civil cases. Some corporations, it transpired, were finding ways to oppose points of view which had the effect of silencing their critics. These often included accusations of defamation, conspiracy, nuisance, invasion of privacy and interference with business.

Such cases, reports Australian academic Sharon Beder, seldom, if ever, reach the courts. Where they do, it is estimated that less than 10 per cent result in a court victory for the corporation involved. The aim, Beder concludes, is to harass, intimidate and distract opponents. The longer that the litigation can be stretched out the greater the expense that is inflicted. It is legal gamesmanship, 'ranging from simple retribution for past activism to discouraging future activism', said one US judge.

SLAPP cases in the US take an average of three years to resolve and even if the person or group being sued wins 'it can cost tens of thousands of pounds, personal and emotional stress, disillusionment and diversion of time and energy,' says Beder. Most SLAPPs do not go to trial because the corporate objective, which is actually to scare off potential opponents, can be achieved merely by the threat of a court case. Company lawyers will usually go to great pains to warn off impending defamation suits.

The battle of words between corporations and their opponents has seldom been more intense. Oil, car, chemical, agricultural, energy and other industries which benefit directly or indirectly from government subsidies have all strongly countered research into ecologically sounder alternatives.

Meanwhile a loose group of journalists and academics referred to as 'contrarians' is providing a useful intellectual critique of emerging radical environmentalists, but is also being used by right-wing organizations for their own purposes. PR corporations like Burston Marsteller and Hill and Knowlton are much employed putting the case of industry in controversial areas.

Far more sinister is the role of the state in silencing criticism against corporations and trying to criminalize opposition to developments. The British government has spent millions of pounds employing a private investigation agency to identify and serve writs on environmental protesters who have opposed road schemes heavily promoted by corporate lobbies. In the past five years legitimate road-protest groups have been raided, phone-tapped, infiltrated and secretly observed by the state security services and undercover police; new laws criminalizing protest and making it harder to demonstrate have been passed and more than 2,000 people in Britain have been arrested for non-violent activities.

There are disturbing details: courts have found men 'not guilty' who have admitted firebombing road protesters while they slept; no official action has been taken against private security firms employed by the state on controversial developments when their employees have been involved in physical intimidation and violence against protesters. The Conservative government, meanwhile, has eroded civil liberties, massively increased the powers of the police and tried to make some civil protests a serious crime, on the level of manslaughter, robbery and rape.

The increasing lack of tolerance of criticism is ominous for the civil society. Corporations have never been more powerful, yet never less regulated; never more pampered by government, yet never less questioned; never more needed to take social responsibility yet never more secretive. The next stage is entering the unknown. Many – like McDonald's – are beginning to buy their stock back from franchisees and institutional investors. Who then will own them? What rights and responsibilities will they then have? To whom will these fabulously powerful self-motivated, self-interested supranational bodies be accountable?

The global society so pursued by the corporations is touted as the harbinger of new freedoms, of new access to information, new societies. The inevitable downside of 'McWorld', the social effects it will have and the consequences of what is becoming a revolution in ideas, lifestyle and morals is little discussed, even less questioned, at boardroom level.

Chapter Seventeen

And It's not just Morris and Steel

'Democratical states must always feel before they can see; it is this that makes their governments slow, but the people will be right at the last.'

George Washington, 1785

On the same afternoon that luminaries at the world business conference in London were earning £ 2 a second for their thoughts on globalisation at the World Business Summit in London, Morris and Steel have a day off from Court 35. Morris takes Charlie to play and Steel joins the group of protesters outside the Mayfair Hotel on Piccadilly. On the other side of Hyde Park, 150 people are gathering outside the Nigerian High Commission. They include among them celebrated writers, academics, environmentalists, human rights and social activists, representatives of charities, journalists and lawyers. All are objecting to the death sentences passed two days previously on Ken Saro-Wiwa and eight other Ogonis by a Nigerian court.

If Nigeria is the immediate subject of their anger, Royal Dutch Shell is the object of their scorn. To recap: the world's second largest corporation has been working the Niger delta for decades. It has extracted an estimated 900 million gallons from beneath the 400 square mile area known as Ogoni.

Ogoni crude has helped fuel Nigeria's development and descent into obscene financial and political corruption. But next to nothing has improved for the 500,000 Ogoni people since Shell found oil there in 1957.

McDonald's is not remotely linked with Saro-Wiwa and the Ogoni but the opposition to Shell and to McDonald's is similar and telling. Many corporations are being targeted not just for what they allegedly do but for what they are seen to represent. Because they are more anonymous than governments and often more financially powerful, they are becoming the *bêtes noires* of new social activists. For corporations the trend should be very worrying; what it means is that their own globalism is being actively turned against them by the emerging global civil society.

The inequalities in Ogoni land are in their own way as startling as those in Court 35. The 500,000 mostly have no electricity, no proper schooling and few health clinics. Their life expectancy is fifty-one, there is one doctor per 65,000 people and one hospital for everyone. Saro-Wiwa and other Ogoni argue that Shell and the oil companies working the delta have brought only the downside of Western modernity: oil pipes to crisscross their farmland, gas-flaring to pollute the air, massive oil refineries to disturb the peace. The Ogoni fields have been devastated by oil spills, their fishing has drastically declined as the water courses are polluted and their lives, says witness after witness before independent tribunals, have physically and mentally deteriorated under corporate development.

The oil corporations, in partnership with one of the world's cruellest and most corrupt governments, accept no social or financial responsibility for this state of affairs, even though they argue that they contribute significantly to schooling and community developments. But why should Shell be legally, financially or morally responsible for the Ogoni? And as a corporation, it is of course not obliged to do anything and it has no right whatever to interfere with the lives of foreign nationals.

In one sense Shell is as unlucky being opposed by Ken Saro-Wiwa and the Ogoni as McDonald's has been taking on Steel and Morris and the McLibel Support Campaign. The 'McLibel two' claim that they represent a whole constituency of opposition; likewise, Saro-Wiwa and the other Ogonis who are charged with him represent for the liberal West far more than a few men taking on a corporation. Saro-Wiwa is a fêted writer, a successful businessman and a good regional politician, but in taking on Shell and the Nigerian government he becomes supranational: a human rights worker, an environmentalist, a social activist – in short a global symbol for a civil society that has few heroes, but is beginning to flex its muscles.

This new phenomenon has been growing for some years. Environmental and social activists around the world tend to be bright and committed to social equity and human rights. Some are linked to groups like Friends of the Earth or Greenpeace, but the vast majority work in their communities or workplaces. Their strength is in their subversion of the corporate image and word, and in their commitment. The price that they pay for opposing hardline governments often hell-bent on selling off a state's resources or throwing out centuries of culture in the name of quick profit is often persecution, imprisonment or worse.

They depend increasingly on the growing political, social and ideological links that they have with each other. The Internet, the fax and the camcorder have been appropriated by grass-roots groups as weapons of resistance to 'McWorld'. The communications revolution led by the corporations for their own ends keeps grass-roots groups in instantaneous contact with each other, and means that they need not depend on the traditional media for anything other than access to larger groups of people. What it also means – as McDonald's UK's President Paul Preston noted – is that flashpoints can spread rapidly around the world and that issues can be highlighted everywhere. Instead of having to deal with a single front of opposition, corporations today may find simultaneous, coordinated action.

Saro-Wiwa knew this well. Detained, placed under house arrest, finally arrested on trumped-up charges of inciting a group of youths to murder, he had known from the start of his campaign against Shell and the Nigerian authorities that the only way his people had a chance of self-determination or betterment was by direct appeal to the global community. If globalism and corporatism in pursuit of the global economy had been the Ogonis' tormentor, so, he reasoned, the same forces could be turned round to save his people, too. He appealed to his own people, of course, but also to those with international voices, to the liberal press, to global environment groups like Greenpeace, to global companies like Body Shop and to global activists like Earth First!.

They were all there that afternoon. Earth First!, young, radical, brave, went first. Just as the McLibel Support Campaign tried to make the links between fast food and the clearing of the tropical forests, Earth First! sees the link between the Ogoni fight for self-determination and the social disillusionment growing in grass-roots Britain. Some feel that the repression of the Ogonis by the Nigerian authorities has echoes of British Home Secretary Michael Howard's crusade against travellers, protesters and animal-rights activists; but also they can see that the oil which Shell has been pumping out of Ogoni land fuels the world's cars and the inevitable destruction and pollution of the countryside.

Nine of them rush the police standing outside the High Commission and padlock themselves to the railings. In minutes they have been hauled away and charged for trespassing on diplomatic territory. They read out the names of the nine Ogonis ordered to die in Port Harcourt.

The next line of attack is the British literary Establishment rallied by International PEN – a distinguished club of free writers who campaign on behalf of imprisoned writers. These men and women are sincere, polite and kissy and almost all over forty-five. Some are well known, others believe they should be. Until this week few have known anything at all about the Ogoni, but they are here on the age-old principle that writers are the voices of society and to silence them is to deny the freedom of speech.

Playwright Harold Pinter is their de facto general and the great man issues by telephone a subjunctive-ridden statement bristling with moral outrage, and then makes his entrance. The troops are out: Tom Stoppard is there, concerned; Michael Frayn is charming; Edward Blishen says he last demonstrated in the 1970s. Lord Longford is appalled, so is novelist and screenwriter William Boyd, who grew up in Nigeria and knew Saro-Wiwa. Nigerian novelist Ben Okri is on his way and Nobel Prize-winning author Wole Soyinka yet again denounces the Nigerian government, this time from Nottingham where he is opening a play.

The liberal troops shuffle around, collars high, some literally creaking from age in the cold. They murmur approval of Yomi Ojetunde, and other London-based Ogonis-in-exile who spontaneously sing: 'Abacha, he's a thief. He should go.' Finally they hand a perfectly composed letter to a lackey at the High Commission, as if they did not know that it would be ignored, and that they were unaware they were dealing with a bunch of thugs and crooks who are about to judicially murder nine men without giving a fig for world reaction . . .

And at the end, defending the culture of the Ogonis and acting like the lightning-conductor of the age, come the poets.

'These companies come and throw confusion in our heads,' says Ugandan Vincent Magombe, coordinator of the African Literature Forum. 'To start with, we think they are good. But they act culturally. They sit in place of our traditions, they change our language, our philosophies, the way we think. It's the indifference that hurts.'

That night there will be a multinational candlelit vigil, and over the next few days the strength and depth of opposition to Shell and the Nigerian government will be seen. Thousands of Shell petrol stations in Europe and America will be picketed. Body Shop will declare corporate war and throw resources behind the Ogoni. When General Abacha finally orders the nine deaths the international outcry will be immense, but despite the political huff and puff and the Commonwealth suspending Nigeria's membership, there will be no official boycott of Nigerian oil. Why? It emerges that the US, the world's largest consumer of Nigerian oil by a long chalk, is already boycotting Libyan, Iranian and Iraqi oil. They cannot risk cutting Nigerian supplies. The Western car corporations that directly or indirectly employ one person in six in the US cannot be threatened. The human right to drive a car cannot be questioned.

When the outcry subsides a few weeks later, the sound of executive relief from the Shell boardroom on the nineteenth floor of Shell House in central London is almost audible. The corporation's British HQ faces north across the Thames, towers over the 'mother of Parliaments' on the opposite bank of the river. Its executives have a weird view of the world, one that bizarrely mirrors the corporation's social myopia: from the nineteenth floor you can see government and the HQs of many other corporations, but it is almost impossible to see people.

Shell, which for fifty years has gone about its considerable business in foreign parts with the assurance and authority of an arm of government, admits privately that it has been woefully out of touch with life on the ground. It is no different from a thousand other US and European companies which have been trading with developing countries for years. Like them, it has people working on the social front line in Africa, the East and Latin America but its management and executive culture, says one of its vice-presidents, is remote, arcane, one of scientists and mechanical engineers, white coats and machines. The corporation works rationally, logically, systematically. Its executives are a culture apart from the street, are not paid to question their social impact. They may be brilliant at analysing money, markets, maps and technical problems, but the corporation, he says, is lousy at appreciating the messy new social agenda that is emerging worldwide.

And just as Ray Kroc could never understand why so many people opposed McDonald's entering communities, and his British President Paul Preston cannot see why groups and individuals oppose the Golden Arches, so Shell cannot understand why so many people around the world are now calling the company 'arrogant', 'aloof' and 'out of touch'. There is little relief in knowing it is not just Shell and that similar charges are being made against thousands of corporations as they enter every nook and cranny of the free-trade world, invited there by politicians in the name of economic development, or gatecrashing on the back of new free-trade rules.

The outrage and the desperation is happening because the corporate Establishment is now a supranational culture, in danger of becoming out of touch with reality, barely listening, unable to understand new agendas, self-referring, culturally anonymous, often ignorant and answerable only to itself. Corporations like Shell or McDonald's, Rio Tinto Zinc, Unilever, Pepsi, Nestlé or Cargills can make heady profits, yet be very unloved; they can increase sales and be despised; provide exactly what people seemingly need yet cease to identify with people's real needs. Issues like justice, human rights, free speech and equity can become irrelevant. Staff may be paragons of personal virtue, upstanding, caring parents, yet when they work for large corporations they are liable to suspend moral reality. The remote, semi-detached culture bred by today's globalism can make corporations alien to communities and, in the words of Charles Handy, author of *The Empty Raincoat*, they are becoming 'increasingly virtual ... dispersed, intermingled ... not necessarily good for the rest of the world'.

And wherever corporations look, they can see Morrises and Steels, Saro-Wiwas and Ogonis and wave after wave of peasants and citizen groups, environmentalists, human rights workers, communities, pressure groups and individuals lining up against them demanding justice; prepared to risk everything, to go to court, to stand on protest lines or to be arrested to halt a deteriorating social and environmental situation. More than that, they have proposals for change, real solutions, they say, for the future.

Saying no to universalizing, economic 'progress' is not new, but what's happening today may be culturally and politically as powerful as colonialism and lead eventually to similar opposition. Where colonialism imposed a new culture of government and law on peoples, so the corporations are changing the world again; not always in overt ways, but by subtler financial, mercantile and cultural means. Generations of social advances and human understanding are being eroded and ours has been called the only century where the sum of human knowledge has actually decreased, given the number of ethnic groups, indigenous peoples, languages and understandings that have been destroyed. The new cultural and economic colonialism, winged in on satellites, mapped out by anonymous financiers, rubber-stamped by pliant politicians and imposed on communities and people without so much as a by your leave, has a speed and a scale of a different order from anything before. What's more, it is materially affecting future generations in that it is putting potentially intolerable stresses on the environment.

The corporate culture is now the bedrock of the Western political culture. There is a growing understanding amongst the rich that the poor are now politically and socially dispensable. Just as the private-mall owners will police their establishments to keep out undesirables, so the political trend is for governments to jail or exclude the people who have been marginalized by their failed policies. And having failed to eradicate poverty, the next step for many societies is to eradicate the poor themselves.

On the larger scale most of Africa can be effectively unlinked from the world economy, say hard-nosed Chicago-influenced economists, or appropriated: and senior executives of the Right-leaning think-tanks seriously propose that groups of multinational corporations should lease the world's poorest countries for a generation to instil 'best practice' economic policies. Just as governments are cutting aid to the world's poorest countries arguing that it is unpopular and does not help, so they propose driving beggars from the streets. The 'average' long-term beggar on the streets of London dies as young as an 'average' Ogoni in Nigeria.

Indeed, the mainstream politician, once viewed by some as the representative of the disadvantaged, has perceivably thrown in the towel on many issues that concern people. Political agendas to put before an electorate every four or five years are reduced to three or four issues where the difference between the parties in contention is increasingly small.

But the new backlash to overarching globalism and government insensitivity has begun. Not long after 300,000 Ogonis had rallied against Shell, 750,000 Indian peasant farmers downed hoes and left their fields to object to American seed companies. Soon after there were grass-roots riots triggered by French nuclear bomb testing, and from Mexico to Malaysia, Indonesia to Peru, Papua New Guinea, Bougainville and Colombia to Guyana and Brazil, there have been demonstrations against the forces of remote authority – transnational corporations, world bodies, mining companies, even banks. Thousands of other protests and human rights abuses have gone unreported. In Britain, Germany, France, Italy and Holland the same dynamic has been working, with protests against supermarkets, road building, open-cast coal mining, toxic wastes, car companies and chemical conglomerates, and mass demonstrations against the European Union or other trade bodies. Even as countries impose austerity budgets and slash social spending to bring countries in line with strict economic criteria for monetary union, seamen, farmers, miners and others are taking to the streets. The demonstrations and civil disorder in Korea are the latest ugly warning about what happens when the thrusting, economically ambitious state obeys only the free market and the corporations, and does not address people's social needs.

The grass roots are jumping, not just at individual corporations and governments but at a system of development that is exclusively geared to crude economic advancement. In almost every country of the world the intensification of farming, of industry or of commerce under the global system favours the elite. It offers no choice to those who do not have the means to respond to it and everywhere the poor are becoming poorer and being pushed to the economic margins, where they have little option but to stand up against the forces that sequester their resources.

On 1 January 1994, the very day that the North American Free Trade Association that gave American and Canadian corporations even greater power in Mexico came into force, the Zapatista rebel army seized several towns in the state of

Chiapas. Like Ogoni land (or perhaps Wales and Scotland), Chiapas is potentially rich, but has been economically marginalized by central governments for decades. The Mexican peasants and indigenous Mayan communities had long objected to fierce economic inequalities stemming, they argued, from a cruel system of land ownership that had seen them progressively disenfranchised. Their land claims were tied up in bureaucratic tangles while large landowners and corporations pressurized government departments to favour themselves. The formal end of land reform had come in 1992 when President Salinas repealed the legislation in order to boost high-tech export-oriented commercial farming in Chiapas. 'In one move Salinas robbed many peasants not just of the possibility of gaining a piece of land, but, quite simply, of hope,' says Stanford University anthropology Professor George Collier. The pressure, he argued, had come from agribusiness, US interests and the multinational donors like the World Bank. If early corporatism (in the form of cattle ranchers) had pushed the peasants off their land, the Zapatistas concluded that the only way to get it back was by the direct occupation of the land.

The Ogonis took up palm leaves, the Zapatistas guns. In Brazil the battle over land between ranchers and the country's fastest growing popular organization, the Movimento dos Trabalhadores Sem Terra, or MST, is intensifying. The Landless Workers' Movement is made up of thousands of disenfranchised people. In the past few years it has become a powerful peasant army recruited among landless farm labourers, the unemployed and the destitute for whom a bit of land on which to grow food represents the only prospect of survival. It is Socialist inspired but like grass-roots movements everywhere today is ideologically independent and apolitical in the sense that it trusts no political party to work for it.

Armed with old shotguns, hoes and machetes, MST followers have been invading ranches in the middle of the night, cutting through the barbed-wire fences and setting up camps. The tattered army of squatters is well enough organized, report Western journalists like Jan Rocha of the BBC and the *Guardian*. 'Its camps fly a red flag, provide food, education, dispense medicines when there are any. The organization is strict, but equable. Group decisions are taken. The life of the camp where 700 families live is decided by committees. Drugs and drink may be banned.'

The struggle of Ogonis, the Brazilian peasants, the Zapatistas, the South Koreans and others have been called the twenty-first-century style of conflict. They are resource based, superficially unconnected to international ideology and localized, and represent an implosion of the sovereign state as the excluded try to regain the resources they need just to survive in a global trading and financial system that works inexorably against them.

Clearly these resource struggles are increasing, as people are forced ever further into the ecological and social margins. Disputes in the Far East have focused on massive mines where thousands of people have been displaced, the destruction of tropical forests or the building of dams, the invasion of ethnic lands, World Bank support for prestige infrastructural development – dams, roads, power stations, agribusiness, irrigation projects – has uprooted millions of people in thousands of communities.

In China more than 5 million people will be moved over the next two decades to poor quality land or into cities to make way for massive projects on the Yellow River and the Yangtse; on the Mekong River hundreds of thousands of lives will be worsened by a series of dams that will deny them their fields; in India several hundred thousand people will be displaced to make way for the $4 billion Sardar Sarovar irrigation plan. Africa is littered with grand, madcap infrastructural failures backed by world bodies or transnational corporations that have disrupted lives for little purpose beyond dreams of aggrandisement.

Sometimes, as in Mexico, Nigeria, Korea, Brazil or Colombia, the disputes are highly visible. Mostly, though, people endure, and watch their families' lives deteriorate slowly as incremental, barely noticed small changes take effect. In Burkina Faso a typical village on the northern plain can have more of its young people scraping a living in neighbouring Ivory Coast or Ghana at any one time than are at home. Why have the young left? Because, says a chief, the land cannot support everyone. Why not? Because the soils are deteriorating. Why? Because the trees have been felled. Why? Because there was no option; the world trading system demands that poor countries sell off their resources. 'The young people are like topsoil,' says one elder. 'Once they go, there is no life in the society.'

What can communities in the way of this sort of 'progress' and economic totalitarianism do? Many protest, marching on town halls, capitals and company HQs, but mostly the response is to move drip by drip. Intensive agriculture, unjust land-tenure systems, global trade and the institutional corruption that follows big money and international projects fuel the flight from the land. The only option for millions today is to leave for the burgeoning world cities which bring with them their own social problems. The refugee migrating from devastated, denied countryside is one of today's new images of poverty.

Shell and other corporations employ the equivalent of 'high priests' and 'soothsaysers' to think ahead, map the future and extrapolate the political and social trends that they think will affect their profits. Their think-tanks – today's equivalent of Roman sheep's entrails – keep coming up with two polarized scenarios. One is of an increasingly globalized, interlinked world, with companies trading freely and profitably across physical and ideological borders and divisions; the other is of endless Chiapases, peasant squatting movements and slow-fuse social implosions. These two scenarios are interpreted as either/ors; the former, they infer, is good, the latter bad for business. The choice for the transnational corporation is always clear – carry on globalizing even more avidly to avoid the latter.

But there is increasing evidence that globalism and localism – what one US writer in the *Atlantic Monthly* coined 'McWorld versus Jihad' – may be intimately linked, opposite sides of the same coin. The more that corporations globalize and lose touch with the concerns of ordinary people, the more that the seeds of grass-roots revolt are sewn; equally, the more that governments hand responsibility to remote supranational powers the more they lose their democratic legitimacy and alienate people. The corollaries are clear: the excluded are forced into the margins of society where governments, unable to heal these social sores, are tempted to cauterize them.

The global bodies, too, peer ahead and see not so much conflict on a global scale, or between countries, ideologies or regions, as endless breakdowns of community, with localized, internecine disputes, civil strife and conflicts over resources. The same globalizing bodies which have arguably encouraged social disease by introducing industrial agriculture, or global trade in their pursuit of economic aggrandisement, now predict increasing disparities of wealth and welfare between rich and poor, a Third World developing in all countries. Says Vandana Shiva, Director of the Research Foundation for Science, Technology and Natural Resources in Delhi, who has studied the cultural impact of industrial agriculture in India: 'It can be clearly shown that the spread of ethnic and religious conflict and the growth of terrorism and fundamentalism can be traced to the social and cultural transformation of agrarian societies' by corporate totalitarianism.

Each global body has its own futurists, its own scenario of nirvana or meltdown. The Intergovernmental Panel On Climate Change sees global warming as the ultimate social disrupter; the Food and Agriculture Organization sees a shortage of land to feed a possibly doubling population; the European Union fears that the starving hordes will invade from the South or the East; and the World Bank and UN think that water will be the source of many future conflicts as communities are forced to share a non-renewable, increasingly fragile resource.

This last is the most certain. You can see potential conflict on the micro-level in an East African safari park where one luxury hotel owned by a foreign corporation and accommodating perhaps a hundred people at a time can be sited in a national park and will use in a month the scarce water normally consumed by a tribe and their animals in a year. It's there, too, in the Philippines and in Thailand where a mania for golf courses or tourist resorts owned by corporations is depriving whole communities of land and water, forcing people off the land and into cities or at best providing unskilled work in a notoriously exploitative industry.

Writ larger, more than sixty countries dispute with neighbouring states their shared river water. Future flashpoints, says the United Nations, include the Middle East, the Nile basin, the Brahmaputra, the Ganges, the Mekong, the Danube and North Africa. The Pentagon and the CIA now accept that environmental factors will increasingly be the source of conflict.

But the rejection of the development models imposed by transnational corporations and governments is just as apparent in Europe and the US. All the outward symbols of

'McWorld' – the motorway, the oil derrick, the satellite TV dish, the massive mine, tank, dam or genetically modified life form – are now being opposed. Noisy, urgent coalition groups are forming to fight everything from poor air quality, intensive farming and lousy water to toxic emissions, invasive car culture, electromagnetic radiation, supermarkets and animal cruelty. On their own the campaigns are small, but when linked up they constitute a sizeable opposition that governments and corporations cannot ignore.

The opposition is now too diverse to be dismissed as single issue, too politically and intellectually broad to be thought of as 'Luddite', 'anti-science' or 'anti-progress'. If anything, protest is becoming a binder of society rather than a divider. The British road protests in the past five years have been remarkable if only because they have shown that broad environmental issues are not the preserve of the middle classes. More than 200 anti-roads groups mushroomed after the announcement of a £23 billion road-construction programme backed heavily by powerful corporations. The sight of the wealthy protester shoulder to shoulder with the homeless and the unemployed was too hideous even for a notoriously insensitive government to contemplate, and the programme was slashed. Similarly, long-running protests against animal cruelty brought people together in a rarely experienced common ideological bond.

A radical but disparate movement is emerging from the grass roots in most countries. It is feeding off widespread social dissatisfaction and a sense of betrayal by governments and institutions. As the old dreams of material success cease to excite people in the same way as they did a previous generation, so increasing numbers search for simpler lives, with less cash or fewer work-oriented goals. Politicians are widely seen to be self-serving or ineffectual, blatantly greedy or corrupt, with decreasing difference between them and no commitment to the real healing of society. Even as the International Labour Organization reports that two-thirds of the world is now unemployed, the media reports massive pay settlements for corporation directors on the back of further redundancies, rationalizations, downsizing and technological advances.

Above all the smug, narrow, corporate and governmental definitions of 'progress' are being seen to be wildly at odds with the aspirations of most people. Slowly the consumer begins to wake up to the fact that what gives a life quality today is very different to what the corporations may propose. Slowly the consumer seeks more intangible products from companies – social responsibility, sensitivity to community and people's everyday needs, ecological awareness. It is no longer good enough for a company to provide a job, or to leave people in the lurch by running off to a cheaper centre of production, or to deskill or casualize a labour force. It may happen, but in the absence of a lead from government companies are being invited to respond to a new social agenda.

Mostly they do not respond. And, imperceptibly at first, then with gusto, the grass roots stir and flex their muscles. When Shell proposed to dump the Brent Spar oil platform in the North Sea the corporation was scientifically, financially and technically correct. It would have been a good decision had it been made fifteen years ago. The corporation could not believe it when the 1990s turned round and bit it. Shell was blind to the fact that the message it was transmitting – that a corporation without any remit except to make profits believed it had the right to dump its rubbish in a resource that belonged to everyone – was now deeply offensive and arrogant. Hundreds of thousands of people objected and Shell, shocked, changed its mind.

Recent consumer boycotts have hurt and have sent many

corporations scurrying to look up phrases like 'corporate ethics', 'social justice' and 'common sense'. Politicians, too, are left wondering what is happening; President Chirac's determination to test nuclear bombs in the Pacific awoke deep global hostility, as much for the environmental outrage as for the totalitarian nature of the nuclear industry and the way the French dependent territories have been kept in miserable colonial thrall. The growth of the McLibel Support Campaign is mirrored in the focused opposition being mounted to dozens of other global companies, Nestlé, British Aerospace, Rio Tinto Zinc, Lloyds and Midland banks, Guinness, Proctor and Gamble among them. You are not a fully global corporation until you have permanent watchdog pressure groups attached limpet-like to your body corporate.

Language is everything. What corporations seem incapable of seeing is that their PR phrases, glossy talk and blandishments about 'stakeholders', 'choice', 'care', and 'service' are increasingly laughable. A public brought up on constant exposure to hype and marketing can instantly deconstruct the sales pitch to find the reality. The more that corporations pay marketing and PR teams to capture the language of social or environmental responsibility to claim they are 'sustainable', 'caring', 'listening', 'green' or 'responsible', the less people believe them. In an era where everyone under the age of forty has been brought up with mass consumerism, there are no more illusions. In a globalized world where people are constantly told that there is infinite choice and the chance of individual prosperity there are few people in the West who now believe that life will really improve for society in general. They might. We won't.

And as Steel and Morris have identified, the gulf between public reality and corporate-speak may be greatest with food. Few people are today connected to the land, even fewer know what can go into a processed ham, a sausage, a bottle of wine or a soft drink. How many people would eat a frankfurter which clearly stated that it was made of blood plasma, powdered latex, artificial spices, mechanically separated meat, genetically modified soya, powdered egg white, animal fats, preservatives, colourings and flavourings? Processed ham regularly includes polyphosphates, nitrites, texturizing proteins, erythrosene; and never mind the herbicides and weedkillers sprayed on to wheat, an industrial croissant might owe its texture and flavour to antioxidants, fatty acids, emulsifiers and odourants.

As more is revealed about the intensification of industry and the ill treatment of animals, and as one food scare follows another, so the public loses trust not just in the food it eats but in the whole agricultural system and those that seek to justify it. Intensive agriculture is seen to have little respect for nature, to have dispensed with people in favour of machines and chemicals; to be uncaring of animals and polluting. The subliminal message that the consumer receives is that a totalitarian system of food production has been developed by a few companies and increasingly the industry must operate in relative secrecy to survive. Even potential meltdowns like BSE have failed to make the industry contemplate change on any real scale: the £3 billion BSE has cost so far has been pocketed with alacrity by a handful of privately owned corporations very well known to government.

If 'McWorld' is built on promises of better tomorrows, then it ensures that its downside is never fully discussed. It amounts to a tacit censorship, endorsed by politicians and corporations. Free trade, say the financial analysts plucking figures out of the hat almost at random, will massively increase the world's wealth. It may be true but no one is employed to analyse the social costs; likewise, the car has been peddled by governments and the largest corporations on earth as a universal ideological good, giving freedom, access and mobility, without anyone having to consider the associated loss of nature, tranquillity or health. Nuclear power was hailed at the start not just as the ultimate deterrent but as the provider of free electricity for ever. Today its real costs – which stretch over centuries – are never calculated. Likewise the 'green revolution' in India certainly increased food yields but at what unquantifiable costs to society?

Corporate censorship mirrors the lack of governmental transparency. Who is told that the real price of those pretty cut flowers on the market stall is Colombian, Peruvian or African women drenched in toxins and dying of cancers and tumours because they have never been educated so cannot read the labels in English that the chemical companies resist even putting on their poisons? Few in the food industry want the consumer to know the significance of what goes into their products and the industry pays lobbyists handsomely to resist labelling or meaningful information. Supermarkets boast the choice of 33,000 product lines but keep quiet about how the food chain that they control limits real choice. There were several thousand varieties of apples, potatoes, fruits, cereals on offer at the turn of the century in Europe. Today only a handful are grown in a big way and the diversity of nature is massively eroded.

But above all the disrespect and lack of trust in the globalizing culture of the multinationals is rooted in disappointment and in the inhuman scale of so much modern development. The glitzy promises of health, wealth and happiness have only materialized for a few. 'Wealth' is now in far fewer hands than it was. When Communism fell, the politicians – West and East – said there would be a new transparency and openness in government, a new era of glowing democracy, a massive peace dividend to eradicate poverty. Within a decade people find civil rights declining, more centralization of power in the hands of governments or corporations, more surveillance of individuals, more people in prison, more access by government or corporations to personal information, less right to protest, fewer full-time secure jobs, less access to public space, less workers' rights and collective bargaining, more crime, tax levels within a whisker of what they were, education and health costs spiralling, pollution better only in a few areas and worse in many, arms spending down by roughly 10 per cent in most Nato countries, but dollar for dollar rising again in many countries.

Failures to take account of what is happening at the grass roots mark a rejection of values as much as anything; the felling of a tree in East London to make way for an urban motorway is immediately interpreted by locals as the remote state bulldozing aside a community; so too the outcry over Prince Philip ordering the felling of an ancient avenue of oaks in Windsor Great Park because he found them untidy. When Daniel Zapata, a Native American campaigner against corporate coal mining in the US, can visit South Wales and be applauded to the rafters for referring to communities there which are threatened by massive open-cast mining as 'indigenous peoples' something is happening. When 'tribes' of homeless motorway protesters identify with the Zapatistas in Mexico, or the Yanomami in Brazil, then something is happening.

The rise of 'localism' around the world mirrors the rise in globalism, and the extremism of the corporations may be matched by the extreme lengths others take to oppose them. 'Localism' may in time be seen as one of two axial principles of the age, a complex political and social phenomenon, linked with both nationalism and tribalism. It has played a part in the disintegration of the Soviet Union and Yugoslavia and in the rise of fundamentalism, and it's there in trumps in many separatist and self-determinist movements in South America, Africa and Asia.

As a rule, though, where social justice is denied to people and citizens are not consulted or made participants in their future, there is an increasingly robust reaction. As in Britain with its new tribal youth movements, road protesters, travellers and social justice groups, so in Brazil, South Africa and the Philippines the global, Western development is recognized as failing ordinary people.

Yet if globalism and localism are emerging as co-equal world forces, they should be recognized as co-dependent, intolerant bedfellows, increasingly unable to communicate with each other. As was seen in Nigeria, and in the responses of corporations, human rights organizations, environmentalists and others, each informs the other, yet each fears and fuels the other's growth; each ridicules the other's belief systems, culture and traditions.

So localism is branded by business and political elites as 'narrow', 'closed' and 'backward', leading to political implosions, repression, intolerance and the breakdown of society; the same charges are flung back at globalism, which is further dismissed for being 'totalitarian', 'violent', 'homogeneous' and 'exploitative'. Globalism's totems – the reactor, the oil derrick, the fast-food restaurant – are welcomed or rejected as the agents of a new colonialism, just as the signatures of localism – the ethnic group, women disarming jets with hammers, the bunch of seeds collected by a family to plant next year, a small boat defying the absolute power of foreign navies – and now the image of Ken Saro-Wiwa hanged but unrepentant or of Morris and Steel taking on McDonald's are dismissed as emotive, irrational, ignorant and populist.

McLibel is a tale of our times. It shows what happens when representatives of two world views emerge and clash. It is a clash of faiths, of philosophies and fundamentals. If McDonald's is dependent on competition, free trade, access to markets, deregulation and the global marketplace, Steel and Morris seem to propose cooperation, a new moral agenda based not on nationalism or a retreat into the past but on respect for people and their predicaments, animals and place. Where corporations like McDonald's seek growth, market domination and maximized profits, the majority of the world are seen to thrive best in sensitivity and transformation, with new visions and goals.

Both sides have all to play for because as national governments lose their legitimacy and willingly or not cede traditional functions to corporations, so both the global and the local can flourish. And just as the transnational corporations have no boundaries and respect no borders, so an infinity of grass-roots movements and non-governmental groups are beginning to stand outside the traditional political structures and effect DIY change.

They argue fiercely that the dominant global economic model is geared to benefit only a few. The trillions of dollars' worth of US corporate stock is owned by about 10 per cent of the country; in Europe the figure is similar. The result, they argue, is massive social problems that cannot be addressed by the market or corporations whose responsibility is to themselves rather than the common weal. Furthermore, with little or nothing to choose between political parties, which are in thrall to corporations or international bureaucracies, they argue that the linked crises in governance, cities, the environment, health, education and welfare are increasing. They conclude that a radical, alternative more humane model of development is needed.

Dismissed as 'one issue' groups by the party politicians, together they may be seen as a realistic new political force, even as the seeds of a new society. If that seems radical it is just a measure of how unfashionable popular idealism has been made to seem by the free market. It can seem radical these days to get on a bus or walk.

The non-governmental organizations (NGOs) have become one of the prime checks and balances to government and corporations and almost the only generator of realism. Their rise as analysts, watchdogs and doers has been swift and has mirrored society's new complexities; in 1909, there were fewer than 200. Eighty years later there are said to be almost 30,000. Their increasing influence on policy agendas is already crucial, for though they may each represent specific concerns, in their proliferation they are making governance more representative and taken together they offer an extraordinary vision of the future. But in the growing absence of real political choice and in the presence of archaic, short-term thinking at the centre, they are increasingly giving up on the politicians and finding their own solutions with or without partners in industry.

This 'civil society' is much the same around the world: it comprises grass-roots activists, voluntary and community associations, human rights, labour, environmental and women's groups, charities, development bodies, liberation theologists and ecologists and Church and consumer organizations. They are becoming the moral backbone of most states, the repository of ethical values and ideas about the common good, and are filling the vacuum left by a disengaged or amoral state.

These days their grass-roots cry – from Ottawa to Ouagadougou – is for respect and consideration; for communities, human scale and for the source of life itself: the environment. There's much bandying around of the devalued phrase 'sustainable development' though few would disagree with the sentiments of the four-hundred-page Agenda 21 document that all countries signed up to at the Rio Earth Summit in

1992, but few have adopted. Nevertheless, spurred on by the Rio process at the Earth Summit, which gave grass-roots groups and new social movements a say, disillusioned by governments that seem unable to find solutions, a realistic alternative agenda is developing in both North and South.

It is rooted not in the politics of the Left or the Right – both of which are seen clearly to have failed – but in the need for equity. A raft of new ideas and responses to the global economy is surfacing. In the North – the belly of the unsustainable consumer beast – comes alternative trading, fair trade, Green consumerism, ethical business, consumer movements, new banking, farming and financial institutions, new ideas for business and community funding. Other parallel microeconomic systems like Local Exchange Trading Schemes, time dollars and people's banks are gathering pace and, with no help from anyone in authority, are establishing themselves at the grass roots.

They all emphasize healing fractured or vulnerable local economies, and are all underpinned by social concern. The economic theory behind them is simple enough: whereas a global economic system leaves the weakest without support, and everyone open to the vagaries of distant speculators and uncontrollable markets, a local system is controllable, understandable, accountable and on a scale that people can understand.

The LETS (local exchange trading schemes) are breaking new ground in self-help circles. The principle of what Jonathon Porritt would call 'manic minusculism' is to establish microeconomic systems where communities, be they geographical or institutional, can trade goods and services with their own currencies. They are fundamentally subversive to the arcane and incomprehensible monetary system that can whizz trillions of dollars around the world in an instant without a nano-thought for its effect. Money is revealed as nothing but a token of exchange, worthless in itself, and notions of debt and credit are seen as functions of inefficient economies.

LETS are marginal to any economy, little more than neighbourhood barter currencies, but their potential for building a sense of community and stimulating debate and 'non-monetary' exchanges between people especially in groups who have little cash but much else to offer, may prove important. Two people may not have money from the cash economy, but the skills and services that they offer – normally exchangeable only with a national currency – can be matched with a LETS economy. These are early days, but in Britain the need for different, community-based finance schemes and new ways through old problems is not doubted: there are more than 450 schemes in Britain and 45,000 people using LETS. Local councils are helping fund them, to establish whether they can be developed to help the old, the poor and even the homeless. They are mirrored in the US and Canada with 'time dollars'.

LETS are relatively new and may not work in large groups, but the credit union, where a community loans money at low interest to members, is an old idea whose time has come. First seen in the nineteenth century, they are increasingly important as a coping mechanism to build autonomy and human capital in areas of high unemployment and social devastation. One of their key criteria is social; before joining, people are asked to prove a 'common bond' with existing members, for instance because they live in the same area, or work in the same firm. Much of northern England is now covered by credit schemes.

Sometimes schemes like these develop into fully-fledged community banking. In the Basque country in Spain, the Mondragon cooperative, which now employs 21,000 people, set up the ethically based Working People's Bank. In Holland, the Triodos Bank is doubling in size every few years, and within two years of opening in Britain has more than 15,000 members. Now it is consolidating in Germany and Denmark. Like the Cooperative Bank in the UK, it specializes in ecological, ethical and small-scale loans.

Coming up smartish in Europe and the US is the great rise in alternatives to the industrial farming system. Organic farming is thriving now as consumers lose confidence in government and industry blandishments about safety and quality. With little help from governments or the massive and much abused European farm-subsidy system, and with no advertising or institutional or marketing support, organic farming is beginning to make real inroads into traditional markets. In Denmark, Germany, Austria and Sweden demand now outstrips supply and whole regions are now proposing that they turn to more sensitive ways of treating the land.

In Britain, where governments studiously ignore the social and environmental costs of industrial farming (despite one in five teenagers being vegetarian and more than 3 million people belonging to environment groups), organic farming is regarded in official circles as marginal. By consistently furthering the cause of the polluters and those who abuse the subsidy system, the government further loses its legitimacy with the grass roots.

This does not stop farm schemes and direct farmer-to-consumer businesses flourishing. There are long waiting lists now for some 'box schemes' where households are delivered a selection of seasonal vegetables each week. In Britain, where only 0.3 per cent of the land is farmed organically, the large supermarket chains are failing to meet the demand for organic produce.

Even the value-free City institutions and corporate establishments are being made to sit up by the success of some alternative initiatives. Fair trade, the simple guarantee to Third World commodity producers that they will be paid a more stable and slightly higher price for their goods, can make enormous social differences. In Britain coffee, tea and some chocolate are available; on the Continent the guarantee is being extended to fruit, nuts, honey, sugar and more.

Fair trade may be the heir apparent to the Green consumer boom of the late 1980s, but because it is far less open to corporation hype and 'Greenwash' it should develop strongly. Next on the socially responsible shopping list? Environment and development groups are moving into retailing; serious trading partnerships are developing between industry and NGOs to develop alternative technologies; other groups like the World Wildlife Fund are helping develop the fishing policies of multinationals.

Meanwhile ethical investments are making fast inroads. If charities, educational establishments and unions which together control more than £60 billion of British pension funds were to move this way one of the last bastions of official ignorance would be breached. It is happening in the US and on the Continent.

The effect of any one of these initiatives is minuscule but they should be seen as seedbeds for less exploitative living. They are, too, politically more important than their parts. Because they have a moral content, they show governments and corporations to be at best amoral, at worst ignorant and impotent. It is not hard to see that what is now an alternative economy could, with the right signals and help, within a generation rival the 'black' economy.

There is a growing appreciation, too, that the South has as much to offer the North as vice versa. As 'Third Worlds' develop in most OECD countries, so policy makers are beginning to see how non-governmental groups in the South have coped with deprived life at the bottom of society. The Grameen bank in Bangladesh was set up in 1976 by an economics professor at Chittagong University. Grameen is a development bank which specifically aims at lending micro-credit to groups of poor people and most especially to women. Its success has astonished commercial banks everywhere. By 1990, almost one-third of all Bangladeshi villages had a Grameen. The repayment rate is 98 per cent. Traditional loans in neighbouring India expect a 20 per cent repayment.

After decades of deliberately ignoring the wealth-creating possibilities at the grass roots, the World Bank has begun backing with micro-credit in the South. The only other global body with a remit to address directly the economies of the disadvantaged is the International Fund for Agriculture and Development. Like the Grameen, this small UN development body has quietly proved year after year that the poor are consistently better at repaying loans and investing in the enterprises that develop. Now governments are seeking to raise $20 billion to massively increase availability of micro-finance and its potential is being explored in rich countries, too.

Despite this the community level is still all but ignored in both North and South. Most policy makers still have not grasped the importance of local action on environmental and developmental issues. Everywhere they remain to be convinced, everywhere there is still enormous faith in the big plan, the big politics, the big theatrical gesture from above, and little remonstration when it fails. Yet wherever studies are made of micro-level community projects, the rate of return in economic, social and environment terms is found to be positive, if difficult to quantify.

Take, for instance, Tamassogo, the community in Burkina Faso where the young men had been leaving. That was five years ago. Today its population has increased, it has built itself three schoolrooms and no one leaves in the dry season when the harvest is over. But there is no magic solution. Plan, a British-based charity employing nationals has provided a bit of help so local outreach workers and rural development graduates can go into the village and teach self-help techniques. The villagers are learning about soil conservation, composting, tree planting, fuel conservation and vegetable growing. They have paid for their own investments, started small, taught themselves. 'It took longer, but the benefits will last longer than if someone gave us everything,' says the village chief.

Tamassogo barely features on the Burkina Faso economic map. Would the World Bank or the IMF be impressed by this attitude? How do you quantify the cultural, economic or social benefit of Alphonse or Hamado or his three brothers staying in the village? The village feels richer for having planted a thousand trees for eventual shade and wood supply, compost and biodiversity, but the market cannot properly quantify it, and attempts by economists to put a monetary value on life end in general nonsense. One of the world's leading economists did his sums and concluded that a life in the rich North was 'worth' more than fifteen times a life in the South.

Micro-enterprises – self-help cultures like that at Tamassogo – are the real backbone of the world economy and the cultural environment. Ninety per cent of UK businesses still have fewer than ten staff. Although 500 corporations now control more than a quarter of world economic output, the main source of employment is still the small enterprise – the very operations that are increasingly at risk from globalization.

Steel and Morris and thousands of others see themselves equally as defenders and promoters of this world. They welcome its diversity, and the choice it offers. Strip away the politics and the past; theirs is a simple enough vision based on giving people control over production and consumption, education, self-determination and social support. It involves rolling back corporate influence, listening to people on every level, trusting them to participate in decisions that will affect their lives and working together. To cynical politicians it can sound dangerous, idealistic, impossible to contemplate in a sophisticated democracy. To corporations it seems freakishly inefficient, to the state it can sound like the Last Trump. To the bulk of people, seeking little more than quality, continuity and prospects, it is fundamental and fair.

Chapter Eighteen

Day 313

'Have you nearly concluded your argument?'
'Mlud, no — variety of points — feel it my duty tsubmit —
ludship.'
– Mr Tangle in the trial of Jarndyce and Jarndyce:

Charles Dickens, *Bleak House*

Nobody comments on the date, but it's Friday the 13th, and
Day 313 of the longest trial in English case law, three times
the previously longest ever libel trial. Outside the law courts
in the Strand, the skies are London-grey.

Inside Court 35 no one is celebrating – not yet, not here,
anyway, though you could guess that the hideously bored-
looking Richard Rampton can't wait to set his mind to a fresh
case, that the hideously overstretched Morris and Steel can't
wait to get their lives back.

Morris is droning smoothly and methodically about
employment. You see, he says, 'Everything Must Go' and he
rereads a section of the offending leaflet. This bit, he says, is
'Fair Comment', that bit 'is Fact'. Sidney Nicholson sits
shaking his head slowly. By osmosis or some other physical
and mental process, the former policeman seems to be taking
on Rampton's characteristics. With finger and thumb he now
smooths an imaginary moustache, now he rubs his jowls,

shakes his head. Two dark-suited men, corporates to their ties, sit at the very back of the court. They neither move nor speak. Only they and Nicholson are obviously from McDonald's. The audience of twenty people consists of brightly dressed new-agers and duller-looking reporters.

Rampton's assistant, Timothy Atkinson, still sits in the row behind his master. He leans forward and whispers into Rampton's ear. He has grown older and richer, has Timothy, but he still looks every bit the swot – specs still slipping down his nose, wig still tipped at a rakish angle. It seems Morris has missed a page. Mr Justice Bell comments caustically, wearily even, that he was wondering whether he would notice. Morris is not put off, still grinds out his case, still believes utterly his points. The subtitles of 'McCancer' and McMurder', says Morris, are 'satire' but 'McDonald's are responsible for torture [of animals]'. Pause. Long pause. 'This Is Fact.' Nicholson harrumphs. 'Ridiculous,' he says aloud.

On the subject of costs, Steel says that McDonald's should be held to what the corporation is quoted as saying in today's *Times* newspaper: that they are not seeking damages. McDonald's, she argues, should get nothing because it printed and distributed 300,000 leaflets, and press releases – it has therefore put its point of view to the public. McDonald's asks for a total of £80–120,000 damages to be paid by Steel and Morris if the company wins.

Morris is back on his feet for one last statement, one last complaint, one last clarification to the world of what he and Steel have done and been through. Yes, he says, the leaflet damaged the reputation of McDonald's and what has been exposed in the trial on employment, nutrition and codes of practice on slaughter shows that the company has broken the law. What the leaflet reveals is damaging, he says, but It Is Also True, he claims. There are long, long pauses now. The judge hardly appears to be listening, leaning back in his monumental red-leathered chair, every now and then looking up a reference. At the back of the court a Robert Morley look-alike has fallen asleep. What is this old boy's part in the theatre? The loyal Dan Mills who has kept the support campaign going for three years says the old boy is a 'court fanatic'.

Rampton stands up and the difference in the court is undeniable. The judge, for one, now pays close attention. Rampton says Morris and Steel have been guilty of 'cynical opportunism'. Mr Justice Bell leans forward and takes notes – he had not even picked up his pen when Morris and Steel were talking. Rampton is in control. My client, he says as protectively as he can of a $30 billion a year corporation, has the right to sue because the leaflet affects its 'trading reputation'. Urbane, smooth, authoritative, and fluent; a liquid speaker, is Rampton.

Nicholson examines a wad of money that he has taken out of a pocket, looks at it, fondles it, folds it, puts it away. Rampton, as if by long habit, darts a snarling, sneering last look across the bench at Morris and Steel. This time, for once, Steel does not pick up the gauntlet, and Morris is blissfully unaware – the two litigants in person are now muttering and giggling together like kids, glad that it's almost over. Any contact the two sides have is curt. Rampton tosses Steel and Morris papers. Morris returns some to Rampton who hardly looks, let alone acknowledges. More press are coming in to the courtroom. More officials sit with or around the judge.

Then, shock. In these, the dying minutes of England's longest trial, Rampton loses his place. Atkinson, playing Prompt, quickly passes up a book but it's open at the wrong page. Before it gets embarrassing and the lion of advocacy is revealed as mortal, Mr Justice Bell leans forward to help, as he had done so many times before with Steel and Morris. The squall passes. Judge and silk talk – a cosy, clubby talk almost inaudible to the gallery – about Article 10 and Strasbourg.

Now Bell seems to be winding up the proceedings. He doesn't know when the judgement will be, he says, he just knows that it won't be soon. This, he hopes, will be the last day in court. There is no fanfare, no curtain call. The clerk declares: 'All rise.' 'Is this the end, is it?' asks one journalist. No one quite knows. Is the long opera over?

It is. Outside the court men clutch mobile telephones. Rampton appears first, immaculately dressed in overcoat and white silk scarf, flanked by his team. He hesitates just slightly when he sees a film crew, but they are not waiting for him. He exits, fast, over the pedestrian crossing. More media arrive. Morris and Steel walk out. Smiles. Watch Morris. He's got a dead cheeky look on his face. He stops, huge grin for the cameras.

And, in a loud voice says: 'So. Anyone wanna leaflet?'

Chapter Nineteen

Judgement Day

'To disarm the strong and arm the weak would be to change the social order which it's my job to preserve. Justice is the means by which established injustices are sanctioned.'

Anatole France

19 June 1997: It has been a long winter since Court 35 adjourned, and a glorious spring has turned to high summer. For many, there seems real hope for change in Britain. After eighteen years of avowed rightwing government, the country has booted out Thatcherism and its paler but no less rabid sucessor under Prime Minister John Major. A squeaky-clean new Labour administration has been elected with a massive majority.

But there is little sense of impending change at the grass-roots where the election seems to be an exercise in power. Alarming figures, mirrored in many other countries, show the rapidly growing gap between rich and poor, the greatest in Britain since 1886. The richest 10 per cent of the population earn as much as the poorest 50 per cent; education and health are in financial crisis. The development process still favours growth at any cost, there is little sense that the disadvantaged are on the political agenda, the countryside is no better protected, the cities are crumbling and polluted. Meanwhile young protesters against new roads and big developments are occupying quarries and trees, anddigging tunnels under airports.

And after six months in purdah, Mr Justice Bell is ready to give his verdicts on McLibel. Not a man to be hurried, he has pondered long and barely looked up. Did he chuckle at a painstaking three-hour television miniseries dramatisation of the McLibel trial while he was deliberating? Has he been aware that McDonald's has had a pretty mixed year, including stagnating US sales, angry franchisees and promotional flops? It has been widely rumoured that Bell's judgement, as befits one of the longest cases in the world, is to be epic.

Word filters out of the Royal Courts of Justice that it will be 800 pages long, and that Bell will read a 45-page summary.

High noon: Court 35 has moved on to its more usual fare: divorce, trademark infringement, negligence. McLibel's final act is to be played out next door, in a slightly larger, even more austere Court 36. Outside the courtroom dozens of people are crowding to get in. Inside, it is as if the assigned space has been double booked by two family groups; the visual symmetry of their differences is stark.

McDonald's—corporation and British operation, respectively the first and second plaintiffs—as before, sits to the right of Mr Justice Bell's dais. The clan knows to wear darkish suits for these public occasions, flowery ties, thin smiles. Paul Preston is there at the front, leading his troops, a company paper bag at his feet. He is deep in conversation with an avuncular, weary-looking Richard Rampton. The quintessential Englishman and the American who has lived in Britain most of his adult life, chat not of courtroom tactics or case detail or strategy, but of fly-fishing in Scotland. It seems it's good this time of year. 'Have you ever caught a land-locked salmon? . . . ' Rampton asks. Preston's reply is inaudible as the courtroom fills.

'Are you going to put the judgements in there, Mr Preston?' breaks in the Associated Press man, sitting six feet away in the press benches and pointing to Preston's bag. Preston quips back: 'Strong as they are, they are not designed to carry 800 sheets of paper.' Patti Brinley-Codd, the company lawyer in lime green, coos and organises. Timothy Atkinson's wig, as always tilted, has a cloud of split hairs at the back, giving it an air bouffant. Sid Nicholson who sent in the spies to London Greenpeace, sits behind him, ruminating as the suits line up in the pews. Shelby Yastrow, the corporation man from Illinois who was sent to offer a deal with Steel and Morris years ago, is there to represent the first plaintiff; young executive puppies sit, well-behaved, shoes shined, expectant, behind and around him. There is a whiff of Homme Sauvage perfume.

On the other, left hand, side is a wide range of people, young and old, mostly casually dressed, many in sweatshirts and trainers. Steel and Morris's supporters, all taking the day off, have arrived early from around the country and look, as ever, on another planet to the McDonald's men. Keir Starmer, the unsung legal hero who has advised Steel and Morris since the very beginning, is there. So too are other sympathetic lawyers. It is a rainbow, alternative collective. Environmentalists, concerned professionals, justice groups, parents, defence witnesses, ex-McDonald's workers, idealists, hopers, ordinary people.

Enter, stage left, Steel and Morris. Morris has a priestly, beatific air this morning, a white shirt sticking above his grey jumper like a dog collar. He carries a small briefcase. He raises his eyebrows, glances around at the assembly, nods to the twenty or more reporters on the two press benches and another thirty corralled by the door. Steel greets the people she recognises. The two defendants, as ever, sit on their own. They look more relaxed than in December when they were last in court. The long suffering and self-denial are mostly over.

Imperceptibly, the focus of the court moves and the volume of chat drops. Enter the judge's clerk in black pinstripe suit and two-tone shirt. The court arises. Bell, as ever the headmaster, comes in swiftly, papers under arm. There is no small talk, no nonsense, no hint of what is to come. And there is no greeting, even recognition, of the small cast of characters who have occupied his waking life for so many years. His first words are to the effect that people may come and go. No one stirs. He starts to read his verdicts.

And for the next thirty-five minutes Steel and Morris and their tribe look askance while Preston and his nod their heads in approval. To start at the beginning. Were Steel and Morris even responsible for the offending leaflet? Should the case have ever been brought? Steel, remember, was not even involved in the London Greenpeace group at the time in question, let alone the campaign. Morris participated in the leaflet's production in 1986, says Bell. He is clear:

'Anyone who causes or concurs in or approves the publication of a libel is as liable for its publication as a person who physically hands it or sends it off to another. It is not necessary to have written or printed the defamatory material. All those jointly concerned in the commission of a tort (civil wrong) are jointly and severally liable for it'

But did the plaintiffs—McDonald's corporation in the US and its British operation—consent to publication of the disputed leaflet when they sent the spies into the group? They had infiltrated London Greenpeace back in 1989/90 and there was evidence that they handed out some of the leaflets. Bell: 'There is no evidence that anyone employed [by McDonald's] authorised or consented . . . it is clear that the enquiry agents did what they did the easier to remain apparent members of the group . . . The defence of consent to publication fails. The whole idea of either plaintiff consenting to, let alone encouraging, the publication of the leaflet is bizarre.'

Bell moves to general principles. The words in the leaflet are to be read in the context of the satirical cartoons and graphics. Was it a defence that Steel and Morris were merely repeating what they had been told, or that they believed what was said was true? No. Bell: 'The meaning intended to be conveyed by the author or publisher of the material complained of is irrelevant.'

Was any of the leaflet fair comment, a crucial argument of the two defendants? 'The defence of fair comment is available only in relation to statements that are expressions of opinion and not defamatory statements of fact. Save for one sentence [in the leaflet] I have come to the conclusion that the defamatory statements . . . are statements of fact, and not comments or expressions of opinion.'

The Defendants appear stunned at this ruling. McDonald's visibly relax. Preston turns to Rampton and the whispers are not about fishing.

Bell moves smartly on to the six main areas of alleged defamation. Here, remember, McDonald's didn't have to prove that the allegations were false. Rather, the hideously unresourced Steel and Morris had to show with primary, original evidence in the witness box that they were true.

Bell addresses the first main issue: rainforest destruction and starvation in the Third World. Was McDonald's responsible? Directly? No. 'Neither plaintiff has ever bought or owned vast tracts of land in poor countries in the Third World. They have not themselves evicted small farmers or anyone else from their land, nor directly caused anyone else to do so'; 'Even in Brazil where the evidence of dispossession of small farmers and tribal people for cattle ranching generally was stronger, I am unable to draw the inference that any cattle ranchers whose cattle have gone on to make McDonald's burgers have been implicated.'

By and large, Bell has ignored the fact sheet's criticisms of multinationals and the food industry in general. He has also interpreted that the word 'rainforest' means more than 'tropical forest'; it is "luxuriant broad-leaved, evergreen, very wet canopy forest.'

Steel and Morris's argument that McDonald's has stimulated markets for beef from former rainforest lands does not wash either. Bell: 'Where the hamburger industry goes from here may be a matter of some concern . . . but in my opinion McDonald's alleged part in an alleged worldwide hamburger connection does not justify the defamatory allegations as far as starvation and destruction of rainforest are concerned.' And did McDonald's use lethal poisons to destroy 'vast areas of Central American rainforest to create grazing pastures for cattle to be sent to the US as burgers and to provide fast food packaging?' No.

Rampton smiles. Preston leans back. Everything so far has gone for the corporation and its British subsidiary. These were some of the hardest areas for Steel and Morris to prove, if only because collecting primary evidence without resources from a country 5,000 miles away was fiendishly difficult. Bell has only the evidence presented to him to go on. Moreover, he has acccepted McDonald's' interpretations of the meanings which the Defendants had argued the factsheet just did not say.

The verdicts move on to recycling. Were Steel and Morris's arguments and detailed mathematics about the amount of forest needed to produce McDonald's packaging enough? The leaflet had stated 'Don't be fooled by McDonald's saying they use recycled paper: only a tiny per cent of it is.' Bell rules that this was an allegation that McDonald's was lying when it claimed to use of recycled paper. Bell: 'Many paper items appeared to have no recycled content in the late 1980s, but paper carry bags, napkins and trays contained substantial proportions . . . . The recycled fibre in those items makes it impossible for me to hold that only a tiny percentage of the paper which UK McDonald's used during the 1980s was recycled.' It was, he ruled, 'a small, but nevertheless significant proportion.' There was evidence that McDonald's publicity material was 'misleading' about some packaging in England being recycled when it was not, but the defamatory charge that McDonald's was lying was not justified.

What about the litter in the streets outside McDonald's stores. Was the company responsible? No. Bell rules that although the system of litter patrols often broke down, that did not make McDonald's culpably responsible for what was left on the streets away from the store fronts. The blame should be on 'the inconsiderate customer.'

But what has happened to the issue of climatic pollution caused by CFCs and HCFCs or pentane gases used to make polystyrene foam packaging, and its non-biodegradeability, and the chemicals used in the production of paper packaging? Bell rules that they are not 'referable' to any defamatory statement about which the Plaintiffs complain, so the evidence heard is judged to be irrelevant. As is methane generation from cattle emissions. So is the one and only piece of comment, the one sentence claiming that McDonald's was 'wrecking the planet', fair? No.

There is a perceptible pause. The core issues are still to come. Bell moves on to the alleged links between McDonald's food, heart disease and cancer of the breast and bowel. Steel and Morris had maintained that the entire nutrition section of the factsheet had been admitted by McDonald's own witnesses, but McDonald's had moved the legal goalposts by changing its claim against the Defendants and made the Defendants prove a more severe meaning than the one originally claimed over.

Bell is unforgiving. It was not true, he said, that eating McDonald's food might well make your diet high in fat, animal products and salt, let alone vitamins and minerals: 'It is only true in relation to a small proportion of people who eat McDonald's food several times a week.' He continues: 'It cannot be right to say that eating McDonald's food will bring the very real risk that you will suffer cancer of the breast or bowel or heart disease as a result of making your diet high in fat, sugar and animal products . . .'

But Bell has gone on to ask whether it had been proved that a diet high in fat and animal products and salt and low in fibre leads to a 'very real risk' of degenerative diseases: '. . . sustained over very many years, [it] probably does lead to a very real risk of heart disease in due course . . . it means that the small proportion of McDonald's customers who eat McDonald's food several times a week will take the very real risk of heart disease if they continue to do so throughout their lives, encouraged by McDonald's advertising.' He finds further that 'it is strongly possible that such a diet increases the risk of cancer of the bowel and the breast to some extent. But that it follows that McDonald's food is not very unhealthy as stated in the leaflet.'

The spell is broken. The left-hand side of the court erupts in laughter. Bell continues: 'I find that various advertisements, promotions and booklets have pretended to a positive nutritional benefit which McDonald's food, high in fat and saturated fat and animal products and sodium, and at one time low in fibre did not match.'

It was Steel and Morris who now looked relieved. These were big points. After all, McDonald's had stated that something approaching 75 per cent of its US business came from heavy users of its stores. The verdicts could be interpreted to mean to mean that the relevant section of the leaflet unjustly defamed McDonald's because many people did not eat there often enough to suffer the ill effects.

What about McDonald's courting of children, with a considerable part of its $2 billion a year advertising and marketing being used for this purpose? Bell: 'McDonald's advertising and marketing is in large part directed at children with a view to them pressurising or pestering their parents to take them to McDonald's and thereby to take their own custom to

McDonald's. This is made easier by children's greater suscep-
tibility to advertising which is largely why McDonald's adver-
tises to them so much.'

According to Bell, McDonald's does use gimmicks, but not,
as stated in the leaflet, to cover up the true quality of the food.
'The food is just what a child would expect . . . There is no
cover up of the true quality of the food,' he says. 'But the sting
of the leaflet to the effect that McDonald's exploits children
by using them, as more susceptible subjects of advertising, to
pressurise their parents into going to McDonald's is justified.
It is true.'

But there is more. 'McDonald's advertising and marketing
makes considerable use of susceptible young children to bring
in custom, both their own and that of their parents who must
accompany them, by pestering their parents.'

The reporters on the press benches have their headline:
'McDonald's exploits children.'

Worse is to follow for McDonald's. Bell moves on to animal
welfare. The leaflet, he says, means that McDonald's was 'culpably responsible for cruel practices in the rearing and slaughter of some of the animals used to produce their food.' Had
Steel and Morris proved this in fact? Bell: 'Laying hens used
to produce eggs for McDonald's spend their whole lives in
battery cages without access to open air or sunlight and without
freedom of movement . . . I do not find the lack of open air
or sunshine to be cruel, but the severe restriction of movement
is cruel and McDonald's are culpably responsible for that cruel
practice.'

'Broiler chickens which are used to produce meat for
McDonald's also spend their whole lives in broiler houses
without access to open air or sunshine. I do not find this in itself
cruel. However they spend the last few days of their lives with
very little room to move. The severe restriction of movement
over those last few days is cruel and McDonald's are culpa-

bly responsible for that cruel practice.'

He says that many cattle were frightened by the noise and unfamiliar surroundings of the abattoirs in which they were slaughtered, but the charges in the factsheet that animals waiting to be slaughtered often struggle to escape and that cattle become frantic as they watch the amimal in front of them in the killing line being prodded, beaten, electrocuted and knifed were not justified.

Nor, he says, was it shown that cattle or pigs used to produce McDonald's food were frequently still fully conscious when they had their throats cut. But 'a proportion of the chickens killed for McDonald's are still fully conscious when they have their throats cut; this is a cruel practice. The proportion of such chickens is small but the number is so large that the allegation that animals are still frequently fully conscious when they have their throats cut is justified.'

The press is loving it: 'Facts: McDonald's exploits children, is cruel to animals.' Another section is going almost completely to the defendants.

Bell rubs in the message: 'There are other cruel practices affecting chicken: calcium deficit resulting in osteopaenia in battery hens, the restriction of broiler breeders' feed, leg problems, rough handling, and pre-stun electric shocks suffered by broilers on their way to slaughter.'

There is brief respite for the $30 billion a year company whose practices, they had always maintained, were the best in the business. On food poisoning, Bell says that on the evidence that he has heard, the risk of food poisoning from eating McDonald's food is 'minimal.' 'From time to time people will no doubt get food poisoning from eating McDonald's food, but the risk is very small indeed.' But there was no evidence, he said, that pesticide residues or antibiotic or growth-promoting hormone drug residues had been found in McDonald's food.

Judgement Day

The last of the major rulings are around working conditions, pay and unions. The leaflet, Bell says, alleged that McDonald's paid their workers low wages and provided bad working conditions, helped to depress wages in the British catering industry, were only interested in recruiting cheap labour and exploited disadvantaged groups, women and black people especially, as a result; and that they have a policy of preventing unionisation by geting rid of pro-union workers.

There is more dynamite. The British McDonald's operation, he says, pays low wages and hence depresses wages for other workers in the industry. But, he says, there is insufficient evidence to prove that the corporation in the US pays low wages, too.

Some verdicts go to McDonald's. It was not true to say that they were only interested in recruiting cheap labour, and that they exploited disadvantaged groups, women and black people. 'Both Plaintiffs are interested in inexpensive labour, but they are also keen to have people who will work well and appear cheerful to please their customers. They treat women and black crew members the same as the rest as far as pay and other conditions go.'

Bell: 'Despite the hard and sometimes noisy and hectic nature of the work, occasional long, extended shifts including late closes, inadequate and unreliable breaks during busy shifts, instances of autocratic management, lack of third party representation in cases of grievance and occasional requests to go home early without pay for the balance of the shift if business is slack, I do not judge the Plaintiffs' conditions of work, other than pay, to be generally 'bad', for its restaurant workforce.'

But McDonald's comes in for some stiff criticism. Breaks are subject to the demands of custom: 'This means they are often taken early or late in a shift, or cut short. Adequate drink breaks are not always easy to come by. The result is that crew can work hard for long periods without adequate breaks.' One of the most unacceptable practices, Bell said, was that of managers 'inviting' people to go home without payment for the rest of their shifts.

Bell: 'From time to time UK crew are invited to go home early if a restaurant is quiet. Sometimes crew are sent home for reasons that would not have bitten if the restaurant had been busy . . . sometimes direct and unfair pressure has been put on crew . . . This practice is most unfair . . . it should not happen at all and in my Judgement it shows where the ultimate balance lies . . . between saving a few pounds and the interest of the individual, often young employees. I had no direct evidence of the extent to which it happens in the US, however it is the kind of systemic practice which is passed from an international holding company to its national offshoot, and on that basis I find that it probably happens in the US, too.'

Moving on to unions, the Judge finds 'as a fact' that [McDonald's] are 'strongly antipathetic' to any idea of unionisation of crew in their restaurants.' But he then rules that the Defendants had libelled McDonald's because they had failed to prove that McDonald's had a policy of preventing unionisation by getting rid of pro-union workers.

There are two issues left to resolve. The first is the defendants' counterclaim, which has run parallel to McDonald's claim throughout the action. Steel and Morris had countersued McDonald's, remember, after the company had issued hundreds of thousands of leaflets and press releases on the eve of the trial calling them 'liars'. Bell finds this allegation defamatory and rules that it 'has not been justified' by McDonald's. He considers that part of McDonald's motive in publishing the leaflets and press releases 'was to discredit the defendants' and that 'there was considerable ill will towards the Defendants' by that time. But, he rules, McDonald's was legally protected in publishing the defamatory statements. It could rely on a defence of 'qualified privilege in the form of the right to reply to an attack', because the company had been publicly attacked in the strongest terms by Steel and Morris for bringing the case. Therefore, 'The counterclaim must fail.'

Steel and Morris, the unlikely 'attackers' of the defenceless $30 billion a year company, look gobsmacked.

And costs? Some of the libellous statements are 'particularly damaging' and 'serious', repeats Mr Justice Bell, but as other allegations have been shown to be justified, McDonald's, instead of being awarded £ 120,000 that they sought, should get half.

After nearly two hours' reading, it is over. Bell turns smartly and leaves. So does the McDonald's group. Steel and Morris's supporters, more untutored in the law, mill around, still unsure of the full significance of the verdicts and the legal language they are couched in. Keir Starmer speaks succinctly: 'It is a triumph', he says. 'Steel and Morris have won handsomely in three sections, more than anyone might have thought possible in the circumstances. McDonald's has lost outright the core of its case, how it treats its workers, its animals and children. Without a jury and with no legal resources, they have achieved something extraordinary.'

The scrum of people surrounding, almost carrying Steel and Morris, moves outside. Morris pins a handwritten poster on his briefcase. 'Judge for Yourself', it reads. Hundreds of people waiting for them cheer as they pause for a moment on the steps, temporarily overwhelmed. At least 50 camera crews and photographers, along with the reporters surrounding them, fire a barrage of questions. In seconds, the 'McLibel 2' make their feelings clear as they distribute more What's wrong with McDonald's leaflets.

Two press conferences follow. One, round the corner in the London School of Economics is open to all and 400 people crush in. It is a two-hour occasion of banners, bunting and celebrations, rousing speeches by the head of Friends of the

Earth, Michael Mansfield QC and others. There are fulsome thanks, compliments and congratulations. The McLibel 2 seem elated and defiant. How are Steel and Morris going to pay the damages? Steel: 'We're not going to pay the damages. McDonald's don't deserve a penny, and in any event we haven't got any money.' Morris: 'The Judge is entitled to his opinion, but so are we and hundreds of millions of other people round the world.'

The other meeting is a sombre, ill-tempered 30-minute affair, well away from the courts of justice and open only to accredited press who must sign in. Paul Preston, McDonald's spin doctors at his arm, fends off hostile questions. How can McDonald's claim to have won? 'McDonald's are broadly happy.' Will they press for damages? 'Not to bankruptcy.' Do you accept that McDonald's is cruel to some animals and that they exploit children? 'We will consider the verdicts.' An enquiry is to be launched, says one McDonald's aide. Will the company make it public? No comment. Will they change their practices, will they withdraw all chicken meals until they have completed their enquiry? No comment.

The media, well-versed in the issues, is quick to have its say. The interpretations are unanimous and damning. McDonald's has won its case, but it is, at random, 'a Pyrrhic victory', 'a case that should never have been brought', 'a PR fiasco', 'an action that takes the prize for ill-judged and disproportionate response to public criticism', and 'a pounds 10m McBlunder' with the 'Burger giant tainted'. It is front-page news of most papers, the top or second story on the televisison and radio news. There are calls for widespread reform of the legal system.

The international press has a field day as the Burger giant is seen to have tripped up badly, winning on legal points but losing fundamental issues. The significance of the verdicts begins to sink in; for the first time ever, the core practices of the world's largest food retailer, a $30 billion a year company with all the political, financial and media muscle in the world, have been found seriously wanting in a court of law. The three phrases ring out: 'Exploitation of children', 'Cruelty to animals', 'Low pay'. How much more damning could it have been?

Steel and Morris are jubilant. Two days later they help distribute 2,000 leaflets outside their local McDonald's store as part of a global protest and 'Celebration of Victory' by thousands of people. More than 500 McDonald's stores out of 750 in the UK are leafletted. Groups in at least twelve other countries join in and at least 500,000 leaflets are distributed.

Within a week, Steel and Morris say they will appeal against the parts of the Judge's verdict which went against them and over some of the legal aspects of the case. Following this, they intend to take the British government to the European Court of Human Rights to overturn the UK's libel laws, challenge their denial of legal aid and a jury trial, and laws stacked in favour of Plaintiffs. They say that they will argue that multinational corporations should no longer be allowed to sue for libel. They also intend to sue for a contribution to the damages from three of the McDonald's spies who had testified to distributing the factsheet.

McDonald's says nothing. The corporation, based in Oak Brook, Illinois, refuses to comment on the verdict, claiming that it is a UK issue. This is despite the fact that they were the first and leading Plaintiff in the action, that they called top US executives to give evidence and twice flew over other executives during the trial for secret settlement meetings with Steel and Morris. It is interpreted as a damage limitation exercise.

And then McDonald's capitulates. On Thursday 17 July, the four-week deadline set by Mr Justice Bell for any final legal applications by the parties passes without McDonald's asking for an injunction or costs. The company thereby effectively abandons all legal efforts to stop the distribution of leaflets or collect any of the millions of pounds it had spent on the case. It is also quoted as saying it will not attempt to collect any of the damages.

Meanwhile, on the back of the verdicts, the National Food Alliance has called for a ban on food advertising targeting children. The UK Farm Animal Welfare Network and the People for the Ethical Treatment of Animals on behalf of its 500,000 members are demanding immediate action to end the cruel practices identified by Mr Justice Bell. Trade unions and labour activists step up their recruitment drive in the catering industry and their campaign for a guaranteed minimum wage, and local residents' associations broaden their objections to new McDonald's stores to include concerns regarding the targeting of local children and the lowering of local wage levels.

Was it worth it? The biggest bun fight in history. The longest, most tortuous case in civil case history. Did the truth emerge, or rather two irreconcilable worldviews, two value sytems each eloquent of their age? Was McLibel really an exercise in justice or in censorship? Was right done? In the end, the law—whether British or American, Canadian or Australian—is very human in its limitations. Let us leave it to Michael Mansfield QC, one of its most eloquent exponents, to put in perspective the wider debate that McLibel has opened, and to make a few incontrovertible points.

'It is timely to be reminded that those without financial resources have fought uncompromisingly for a global value system which has at its heart human, animal and environmental welfare. Helen Steel and Dave Morris have done just this, knowing far mightier organisations have taken the shorter course when faced with the McWrit. No doubt each withdrawal or apology in the past has been a bargain with its own economic necessity. But what this case has demonstrated, through all the verbiage, the statistics, the claims and the counter-claims, is that capitulation is not a political inevitability. Additionally, Steel and Morris have provided inspiration to a generation which has witnessed a relentless descent into moral bankruptcy. They have rekindled an agenda of which we should be proud, and we all owe them a debt of gratitude for being prepared, at great personal cost, to stand where others have fallen. Issues concerning nutrition, diet, health, the exploitation of children, workers and animals and environmental damage are issues which touch upon our daily lives and for which we have a joint responsibility. We cannot afford to turn a blind eye, to turn our backs and pretend that there is nothing that can be done.'

Chapter Twenty

Last Words

'Whereof one cannot speak, thereon one must remain silent.'
–Ludwig Wittgenstein

The dust settles. McDonald's rides out the storm, but what of the promised debate? After several phone calls, Mike Love, head of communications at McDonald's UK, agrees to consider contributing to *McLibel* and answering several questions: Dear Mike, I would welcome McDonald's contribution to a summing up of the trial for inclusion in a last chapter of *McLibel*. Within reason it can be done on your own terms. This mammoth case raises many important points which must be in everyone's interests to discuss, not least about the conduct of individuals and corporations and the relationship between companies and their critics. If only for historical record, your thoughts would be welcome. It's your choice. Please consider this carefully.

As suggested by yourself, I enclose a few questions.

1. Given that the leaflets were being distributed in the USA, why did McDonald's Corporation sue activists in the UK rather than in the Corporation's home country? What view does McDonald's Restaurants Limited (the Corporation's UK subsidiary), and the Corporation itself hold about having had to defend the transnational company's global record in a English courtroom?

2. McDonald's mostly refused to speak to the media during the case, stating frequently that it would comment after the conclusion of the trial. Why did McDonald's decline to comment then, and now that the case is over why is the company still reluctant to talk in an open interview?

3. Does McDonald's take seriously Mr Justice Bell's findings of fact that McDonald's is 'exploiting children' through its advertising, 'helping to depress wages in the catering industry', deceptively promoting company food as 'nutritious' and 'culpably responsible for cruelty to animals', and what changes, if any, will you be making in Corporate policy and practice?

4. Approximately how much have McDonald's spent on the McLibel case since preparations for legal action were first initiated in August 1989? Will the company try to recover any of its costs or damages from the defendants, and if not, why?

5. After your experience in the case, would you say that defamation hearings are the best way to deal with disputes between companies and their critics and can you suggest alternative ways in which the issues in this case could have been aired and resolved without recourse to the courts?

6. Do you think there is a case for the British libel laws in particular to be reformed, if only to avoid such a lengthy trial?

7. Do you feel that the accessability of the full transcripts of the proceedings and the Judgement on the Internet is beneficial, detrimental or irrelevant? I understand that campaigners are continuing to distribute leaflets in many countries, including the UK, as they see it, to counter McDonald's $2 billion annual advertising spend. Do you welcome any public debate and discussion that may be stimulated as a result?

I would welcome answers, or if this does not appeal, could you please make a 'contribution to the debate' in about 2,000 words. A third option might be an interview with Mr Paul Preston? A fourth would be a contribution by Mr Preston himself.

The ball is in your court and I will genuinely try to reflect your point of view which is valid and important,

Yours, John Vidal

Three weeks later Mike Love responds: 'We are grateful to you for giving us the opportunity to contribute. However on consideration I can confirm that our position is unchanged and that we do not feel that there is anything we wish to add to the statement by our chairman Paul Preston issued at the press conference on Judgement day. . . '

It reads: 'We are, as you can imagine, broadly satisfied with the judgment. For the sake of our employees and our customers, we wanted to show these serious allegations to be false and I am pleased that we have done so.

'There are aspects of the ruling which we will have to review and we will do so when we have been able to study the full ruling in detail. However it is clear that the judgment confirms what we have always known, that the allegations are untrue.

'The fact that it has taken three years out of our lives also gives cause for concern. The length of the trial raises important issues about the cost of justice and the speed with which it can be dispensed. We welcome the public debate over proposals to reform the Civil Justice system, especially with regard to the recommendation to allow the judiciary to limit the cost and length of civil litigation. There is a difficult balancing act between fairness and speed but anyone who has been to court knows there is both a financial and emotional cost to litigation; this must be considered when examining how the sytem works.

'We brought this case to protect a reputation trusted by millions of customers every day. The judgment represents a thorough audit of our business. Based on the overwhelming evidence given in support of our case, we believe that our employees and customers will be reassured by the judgment.'

Last Words

The same offer and a request for a verdict on the verdicts is made to Steel and Morris, who reply: 'We're exhilarated by what we, and the Campaign, have been able to achieve over the last few years. By standing up to the company's bullying we turned the tables on them and all their dirty laundry was aired in public, exposing the reality behind the glossy image. The case was transformed into what may have been the first ever public tribunal on the business practices of a multinational corporation. And of course leaflets are circulating worldwide in ever greater numbers.

'The evidence coming out of the courtroom has completely vindicated the critics of the fast food industry in general, and McDonald's in particular (its largest and most prominent exponent). There's no doubt that the only reason we didn't win on all points was due to technicalities—controversial legalistic and semantic interpretations of the meaning of the What's Wrong With McDonald's? factsheet, which therefore increased the burden of what we were expected to prove. The judge adopted virtually all McDonald's extreme arguments about this. And his failure to find for us over our Counterclaim was probably the biggest scandal of them all.

'However, despite being up against oppressive and unfair laws stacked in favour of Plaintiffs, the denial of Legal Aid, a huge imbalance in the resources of the two sides, and the denial of our right to a jury trial, we won on the issues that go to the very core of McDonald's business. The Corporation must be devastated to have been found guilty of "exploiting children", of deceptively promoting their food as "nutritious" and putting the health of their most regular, long-term customers at risk, of paying "low wages" and of being "culpably responsible" for cruelty to animals.

'It couldn't have been made more difficult for us—for example, the factsheet repeatedly criticised the fast food industry and multinationals in general, but the Judge ruled, at

McDonald's' insistence, that we had to prove that McDonald's *itself* was directly to blame for each problem identified (e.g., Third World hunger). He also agreed with McDonald's that all the comments and opinions in the factsheet (bar one phrase) were "statements of fact" which would therefore have to be proven from primary sources of evidence.

'One thing the case has clearly shown is how inappropriate it is for a single Judge to be deciding what issues can be debated in the public arena. Issues such as whether consumers should worry about pesticides and their diet, whether working conditions and pay are bad, whether advertising is exploitative and who is responsible for environmental damage, should be freely debated, without people fearing that if some Judge were to hold a different opinion to them, they could be saddled with thousands of pounds to pay in damages, and even if the Judge agrees with them they have had to spend a huge amount of time and money to fight a case. Such fears prevent open, uninhibited debate which is necessary for progress to be made.

'We don't believe that multinationals should have the right to sue for libel over public interest issues which affect people's everyday lives, but while they do, cases should at minimum be tried by a jury, who, as ordinary people, may be less ready to swallow the line of establishment organisations and those in power.

'The "meanings" decided in a libel case are supposed to be meanings which a notional "ordinary, reasonable, reader" would take from reading the leaflet. So why not have "ordinary" members of the public decide those meanings? We believe a jury would have been very unlikely to adopt the extreme meanings put forward by McDonald's, and in fact would more than likely have thrown the whole case out early on, viewing it as oppressive and contrary to the public interest.

'The day after the McLibel verdict was given, the Jonathon Aitken libel case fell apart after the former Government minister was exposed as a bare faced liar. Commentators asked how he expected to get away with lying in court, and answered by saying that when it came down to the word of a former Tory minister against that of a journalist, he could safely assume, having successfully applied for trial by Judge alone, that the courts would believe his word, particularly since as a Plaintiff legally he didn't have to prove anything under UK libel laws.

'The situation in our case is much the same. Having been denied a jury, the Judge has in the main chosen to prefer the evidence of those representing the establishment or status quo. But, based on our experience at pre-trial hearings, we had expected this to happen and so from the start of the trial we adopted a strategy of gaining admissions from McDonald's witnesses, so that it thereby became not just "their word against ours" but also "their word against their own." Having to break down the slick PR speak to gain these admissions length-ened the trial considerably, but it meant that most of the find-ings of fact went in our favour (it was the *interpretation* of the factsheet that we "lost" on). And it ensured that the truth could not be brushed under the carpet.

'The admissions of McDonald's' witnesses during testi-mony, and the revelations from the official documents we managed to force them to disclose on all of the issues, we hope will stand against them for all time. To a great extent the Factsheet, written in 1986 and out of print before the writs were served on us, is irrelevant, as is any judgement based solely on bizarre interpretations of its text, graphics and design—what really counts are the current leaflets of which over 3 million have been distributed. However, what *is* important is the real issues in dispute in the courtroom, as covered in the earlier chapters in the book.

'So why didn't we win all the points? The burden of proof was entirely on us, so we had to succeed in convincing the judge to rule for us, or else it would be "not proven". McDonald's didn't actually "win" any of the issues. The media proclaimed that McDonald's didn't "poison their customers", "evict Third World peasants" or "cut down rainforests". But we never claimed they did! This was based on the McDonald's interpretations of the factsheet, adopted by the judge.

"Nutrition. We won most of this issue, and should have won the lot. McDonald's key witness had admitted the text of the factsheet (about links between diet and ill-health) was "a very reasonable thing to say", and the judge during the closing speeches had basically agreed. However, he ruled that the satirical cartoons and graphics in the fctsheet meant we would have to prove a much more narrow severe meaning. So we failed to "win".

'Food Safety. In his verdict the Judge agreed that this section of the factsheet (about general food safety concerns associated with modern factory farming methods), taken literally, could be viewed as "inoffensive". But he then ruled that the "context" of the factsheet (antipathy to McDonald's) meant that we actually had to prove that McDonald's "expose their customers . . . to a serious risk of food poisoning"—something the factsheet had not said! In his full judgement, he acknowledged the evidence of routine use of anti-biotics, growth promoting hormones and pesticides in the industry (which was what the factsheet had said). However, he decided that we had not brought sufficient evidence to prove that any of this posed a serious risk to consumers. This is despite widespread concern in many countries over these unnatural practices, and the fact for example that the EC banned the use of hormone growth promoters in Europe because of fears over their safety. The judge also acknowledged the widespread presence of salmonella and campylobacter in poultry raised for McDonald's products, and current concern over E Coli 0157 in beef products. Commenting on McDonald's' argument that cooking products adequately was the one guarantee that pathogenic organisms would be destroyed, he said in his judgement "the risk [of undercooking] is endemic in the fast food system, whatever protective measures the Plaintiffs put in place". But it was not enough for the judge, so again we failed to "win".

'Most of the findings of fact on the issue of workers were in our favour, but the judge decided that he found acceptable what many people would view as exploitation. He ruled that the factsheet's reference to "bad" working conditions was not an "opinion" but a "statement of fact" which he believed had not been "proven". He ruled that McDonald's "are strongly anti-pathetic to any idea of unionisation of crew", but then said we had "lost" this issue because we hadn't proved that "McDonald's has a policy of preventing unionisation by getting rid of pro-Union workers". This was despite the company's former Head of Personnel testifying that employees "would not be allowed to carry out any overt Union activity on McDonalds' premises", and that "to inform the Union about conditions inside the stores" would be a breach of the employee's contract, "misconduct" and, as such, a "summary sackable offence." If that's not a "policy" then we don't know what is.

'The judgement on the "Damage To The Environment" section of the case hinged entirely on the extreme and limited meanings the judge attributed to the words in the factsheet. He ruled out weeks of evidence about the damage caused by the production and disposal of the mountains of McDonald's packaging, saying it was not "relevant". The text criticised multinational corporations in general (which included McDonald's—the world's largest promoter of beef products, and largest food service organisation) for being collectively reponsible for creating an international "cash crop economy" which resulted in land dispossessions and hunger in the Third World. But the judge ruled that we had to prove that

McDonald's itself was directly "causing starvation" in the Third World. Anything less was deemed irrelevant.

'Likewise the Factsheet criticised the hamburger industry in general, and McDonald's as "one of many US Corporations" responsible for the destruction of tropical rainforests. But the judge agreed with McDonald's' submissions that we had to prove that McDonald's *itself* had bought vast tracts of land for cattle ranching, and *ITSELF* used lethal poisons to destroy vast areas of rainforest (which he defined so narrowly as to exclude most of the tropical forest which had been deforested to make way for beef). Therefore, despite the evidence demonstrating McDonald's contribution to environmental damage and social inequality, we failed to win the issue. The decision that we had "libelled" McDonald's because they used a "small" amount of recycled material in their packaging, rather than a "tiny" amount, as the factsheet said, is ridiculous.

'But the most amazing part of the judgement must be the judge's ruling over our Counterclaim. Despite issuing 300,000 leaflets and press releases on the eve of the trial denouncing us, and criticisms of the company as "lies", McDonald's had failed to bring a single piece of evidence to substantiate their defamatory assertions that we had deliberately circulated false information. We should clearly have won our Counterclaim, which would have ensured that the overwhelming majority of the Judgement would have been in our favour. The judge indeed ruled that these company leaflets and press releases contained allegations which were "defamatory", "unjustified", which McDonald's knew to be untrue and that "part of the motive . . . was to discredit the defendants".

'But, astonishingly, he ruled that this was legally permissable as McDonald's had the right of self-defence to protect itself due to being under "attack" from us! He ignored our submissions during closing speeches that if any "right of self-defence" existed, it should not apply to a huge company but instead to members of the public raising valid concerns about corporate domination of people's lives, communities and the environment.

'This is staggering legal hypocrisy and blatant double standards, where the full protection of the law extends to a corporation but comes down heavily on the public. We believe strongly in the public's right of self-defence and for that reason encourage the public to refuse to respect or obey any oppressive, unfair or biased laws which stand as an obstacle to progress. For those who believe in the scales of "justice" we wish to ask: having found McDonald's guilty of deceiving the public about the nutritional value of its food, exploiting the hundreds of millions of vulnerable children it targets, exploiting hundreds of thousands of non-unionised workers with low pay, and causing cruelty to millions of animals, what action will the courts take to end these unacceptable practices? The answer is "none". It's up to you and me.

'The court has imposed no punishment, no sanctions on the McDonald's Corporation. The £ 60,000 damages award against us was considered "derisory" but in any event we would never pay a penny to such an organisation. We would like to move on to other issues and activities but there is still the unfinished business of Appeals, European Court, suing McDonald's' spies and so on. Of course we also wish to participate in the growing campaigns to challenge and eventually abolish multinationals, including McDonald's and we look forward to celebrating the McLibel campaign's success on future world days of action.

'When McDonald's served writs on us they effectively declared war against campaigners and all those who believe in progress towards a more fair and just society. McDonald's lost that war. One reason is that propaganda, no matter how sophisticated or inflated by advertising dollars, can never even approach the power of the truth. A second reason is that the public ARE concerned about their lives, their society and their planet and are not just gullible consumers who only think as far as the next purchase. And thirdly, when people are as organised and as determined to fight for justice and progress as the McLibel Support Campaign and the thousands of grassroots activists around the world are, then they realise that they don't have to lie down and accept the status quo, but can fight back. When millions of people begin to stand up for themselves, injustice and oppression can be swept away.'

And what of the public, the ordinary people courted by McDonald's and appealed to by Steel and Morris, who were not allowed to pass judgement because the issues of McLibel were deemed too complex and scientific? They, too, have an opinion on the trial, best seen on the internet. The "McSpotlight" site (http://www.mcspotlight.org/) has, by July 1997, been accessed over 15 million times since its launch and 2,191,828 times in the month of the verdicts alone. The public comment that it invites is overwhelmingly in favour of Steel and Morris. It includes the occasional detractor ('Go move to Red China for all I care, but leave my Big Mac the hell alone') but most contributions are in the vein of this e-mail: 'The poor little average citizen can eat at a McDonald's but can not have a valid opinion about whether it is a good idea.' McDonald's' web site (www.mcdonalds.com) does not mention the trial. On the day after the verdicts, it was advertising a special deal on a breakfast sandwich.

The storms pass and the cast of characters, battered after 5 years' stress and continual confrontation, pick up their lives. Mr. Justice Bell, his reputation enhanced, goes straight to Bristol to handle a murder trial and then he has his first holiday in three years. Richard Ramton is back on the London libel court circuit, most recently working for a small political party set up as a corporation. The mood at McDonald's London HQ is general relief that the episode seems more or less closed.

Last Words

No one has been fired, and nobody held to account, but Sidney Nicholson has retired.

The enterprise is still hell bent on growth, obsessively opening new stores every few days in England and every few hours around the world. It is business as usual, and, as usual, McDonald's is still being opposed by community groups and individuals wherever it goes. Has it changed its practices in any way since the trial? If any internal investigation of the way it pays people, looks after animals or promotes its goods to children has been made, then nobody has been told and nobody has been consulted. McDonald's legal department, too, is still busy. Elsewhere, Keir Starmer has moved on to high-profile public interest cases challenging governments over prisoners on Death Row in the caribbean and deaths in police custody.

For Steel and Morris, off the front line for the first time in years, the prospects are good. There is still unfinished McLibel business but the case has left them, they say, clearer, even wiser about the role of corporations and how people can stand up to them. Where once observers feared that the single-mindedness and sheer concentration needed to take on McDonald's was threatening to make the as unyielding as the object of their scorn, they now seem more relaxed, at ease with themselves and others. Neither have full-time work, but both are still activists working in their north London communities. They say they are not thinking too far ahead. Steel has the time to walk again in Scotland and has taken on an allotment to grow vegetables. Morris is making up the ground with Charlie, taking him camping and to concerts.

We all laugh a lot more now, he says. McDonald's? Yes, they're laughable.

Diary of the Trial

1985

January London Greenpeace launches a campaign 'to expose the reality' behind the advertising mask of the McDonald's Corporation.
April First international day of action against McDonald's (around the thirtieth anniversary of the McDonald's Corporation).

1986

London Greenpeace publishes a Factsheet entitled 'What's Wrong with McDonald's? – Everything they don't want you to know'. It is critical of the corporation in its treatment of animals, promotion of unhealthy food, effects on the environment and exploitative employment practices.

1987

A campaigning group from Nottingham called Veggies is threatened by McDonald's with legal reprisals if it continues to use the words 'murder' and 'torture' to describe the rearing and slaughter of animals for McDonald's' products in a copy of the London Greenpeace Factsheet. Veggies changes these words to 'slaughter' and 'butchery' and amends the 'destruction of the rainforest' section to refer to the burger industry in general, not specifically McDonald's. No more is heard from McDonald's' legal department and Veggies continues to distribute the Factsheets in bulk.

October 1989 to spring 1991

McDonald's sends private investigators to infiltrate London Greenpeace. The 'spies' take minutes of meetings, answer letters and make friends with members of the group.

September 1990

The McDonald's Corporation issues writs for libel against five members of London Greenpeace considered responsible for distributing the 'What's Wrong with McDonald's?' Factsheet.

Late 1990

The McLibel Support Campaign is set up to generate solidarity and financial support for the McLibel defendants.

1991

January Three members formally apologize. Helen Steel and Dave Morris refuse and decide to represent themselves. They unsuccessfully take the British government to the European Court of Human Rights, demanding the right to legal aid or the simplification of libel procedures.

Late 1993 to early 1994

McDonald's replaces its barrister with Richard Rampton QC, one of Britain's top libel lawyers, who applies for a non-jury trial, submitting that the scientific testimony necessary to examine the links between diet and disease will be too complicated for a jury to understand, and the judge agrees. Morris and Steel apply unsuccessfully to the Court of Appeal and the House of Lords to reinstate the jury. McDonald's also applies for an order striking out certain parts of the defence on the grounds that the witness statements gathered by the defendants do not sufficiently support those areas of the defence. The judge agrees with McDonald's. However, in a landmark legal decision, the Court of Appeal restores all parts of the defence on the basis that the defendants are entitled to rely on the witness statements, on future discovery of McDonald's' documents and on what they might reasonably expect to discover under cross-examination.

1994

March McDonald's publishes 300,000 copies of a leaflet entitled 'Why McDonald's is going to court' and distributes them to customers via its burger outlets. In the leaflet McDonald's says: 'This action is not about freedom of speech; it is about the right to stop people telling lies.'

April Dave Morris and Helen Steel issue a counter-claim for libel against McDonald's. McDonald's now has to prove that the statements contained within the London Greenpeace Factsheet are 'lies' and that the defendants knew them to be so. Under the original libel suit brought by McDonald's, Morris and Steel have to prove that their claims in the Factsheet are true or fair comment, and are required to provide 'primary sources' of evidence to substantiate their case, which means witness statements and documentary proof but not press cuttings or common conceptions.

June By now the defendants have attended twenty-eight pre-trial hearings.

28 June The full libel trial, presided over by Mr Justice Bell, begins in Court 35, High Court, the Strand, London. Richard Rampton QC for McDonald's presents his opening speech.

29 June The defendants present their opening speech.

6 July Evidence begins on the environmental effects of McDonald's' packaging.

18 July Evidence begins on McDonald's' nutritional record.

26 July Evidence begins on McDonald's' animal welfare and food-poisoning record.

September Operation 'Send-It-Back' is launched in Nottingham by Veggies.

12 September Dr Sydney Arnott, McDonald's' expert witness on cancer, unwittingly admits that a statement made in the allegedly libellous Factsheet connecting diet with disease is a 'very reasonable' assessment.

1 October McDonald's UK's Twentieth Anniversary Birthday Celebrations, in Woolwich, south London, are countered. London Greenpeace supporters hand out 4,000 'What's Wrong with McDonald's' leaflets to passers-by.

14 October Operation 'Send-It-Back' is launched in London by the McLibel Support Campaign: fifty demonstrators picket McDonald's' European HQ. The demonstrators return thirty sackfuls of the company's litter picked up from the streets.

15 October National March Against McDonald's: about 500 protesters march through central London.

16 October The Tenth Worldwide Anti-McDonald's Day is the focus of independent protests all over the UK and the world: seven benefit concerts are held in Australia.

28 October Evidence begins on McDonald's' use of advertising techniques.

1995

13 March The 102nd day in court breaks the record for a British libel trial (beating the 101-day record set by *Daily Mail* vs. The Moonies in 1982).

April Evidence begins on McDonald's employment record.

15 April The fortieth anniversary of the McDonald's Corporation. The defendants are invited to the United States to attend an anti-birthday celebration outside the first McDonald's burger bar (now a McDonald's museum) in Des Plaines, Illinois. McDonald's abandons plans to hold a birthday celebration in the museum on that day. Anti-McDonald's demonstrations are held in over twenty countries around the world.

26 May At the McDonald's Corporation Annual General Meeting in Chicago, Michael Quinlan, Chair and Chief Executive, attempts to placate a concerned shareholder by stating that the libel case would be 'coming to a wrap soon'.

6 June McDonald's hires Ruskin Park in South London for three days in order to shoot a television advertisement. The project is abandoned at a cost of £100,000 after demonstrators keep popping up in front of camera with 'McGreedy' banners.

28 June The first anniversary of the trial. The national media reports that settlement negotiations between McDonald's and the defendants are under way. Steel and Morris read a statement outside the High Court which says that McDonald's initiated settlement discussions and on two separate occasions flew over members of the US Board of Directors to meet them. McDonald's offers money to be given to a third party if the defendants undertake a legally binding agreement not to criticize the corporation again. The defendants refuse to terminate the trial.

3 July McDonald's ends an agreement in which a copy of the official court transcripts (which it pays for) is passed to the defendants, citing the amount of court evidence finding its way into the national and international media.

26 July Summer recess begins.

25 September The trial recommences.

12 October The third anniversary of the death of Mark Hopkins, an employee electrocuted at McDonald's' Arndale store in Manchester, and a Day of Solidarity With McDonald's Workers in the UK. Mark's mother Maureen organizes a picket at the Arndale Centre store which forty people attend, and there are protests and leafleting in many places.

16 October Eleventh Annual Worldwide Day of Action Against McDonald's (also UN 'World Food Day'). In the UK, about half (300) of McDonald's' stores are leafleted. Protests in at least twenty other countries.

18 October The defendants begin calling their employment witnesses: over thirty ex-employees of McDonald's together with trade union officials and activists from around the world.

1996

16 February The McLibel defendants launch the McSpotlight Website outside the McDonald's store at Leicester Square, in central London.

22 February The section of the trial on the connections between McDonald's and rainforest destruction (particularly in Central and South America) begins.

2 April The Court of Appeal refuses to grant the appeal brought by the McLibel defendants against the judge's ruling on the meaning of the London Greenpeace Factsheet in relation to nutrition.

10 June The first of the 'Enquiry Agents' employed by

official court transcripts (which it pays for) is passed to the defendants, citing the amount of court evidence finding its way into the national and international media.

26 July Summer recess begins.

25 September The trial recommences.

12 October The third anniversary of the death of Mark Hopkins, an employee electrocuted at McDonald's' Arndale store in Manchester, and a Day of Solidarity With McDonald's Workers in the UK. Mark's mother Maureen organizes a picket at the Arndale Centre store which forty people attend, and there are protests and leafleting in many places.

16 October Eleventh Annual Worldwide Day of Action Against McDonald's (also UN 'World Food Day'). In the UK, about half (300) of McDonald's' stores are leafleted. Protests in at least twenty other countries.

18 October The defendants begin calling their employment witnesses: over thirty ex-employees of McDonald's together with trade union officials and activists from around the world.

1996

16 February The McLibel defendants launch the McSpotlight Website outside the McDonald's store at Leicester Square, in central London.

22 February The section of the trial on the connections between McDonald's and rainforest destruction (particularly in Central and South America) begins.

2 April The Court of Appeal refuses to grant the appeal brought by the McLibel defendants against the judge's ruling on the meaning of the London Greenpeace Factsheet in relation to nutrition.

10 June The first of the 'Enquiry Agents' employed by

locations around the UK, including a large picket in Manchester organized by the Hopkins family.

16 October Protests in twenty-five countries to mark the Twelfth Annual World Day of Action against McDonald's. About 250 of McDonald's UK stores are leafleted.

17 October Court of Appeal refuses to give the defendants leave to appeal against Mr Justice's Bell's ruling that they must go first in the closing speeches and that they can be given no more time to prepare.

21 October The McLibel defendants start their closing speech.

1 November The McLibel trial becomes the longest trial of any kind in English history on Day 292. The previous longest trial was the Tichborne personation case, which lasted 291 days, ending in 1874.

19 November On Day 303 the trial becomes three times as long as any previous English libel trial (the previous longest being a mere 101 days!).

28 November The defendants finish their closing speech and Richard Rampton QC hands his in in written form.

3, 4, 6 December The judge asks Mr Rampton questions about his closing speech.

11, 13 December The defendants present their final legal arguments. On Day 313, they submit that English libel laws in general – and in this case in particular – were oppressive and unfair, particularly the denial of legal aid and a jury trial. The defendants argue that multinational corporations should no longer be allowed to sue their critics in order to silence them, and cite European and US laws which would debar such a case. They further argue that the McLibel case was beyond all previous precedent, was an abuse of procedure and of public rights and that there was 'an overriding imperative for decisions to be made to protect the public interest'.

13 December Day 313, the last day of final submissions. Mr Justice Bell: 'I will say now that I propose to reserve my judgement. It will take me some time to write it. I don't mean to be difficult when I say I don't know when I will deliver it because I don't know.'

1997

16 February On the first anniversary of the launch of McSpotlight, the Website doubles in size overnight with the addition of all the official court transcripts and Richard Rampton's closing submissions. The Site was accessed over 7 million times in its first year.

26 February Copex, an arms trade exhibition company, abandons its libel action against Peace News and Campaign Against The Arms Trade (who had been encouraged by the McLibel Support Campaign), paying out £ 32,497 costs.

April McDonald's Corporation 1996 Annual Report announces 'Systemwide sales exceeded $30 billion for the first time, and net income crossed the $1.5 billion threshold'.

4 June John Lewis plc abandons its libel action against the National Anti-Hunt Campaign after a national defiance campaign and public support and legal advice from the McLibel 2.

19 June Mr Justice Bell give his long-awaited McLibel Verdict, reading out a 45-page summary of his 800-page Judgement. He fines the defendants pounds 60,000 for 'serious' and 'important' libels, but finds McDonald's responsible for 'exploiting children', 'cruelty to animals', deceiving customers about the nutritional qualities of their food, and paying 'low wages.'

21 June McLibel 'Victory Day Of Action' sees 400,000 What's Wrong With McDonald's? leaflets distributed outside over 500 of McDonald's 750 UK stores, and solidarity protests in over a dozen countries.

July A full-length documentary "McLibel: Two World's Collide" has been completed by One Off Productions (oops@

spanner.org). Videos are available. The 'McSpotlight' Internet site (http://www.mcspotlight.org/) is accessed 2,191,828 times in one month. It is updated to include the full 800-page judgement.

13 July *Sunday Times* (UK) reports that Ed Rensi, President of the McDonald's Corporation, has been removed as Chief Executive following falling US market share, promotional flops and franchisee discontent.

17 July Final deadline passes having been set by Mr Justice Bell for any further applications including costs or injunctions. McDonald's effectively abandon all legal action to try to prevent the dissemination of leaflets and recovery of costs (estimated at £ 10m). They are quoted as saying they will also not attempt to recover any of the damages they were awarded.

5 August McDonald's announces it has withdrawn their planning application to build a drive through at Alexandra Palace Park in Haringey, North London. The plan had encountered widespread local opposition, including from the McLibel 2 (Haringey residents).

August Steel and Morris lodge Appeal to the UK Court of Appeal.

11-18th October Projected global week of action against McDonald's.

Thanks to SQUALL magazine which originally produced 'Diary of the Trial' in a longer form as 'Diary of a Stance'. SQUALL has covered the McLibel case on a regular basis and can be obtained from PO Box 8959, London N19 5HW, telephone 00 44 171 561 1204. Website: http://www.phreak. co.uk/squall/

Afterword from the McLibel Two

Freedom of Speech and Libel

Few people have any idea of the nature of libel laws and the way in which they are used. It was the same for us when we first got the writs. Despite not being the authors of the London Greenpeace Factsheet we found the burden of proof was put on us, that there was no legal aid, that we could not rely on previous reports, no matter how authoritative, and that there was no protection of freedom of speech whatsoever.

Most people (including us) generally believe what they read or are told *unless* they have some reason not to believe it. When we read the Factsheet and other subsequent leaflets about McDonald's we had every reason to believe their contents. They were exactly the kind of thing we'd read in any number of places before, including statements made by those most prominent in the respective fields. Yet now it was down to us to prove it all true.

Imagine (you may not need to) that a factory in your neighbourhood is pumping out pollution which is affecting people's health. You decide you want to stop this, and you get together with neighbours to start a campaign. A leaflet is produced which repeats information reported in newspapers and scientific journals about the relevant chemicals or substances being released into the environment, and the effect that it's had or may have on people's health. The company slaps a writ on you claiming it has been libelled. You may or may not have helped with writing the leaflet, but it's now your responsibility to prove to the satisfaction of the English libel courts that those chemicals or substances do have those effects, and even if you can prove that, that it's actually had that effect in your neighbourhood.

What do you know about how to file a defence to a libel claim? Probably nothing. How many libel lawyers do you know? Probably none. If you're lucky you may have access to a library with a good stock of law books, and you might just be able to puzzle out how to file that defence.

But even if you can get as far as filing a defence, think, as an ordinary person, how difficult it is to prove something true. Particularly on matters of health. How do you actually *prove* that the pollution has made or may make somebody ill? First you have to find some eminent scientists in the field – the courts won't take notice even of scientific reports without an 'expert' in court to back them. But how many eminent scientists do you know? And even if you can get hold of one, you're entirely reliant on their goodwill, you couldn't afford to pay their fees to produce a report for you. Meanwhile the company concerned has plenty of money with which to pay for reports saying that the amount of chemicals released are negligible or that there are no ill effects. There's always at least one scientist whose point of view coincides with the company.

We were fortunate that when we got the writs we were put in touch with a barrister, Keir Starmer, who had experience in the field of libel law (most lawyers don't). Without him, it's unlikely we would ever have got our defence off the ground, because the laws and procedures are so complex. We were fortunate that some experts did step forward to give evidence on our behalf without the standard fee for preparing a report and testifying. And that so many ex-employees too found the time to come to court. We were also fortunate that people sent in enough money to enable us to pay photocopying and phone bills, and for our witnesses' fares to court. But it could have been different.

It should be different. Companies which have such power and influence over the lives of ordinary people should not be able to use libel laws against their critics. It is of vital public importance that matters which affect people's lives and health are areas of free, uninhibited public debate. Even the House of Lords recently admitted that the threat of a libel writ had a 'chilling effect on freedom of speech' and therefore ruled that it was in the public interest that governmental bodies would no longer be allowed to sue for libel. So why should multinational corporations? They are often more powerful than local or national governments, and even less accountable.

In the USA companies and public figures have to show that the critic *knew* what s/he was saying was false before they can even begin an action for libel – if adopted here that would be a start. Then at least campaigners who produced leaflets based on information reported in newspapers and/or scientific journals could not be sued.

When we got beyond the initial panic of trying to file a defence it became apparent that it was important to fight the case not just as a battle with McDonald's but as a fight against this country's oppressive libel laws. We became aware of the widespread unseen censorship going on. Most libel cases don't even make it to court because defendants face years of long, drawn-out, unfair, complex and archaic proceedings and there's no legal aid available, so generally a humiliating apology or settlement is made to avoid the massive costs of a case. These settlements inevitably include an undertaking not to repeat the criticism, and on top of that the fake 'apologies' are paraded around as if they vindicate the reputation of the plaintiffs. The result is mass censorship, and no one knows what's really going on behind the scenes.

Additionally, every day campaigning groups, newspapers and publishers censor what they want to say. Not because they don't believe it's true. Not even because they're not sure if they have the evidence to prove it. But simply because they don't want to risk getting a writ. It costs an enormous amount to fight a case and most don't want to have to try to find that sort of money, many simply can't.

Is such self-censorship in the public interest? No. These companies have the resources to put out their own leaflets or adverts putting what they see as their side if they feel they have been misrepresented or slighted. They can very easily 'defend' themselves.

People should have the right to put forward their honestly held beliefs to draw attention to what they see as the problems with the way society is run. It is only through the expression of alternative views and ideas that injustice is remedied and society progresses. It is in the public interest that there be the widest possible dissemination of critical information about those institutions which dominate our lives and environment. There also needs to be vibrant public debate about what is really happening around us, and about the alternatives.

If companies do choose to use oppressive laws against their critics then court cases do not have to only be about legal procedures and verdicts. They can be turned into a public forum and focus for protest, and for the wider dissemination of the truth. This is what happened in the McLibel case.

Any unjust law can be made unworkable by organized public noncooperation and defiance, as has been shown by so many struggles throughout history. One of the most recent in the UK was the successful mass non-payment of the Government's 'poll tax', leading to its abolition. The right to criticize rich and powerful companies and institutions is an absolute necessity. Society should never tolerate the censorship of genuine and alternative voices for the truth.

How were we able to fight such an 'impossible' battle as McLibel? Ordinary people's strength comes from their sense of justice and feeling of solidarity with others, from the expression of their views and from having confidence in themselves. Our own awareness and strength has been gained from the experiences we've had in the many activities, campaigns and movements we've participated in over the last twenty years. And of course from all the help we've had. Thanks are due to all the witnesses, experts, legal helpers and everyone else who contributed in any way to the case or campaign. The dedication of unpaid volunteers at the McLibel Support Campaign and at the McSpotlight Website (www.McSpotlight.org) has ensured a wider and more detailed knowledge of the case.

Alternative views are not abstract ideas. Most have been discussed, developed and fought for throughout history. We brought our own personal experiences with us into the courtroom. We are absolutely exhausted after defending ourselves throughout the mammoth case, but exhilarated by what we were able to achieve. Maybe for the first time in history a powerful institution (it just happened to be a fast-food chain, but in some ways could've been any financial organization or state department) was subject to lengthy, detailed and critical public scrutiny. That can only be a good thing! We hope McLibel has demonstrated how ordinary people can get together and stand up to even the most powerful adversary.

As for us two – can we have our lives back, please?

News of the verdict and any subsequent appeals can be obtained from the McLibel Support Campaign, 5 Caledonian Road, London N1 9DX or www.McSpotlight.org

References

The Politics of The Real World – Michael Jacobs (Earthscan)
McDonalds' Behind the Arches – John F. Love (Bantam Press)
Grinding It Out – Ray Kroc
The Politics of Industrial Agriculture – Tracy Clunies-Ross, Nicholas Hildyard (Earthscan)
When Corporations Rule The World – David C. Corten (Earthscan)
A New World Order – Paul Ekins (Routledge)
The Power of the Machine – R. A. Buchanan (Viking)
Liberation Ecologies – ed. Richard Peet – Michael Watts (Routledge)
The Last New World – Mac Margolis (Norton)
Future of Progress – Goldsmith et al. (Green Books)
The McDonaldization of Society – George Ritzer (Pine Forge Press, California)
Short Circuit – Richard Douthwaite (Green Books)
The State We're In – Will Hutton (Vintage)
Science For The Earth – ed. Tom Wakeford, Martin Walters (Wiley)
The Power In Our Hands – Tony Gibson (Jon Carpenter Books)
Bleak House – Charles Dickens (Penguin)
McDonald's Fact File 1996 – (McDonald's Communications Department, London)
The Globalisation of Agriculture – Vandana Shiva (Research Foundation for Science, Technology, Delhi)

John Vidal would also like to thank other publications including *The Ecologist Magazine* and the Institute for Environment and Development (London), The World Resources Institute (Washington), and the New Economics Foundation (London).

Index

345

Index

Index

Index

Index